FOURTEEN
Talks
BY
Age
FOURTEEN

FOURTEEN

Talks

BY

Age

FOURTEEN

The Essential Conversations You Need to Have
with Your Kids Before They Start High School—
and How (Best) to Have Them

Michelle Icard

Harmony Books
New York

Published in the United States by Harmony Books,
an imprint of Random House, a division of
Penguin Random House LLC, New York.
harmonybooks.com

Harmony Books is a registered trademark, and the Circle colophon
is a trademark of Penguin Random House LLC.

Library of Congress Cataloging-in-Publication Data
Names: Icard, Michelle, author.
Title: Fourteen (talks) by (age) fourteen : the essential conversations you need to have with
your kids before they start high school - and how (best) to have them / Michelle Icard.
Other titles: Fourteen talks by age fourteen
Description: First edition. | New York : Harmony Books, [2020] | Includes bibliographical
references and index.
Identifiers: LCCN 2020007814 (print) | LCCN 2020007815 (ebook) |
ISBN 9780593137512 (hardcover) | ISBN 9780593137536 (epub)
Subjects: LCSH: Parent and child. | Communication in families.
Classification: LCC HQ755.85 .I34 2020 (print) | LCC HQ755.85 (ebook) |
DDC 306.874—dc23

ISBN 978-0-593-13751-2
Ebook ISBN 978-0-593-13753-6

Printed in Canada

Editor: Marnie Cochran
Book Designer: Ashley Tucker
Jacket Designer: Anna Bauer
Production Editor: Serena Wang
Production Manager: Heather Williamson
Composition: North Market Street Graphics
Copy Editor: Alison Hagge
Indexer: Jay Kreider

10 9 8 7 6 5 4 3 2 1

First Edition

For Travis.

I've never met anyone who's collected more interesting conversations,
or who finds people more genuinely fascinating, than you. Thanks for
twenty-six years of intriguing, weird, profound, and funny conversations.
I'd like to have a million more.

And for Ella and Declan.

I love you. Anytime you want to talk, I'm here to listen.
I'll bring the snacks.

CONTENTS

Who Am I to Say?

Chances are you've come to this book because you're at a loss for words—or at least at a loss for words that resonate with the young adolescent in your house who no longer wants to talk or listen to what you have to say.

I'm here to put you at ease.

But, who am I to say, "Don't worry," and "It will be okay," and "You can have great conversations despite the overwhelming, disheartening stereotypes about surly, disconnected teens"?

I've spent the past sixteen years working with middle schoolers and their parents. I run leadership programs for middle schoolers, conferences for parents and kids, and an online group of more than 6,000 parents of middle schoolers. I'll share stories from my work with you here, although I've changed people's names and identifying information to preserve their privacy. I also write for several national outlets, and my first book, *Middle School Makeover: Improving the Way You and Your Child Experience the Middle School Years,* is a primer for the social and emotional changes both you and your kids will navigate when midlife meets middle school under one roof.

That's my resume, but perhaps more important, I'm drawn to this work, in part, because I remember my own early adolescence with unforgiving clarity.

I'd like to say I had the natural good looks, style, and poise of a sixth-grade A-lister. In reality, I sported oversized glasses, a choppy bowl cut–mullet combo hastily engineered by my mother, and I was in desperate need of orthodontics. While other kids my age were successfully pulling off Madonna- and Run-DMC–inspired looks, my closet had big Bea

Arthur vibes. Yet somehow, I remained oblivious to how off-the-mark my choices were. By eighth grade, I'd achieved a level of self-confidence that can best be measured by my brave decision to pin a giant brooch on my corduroy suspenders for picture day. Why my classmates didn't copy my awesome outfits like they did my tests, your guess is as good as mine.

The point is, I work with young adolescents because I know what it feels like to be on the fringe, and all adolescents, no matter how seemingly confident or popular, feel on the fringe in one way or another. The same is true for parents of adolescents. Even the ones who show up as the happiest of families on social media will tell you their kids make them feel like complete strangers at times.

Also, I'm someone who likes to study. Ever since middle school—the time when I felt most detached from both peers and family—I've been studying how people connect. I gobble up all the research I can on adolescents but I also just pay attention: to the kids I work with, to my own teens, to their friends, to my friends, to characters on TV, and to strangers at the grocery store, absorbing the subtleties of what works and what doesn't in as many social situations as possible.

This book divulges all I've learned about what works best in keeping parents and kids connected (even when your kid is fooling you into thinking they want no such thing). It strives to help you talk through important life topics that will launch your child into adolescence and beyond with the confidence, caring, coping skills, and good character that every generation hopes for the next.

Enough About Me ... More on This Book

Why *these* fourteen conversations? Each conversation topic taps into a broad quality, skill, or understanding parents universally want for their kids. By having these early conversations, you will proactively lay groundwork for your kids to be kind, healthy, hard-working, creative, empathetic, and successful people, before they're exposed to the wider experiences and distractions high school brings.

In *Fourteen by Fourteen*, you won't find separate chapters devoted to the latest issue du jour, whether that's sexting, vaping, misusing social media, or whatever may be the next frightening topic in our news cycle. I decided against this approach because if all of the fourteen conversations were warnings, it wouldn't be much fun for anyone, and my hope is that this book makes talking together more enjoyable and rewarding for both parent and child.

That said, I know many parents will come to this book with more specific, burning questions. "How *do* I talk with my kid about not Googling porn? Help!" You absolutely should talk with your kids about the specific issues young adolescents will face, and I won't leave you high and dry. On each broad topic, I've included specific scenarios you might commonly encounter, and I use those as entry points for the larger lessons of the chapter. In the Talking About Sexuality chapter, for example, I'll talk about porn and you'll see dialogues related to middle school dating in one example, consent in another, and bisexuality in a third. In the Talking About Impulsivity chapter, you'll see conversations covering emotional outbursts directed at a sibling and then stick-and-poke tattoos (this one you could easily customize to whichever body-harming trend is big at your kid's school, like the eraser challenge or slap game). The real challenges adolescents face come up in different ways, in multiple chapters, nestled among the broader lessons you want your child to learn.

I understand that trying to convince a middle schooler to listen to you can be exasperating. Often it can feel like the best option is *not* to talk. I've seen many parents of tweens stop talking to their kids about important things because they don't know how to do it effectively, and I've seen many parents of teenagers later have an arduous time reconnecting after a long disengagement. I hear parents lament about the middle school years because it's when kids begin to pull away and think about who they want to be *apart* from their parents. And I hear parents of high schoolers worry about their teens' abilities to make good choices as they find themselves pressing the boundaries of adulthood and brushing up against high-stakes decisions that can have a lifetime of consequences. Not to worry. This book bridges the gap between these stages of parenting, giving you a new language for staying connected.

Speaking of language, here's a vocabulary dilemma: What do we call these creatures you're living with now? Are they tweens, preteens, teenagers, young adolescents, children, kids? The answer is yes to all, inconstantly and unpredictably. Between the ages of ten and fourteen, kids bounce around developmentally. As parents, we think growing up ought to be linear, that kids should make forward progress with important attributes like maturity and responsibility. The truth is, it's one step forward followed by two to ten steps back. One day they're texting their crush and yelling for you to leave their room, and the next they're playing with toys and asking to sleep in your room again. For this very reason, they're hard to label. You'll see as you read, I use all the terms for this age group interchangeably because there's just no easy way to pin them down. I have to admit, it's one of the things I like best about people this age.

One more thing before you dive into the rest of the book. I want to give you an image to keep in mind. Have you ever played racquetball? It can be terrifying at first. It's squeaky and sweaty and the ball zooms around in unpredictable ways at top speed. For beginners, the best case is you'll feel awkward and embarrassed when you miss. Worst case, you'll get hit—and that stings. But with practice, racquetball becomes fun because of the four walls of the court. Think of your conversations as racquetball games. Don't fear the lack of control. Feel safe in letting that ball bounce wherever it may, knowing you have some external walls in place to maintain a positive structure. What are your walls? Well, I don't know. But I can tell you mine.

Since my kids were little, I've protected the four areas of our lives that I think make our home a safe space: sleep, autonomy, unconditional love, and dignity. Sleep is a basic. Without a good night's sleep none of us are our best selves. I wasn't a particularly strict parent, but I guarded bedtime like a hawk. And if things got tense, I could say, "Let's sleep on it and talk tomorrow," which almost always helped. Autonomy is important to me, too. I usually gave choices so my kids could practice thinking for themselves and even when I didn't like what they picked, I felt good knowing they were learning how. My job wasn't to make my kids think or act like me or anyone else for that matter. It was to teach them how to think and act for themselves. My third wall is unconditional love. No matter what, I made it clear that my kids had my support and love, even and especially when they felt nervous about the messy choices and mistakes they made. Finally, I talk often about how all people, not just family members, have inherent worth and we should honor that in our thoughts and actions. With these four walls in place, I felt I could let other stuff move around a lot more freely. Your walls will be unique to your family and I encourage you to spend a minute thinking about them and talking to your family about what they mean to you.

How to Read This Book

You know how to read a book. Front to back, right? Usually, yes, that is the most sensible approach. Unless, that is, you're a parent of a tween or young teen, in which case you've probably come to this book in a state of panic, chaos, or confusion. Most of you will dart straight to the index in search of something specific, which will drop you somewhere in the middle of nowhere, but exactly where you need to be. I'm a fan of this unorthodox approach because the days are short and the to-do lists are long, and sometimes you need an answer quickly. But I will make a small request, please: that you carve out enough time to read the first three chapters contained in part 1 before ricocheting through the chapters devoted to specific conversations (in whatever order you see fit at that point). Part 1 is short, but it will make you a believer in part 2, where the solutions to your conversation conundrums lie.

Once you arrive at part 2, the book becomes a kind of a Choose Your Own Adventure. You can read the Talking About chapters in any order, depending on which topics are most pertinent to your family. Although, if you don't have a pressing issue you need help with right away, you will find it easiest to go in order for the obvious sake of not losing your place and also because I've arranged the topics to give you practice with the simpler ones first, progressing toward the more nuanced. Ready? Let's get this ball bouncing.

PART 1

Getting Ready to Talk

It's Time to Learn a New Language

You and your child have always shared a special language. When they were just an infant, it's how you knew which cry meant "I'm hungry," and which meant "I need a diaper change." It's how the mysterious squeal "Bargdor!" that stymied babysitters or grandparents was instantly clear to you as your two-year-old's way of asking for her stuffed dog, Benjamin. From the day they were born, you and your child have been developing your own language, together.

Until middle school.

At around age eleven, kids begin the normal and necessary work of pulling apart from their parents. As tweens set their feet on the long path to adulthood, the first and most important thing they do is begin to establish their own identity. Simply put, this means figuring out who they are *apart* from you.

Just as the job of language is to tie groups together, the job of tweens is to break ties apart. Although the process can be painful, kids who don't begin to assert their independence in adolescence have difficulty establishing healthy partnerships later in life. A key element to avoiding toxic or codependent relationships is for each party to have a strong sense of self, but this only happens when we allow young people a chance to figure out their own styles, values, interests, and beliefs. While it helps to know this kind of separation behavior is on-track developmentally, and

> Just as the job of language is to tie groups together, the job of tweens is to break ties apart.

your child isn't surly or contrarian for no good reason, it can still feel like rejection, made even more difficult when your child starts being exposed to a wider array of experiences, many potentially dangerous. It's natural that you'll want to protect and support them through it all.

Protecting and supporting are hard to do when kids become tweens, because one of the first things they often do is shut down communication. Parents, often blindsided by this, turn up the volume. They become like tourists in a foreign land trying to figure out how to communicate with the locals. Have you ever witnessed a frustrated adult trying to get their point across to an aloof twelve-year-old? They're reduced to saying the same things over and over again, increasingly more slowly, and loudly with every iteration. "I. Said. To. PUT DOWN. THE IPAAAAAD!" Repeating yourself, shout-talking, or slowing *way* down when trying to get your point across to your middle schooler are the equivalent of an American tourist in Italy adding an "ah" sound to the end of their words. "I likah the pizza pleasah." It doesn't get the job done, and you come off sounding clueless.

So how do we reconcile a tween's need to separate from us with our parental desires and obligations to keep them safe, smart, and connected? We learn to speak a *new* language. This isn't intuitive, but it will be easier than you think. This book will be your guide and translator.

Since I started working with tweens and their parents, a lot has changed. Back in 2005, social media wasn't on anyone's mind, and the most exciting piece of technology a kid could get their hands on was an iPod touch. Suicide rates have risen by 30 percent since 2000 with the highest spike seen in girls ages ten to fourteen. By age fifteen, almost 30 percent of teens have had at least one drink. Middle schoolers who tried vaping increased by 48 percent in 2018. Diagnoses of clinical depression in adolescents have increased by 37 percent since 2005. School shootings have become common news, and lockdown practice is a regular part of your school kid's life. But as the saying goes, the more things change, the more they stay the same. Though the lives of young adolescents seem more complicated than ever, the way to help them remains as simple, predictable, and reliable as ever: Talk with them. Not *to* them or *at* them, but *with* them.

The kids I work with tell me the same thing. They wish their parents would talk with them *more* about these issues. So, what stops parents from doing this? It certainly isn't a lack of desire.

Take, for instance, my friend Sonia, a working mother who always prided herself on her close relationship with her daughter, Elaine. They were the kind of duo who shared private jokes, enjoyed "girl time" on weekends, and chattered away like old friends, whether in the car or sitting together at a school function. But when Elaine hit seventh grade, she started pulling back from Sonia, spending more time away from the family, and resisting her mom's attempts to crack shared jokes. When Elaine began to rush through family dinners, kept her headphones on during car rides, and turned down offers for manicures on the weekend, Sonia started to worry. "I'd offer to do the things she loved, like we always used to do. But she didn't want to do anything. I started offering to let her bring a friend. But she said no even to that." Sonia didn't want to give up on her relationship with Elaine, so she began pleading. Ultimately, her husband made a comment that Sonia was "acting like she was in middle school herself, trying to get the popular girl's attention."

Sonia became so worried about her daughter pulling away that she installed monitoring software on Elaine's phone and read through her texts and social media conversations. She even found Elaine's diary, read it without her knowing, and discovered that a boy in the grade above Elaine had been asking Elaine to send him a picture without her shirt on, as well as Elaine's indecision about how to respond to him. Sonia found herself in a predicament, trying to figure out how to let Elaine know she knew this, without revealing her hand and possibly losing her daughter's trust entirely. This is when she reached out to me, feeling lost and searching for advice on her next step.

Hank, a single dad of both a son and daughter, found himself in a different predicament and came to me when his thirteen-year-old son, Elijah, was caught drinking at a party. Hank felt blindsided when he got the call from the parent who had hosted the party. Hank had talked openly to his children about his family's history with alcoholism and the dangers alcohol presented, particularly given their genetics. Hank felt sure Elijah would have thought twice before drinking—especially at such a young age—but it seemed that his candor about their family's struggle hadn't been a deterrent at all. Since Elijah didn't demonstrate the ability to think clearly when it came to alcohol consumption, Hank opted for the harsh punishment of four months' grounding instead of more talk, hoping that might teach Elijah the lesson he needed to learn about the dangers of alcohol consumption.

Lots of us can relate to these situations. We feel rejected, then worried, then trapped in a chess match with our kids, unsure how to strategize our way out of a corner. Both Sonia and Hank not only had a deep desire to connect with their child, but they had valuable information to share. Yet in each scenario, when their attempts to talk had failed, both parents switched gears, sacrificing conversations for what they saw as the more critical imperative of keeping their tweens safe, which they attempted to do by constant monitoring. Hank kept his son at home where he could always keep an eye on him; Sonia tracked her daughter's conversations online and outright spied on her by reading her journal.

Sometimes, making your tween's world smaller is the best way to keep them safe. This is not a book that shrugs off discipline and boundaries. But sometimes, parents resort to the "shut it down" approach because they feel they lack other viable options. They don't trust that their kids will make smart decisions, so they deny them the opportunity to make *any* decisions. The irony is, kids don't learn how to make smart decisions without practice. Given that kids need to have experiences, good and bad, to learn from, the best thing a parent can do is help them evaluate, process, and reflect on what works and what doesn't. That only happens through good conversations.

In other words, Experience + Conversation = Powerful Learning.

This book gives you a way to talk with your kid, even though your kid has reached an age when they will naturally start to resist. In fact, when that starts happening, it's actually a sign that it's more important than ever to have meaningful conversations. One thing I hear in my work, particularly from parents who disagree with my approach, is "My job isn't to be my kid's friend. My job is to keep them safe." This sentiment often goes hand in hand with a more authoritarian parenting style. Confusing curiosity with leniency, or empathy with a need for approval, is a dangerous mistake. Research and common sense tell us that kids who feel comfortable talking with caring adults about their problems are healthier, happier, more resilient, and better poised for future success.

As you read, you'll learn how to get over the most common hurdles in talking to tweens: knowing what conversations are most important, having a way to get started that won't irritate your kids or scare them off, figuring out what to say and what phrases to avoid, keeping them engaged in conversation, and exiting conversations in a way that keeps them wanting more. Keeping kids safe is all about having the right conversations at the right time.

> Research and common sense tell us that kids who feel comfortable talking with caring adults about their problems are healthier, happier, more resilient, and better poised for future success.

Karen, a stay-at-home mom who regularly attends my monthly Michelle's Meet Ups (programs I host in which parents can submit anonymous questions to me ahead of time), is a walking testimonial for parenting through great conversations. The mother of three kids, ages sixteen to eight, she initially came in search of help with her oldest child, Aidan, a shy guy who she never felt as close to as her other children. She and Aidan had few shared interests throughout his childhood, so she often felt like a chauffeur and cook more than a companion or confidante.

For Karen, it was a relief to learn that a meaningful conversation with Aidan didn't need to sound like it did with her other two. They probably wouldn't linger over dinner, sharing laughs or heartfelt moments over burgers and fries. Short conversations became a game-changer for their relationship. She started with texts, having complete, if condensed, conversations about everything from grades to family dynamics. Once Aidan warmed up to the pattern and predictability of these text exchanges with his mom, and once he trusted they would be nonjudgmental, succinct, and balanced, he opened up to talking with her about more than what's for dinner when they were in the same room.

Aidan is now a high school sophomore, and Karen feels the years of groundwork she put into developing their conversation skills have paid off. "Aidan talks to me about so much now. I hear a lot about what his friends are going through. It's nice to know he trusts me enough to tell me." This trust bodes well for Aidan being able to talk with Karen about more than what's going on in other people's lives. Should Aidan find *himself* in a situation where he needs the insight of an adult, he'll likely feel his mom has proven her ability to be reasonable, and he'll feel comfortable talking with her about his own circumstances.

A BRIEF Model for Conversations

Remember the book *1-2-3 Magic*? It changed our lives because it used a wide variety of crazy-making scenarios your toddler could put you in, then layered a simple counting model over every one to get your child to listen to you. It seems almost impossible that an entire book could be written on how to count to three before instituting a consequence for not following directions, but seeing the model applied to all the scenarios we faced on a daily basis ("No, you can't have that candy bar," "I said shoes on," "Stop touching your brother") showed us how the most patience-thinning parenting challenges could be tackled with a consistent, easy solution.

In the same way, talking to a tween about pornography, vaping, privilege, or social exclusion doesn't require reinventing the wheel every time. Instead, it only requires remembering a simple acronym, a guiding principle for talking with young people that I call "BRIEF." B stands for *begin* peacefully; R is for *relate*; I triggers the *interview* part of the conversation; E reminds you to *echo* what you're hearing; and F is the point at which you can give *feedback*. Applying this structure to the conversation, though the topics are vastly different, will provide some relief to those of us who don't know where to begin—or even end—with such tough topics.

I should also mention something we parents tend to forget when talking with tweens. A conversation is quite different from a lecture, and requires willing participation from two or more people to make it work. You can force a lecture, but not a conversation. This model I use to foster meaningful discussion is meant to break down barriers and encourage participation, increasingly more so with time, trust, and experience. For that

> A conversation is quite different from a lecture, and requires willing participation from two or more people to make it work.

reason, you might read some of the sample conversations in this book and think they seem a little too easy, or that there isn't enough pushback from the kid. That's on purpose. If a kid is pushing back, it's not the time for a good conversation.

Let's take a look at how the BRIEF model works using a scenario in which a parent discovers their tween has been keeping bad grades a secret.

BEGIN Peacefully

I recently asked my online parenting group to tell me what they felt was the hardest part about talking to a middle schooler in regard to something important. The results were nearly unanimous: getting started! A tween is likely to shut you down right away, blow you off, agree with you quickly just to get the conversation over with, or just not understand where you're coming from.

Parents are often so worried about how their kid will react, they talk themselves out of bringing up difficult topics, or they do the opposite and dive right in without a plan. In light of this, I always advise parents to begin things peacefully. In practice, this means begin with an unemotional observation. If, for instance, you need to have a tough conversation with your child about the fact that you know he's been hiding his bad grades, you could start with that unemotional observation: "So, it looks like report cards came out—I saw your grades weren't as we expected."

Another peaceful way to get things started might be to ask if your kid can explain things to you: "Your grades are different from what I expected. Are they what you expected? Is there anything you need to tell me?"

Making a scheduling request so your kid doesn't feel caught off guard is also a peaceful way in: "Report cards came out today and I think we should debrief. Is before or after dinner better for you?"

A common pushback I often hear from parents amounts to "I'm the parent. I shouldn't have to pander to my kids." It's true that there will be times when you can and should be direct and in charge, but it doesn't make for a pleasant start to *every* conversation. The less you use a direct approach, the more likely your kids will straighten up, put down the phone, and take you seriously when you do. Save it for when you need it to count most. An indirect approach to these conversations gives you a better chance of teasing out some initial words when your kid feels the stakes are low, and then, once the silence is broken with a few words, it will be easy to dial up the conversation momentum, as opposed to starting at full speed.

So, start peacefully and then be quiet and wait for your child to fill the space.

RELATE to Your Kid

Internet trolls aside, no one likes getting into a conversation that begins antagonistically. Tweens have a propensity toward defensiveness, and most can't yet read facial expressions or interpret tone of voice well, so they often presume you're angry, even when you're not. To get past this, start with the simplest of peace offerings: relating to your child's experience or perspective, even if it's a stretch for you.

In the case of your child hiding bad grades from you, the words *lying, integrity, laziness,* and *you're grounded* may very likely be on the tip of your tongue. Instead, *breathe.* Your child, smart enough to keep up the deception, was also smart enough to know the jig was up when report cards came out and needed to be signed. They now likely feel scared, anxious, and ashamed. Don't worry about whether they deserve your empathy when they clearly deceived you. Consider the endgame. It's your job to teach them how to do better, and no one learns best when they are scared and anxious and ashamed.

Here are some ways you can relate to your child so they will listen to the rest of the conversation:

- "It's tough when you finally have to be honest, but I find it always feels better to stop hiding things from people who want to help us."

- "This is hard. I'm sure you feel a bunch of emotions right now. Don't worry. Together we can figure out where to go from here."

- "I remember times when my grades dipped and it felt awful to get behind. It will take some hard work to pull your grades back up, but with focus and support you can do it."

INTERVIEW to Collect Data

As they say, there are three versions of every story: yours, mine, and the truth. It's time to get a better understanding of your kid's version of the truth, and they will be more likely to be honest with you because you've established yourself as an ally, or at least an empathetic authority figure. This is where you get to ask your burning questions. This is not the time to try to catch your kid in a lie or teach them a lesson. Consider this a neutral fact-finding mission. Play the part of a good, if slightly detached, district attorney who doesn't have a lot riding on this case, but still needs to gather information from all sides.

- "At what point did you realize your grades were slipping?"
- "What do you think were the biggest reasons for the slip?"
- "Did you consider talking with me about it?"
- "What did you think would happen when I got the report card?"

ECHO What You're Hearing

Every step in the BRIEF model prepares you for the next, all leading up to the final and most important step when you give feedback, but anyone who's tried to start a conversation with feedback knows it usually doesn't go well. For this reason, the Echo step is part validation, helping to pry open your kid's mind to hearing your suggestions (or requirements) in the next stage, and part comprehension check, making sure you've got the facts straight at this point. Echoing might sound like this:

- Start with "It sounds like" or "I'm hearing": "It sounds like you had an idea your grades were slipping, but felt like you could handle it on your own."

- Summarize key facts: "Okay, so you thought your grades were still on track and this comes as a surprise to you, too."

- Use their words in a question: "Am I right that you feel like this is mostly the teacher's fault?"

FEEDBACK

This is the moment you've been waiting for. The Feedback step is where you get to finally offer suggestions, guidance, or make new rules if you need a firmer resolution. I find tweens respond best to feedback when you ask if they're open to it; however, there may be times when you can't wait for your kid to invite your guidance and you have to put strong boundaries in place. In that case, don't ask. Just clearly state the rules.

Feedback should relate directly to the problem you've uncovered through interviewing and echoing. Don't pile on other problems you've been having with the child and escalate the argument to "Well, it's not just your grades, but your room is a mess, you're mean to your sister, disrespectful to me . . ." When you're mad at someone, it's tempting to intensify an argument by including as many examples as possible to illustrate they are Wrong and you are Right, but it's unfair and counterproductive.

In the scenario we've been working through, let's say you discovered during the interview that your child realized their grades were slipping, thought they could handle it themselves, then despite watching math tutorials online, couldn't correct it, panicked, and buried the problem. Feedback might sound like this:

- Summarize the key downfall and state how to avoid it next time: "I appreciate you wanting to handle this yourself, but asking for help sooner is going to get you better results. Next time, I expect you to let me know right away when your grades are slipping, so we can come up with a plan for you to bring them up before it starts dog piling. Think of this like a basketball game. It's so much harder to come back from a huge deficit in the fourth quarter than to change your play early in the game."

- If you can, you might start by asking if your kid is ready for feedback then follow up with guidance: "Are you open to hearing what I think?" Pause. "Okay, we need to put all our focus on how to get you out of this situation. Let's make a plan together. Tell me what you think needs to happen first and then I'll give you my thoughts."

- If you feel the consequence needs to be fast and firm: "You might have been trying to avoid a bigger punishment by keeping this a secret for so long, but now you find yourself in a position where your free time will have to be spent on bringing up your grades. Had you addressed this sooner, you might have gotten off with a weekend of catch-up work. Now we're looking at several weekends of extra work and tutoring. Until we see you have made up all missing work and your grades reflect more effort, you will stay in every weekend and do all your work at the kitchen table where I can monitor you."

Note: Through the first few steps you should have established a rapport to put your kid at ease, and as they warm up to this method, they may even become surprisingly talkative. Long conversations are great, but I do love that this acronym spells *brief*. It's always better to get in and out—having several shorter conversations on a topic—than it is to talk for so long your kid tunes you out or cuts you off when you bring up the same subject a week later because they're afraid of a lecture.

When you're done, quickly change the subject. "Anyway, that's something to think about. So, what's your afternoon look like?" Or "All right, sounds like we've covered this. Thanks for talking with me. Hey, did you see the trailer for the new Marvel movie is out?"

The more you practice BRIEF conversations, the more you'll find your kids opening up and trusting that they can talk with you about anything.

Why the Urgency to Have These Conversations Before Age Fourteen?

One of the biggest shifts in parenting over the last decade is the way in which fear of technology has invaded parent decision making. Worried about pedophiles, mean kids, low self-esteem, and atrophied social skills, we parents frequently fall into playing defense, instead of developing a strong parenting offense. We tend to fear the foreign space in which our kids are growing up and conflate our ability to constantly monitor them with their ability to protect themselves. Of course, monitoring and protecting aren't the same thing. If you're waiting to catch your kid before they fall down a hole, you're missing countless opportunities to talk about when unexpected new holes might appear and how to walk around them. Installing the latest spyware doesn't keep your kid safe. It just alerts you when they've messed up. The truth is that old-fashioned conversations have never been more important than in this digital age.

> We should be thinking of fourteen as the new eighteen. Starting [these conversations] earlier gives parents time to teach instead of cram.

Time has a tendency to get away from you when you're raising kids. One minute they're eight, and the next they're graduating from high school. Setting an intention to start these fourteen conversations by age fourteen is a way of getting a foothold on time and fitting in the important talks you need to have with your child. These conversations can't wait. Further, we should be thinking of fourteen as the new eighteen. Parents commonly start to panic midway through senior year and try to cram their kids full of life lessons on safety, independence, responsibility, *on top of* how to do laundry without shrinking all their favorite clothes. Meanwhile, toward the end of high school teens are often consumed with college applications and then sliding into a senior slump. Starting earlier gives parents time to teach instead of cram.

But the most important case for having these conversations by age fourteen has to do with our kids' developing brains. Research shows us that for boys, fourteen is the most dangerous age of a young man's life. A study of males ages nine to thirty-five, found that the age at which risk taking is the highest is 14.38. A similar study has not been done on females, but since we know that girls enter puberty earlier than boys, we might wonder if the same brain activity that causes increased impulsivity and risk taking in boys strikes girls earlier as well. Additionally, the adolescent brain begins to prune away information it deems unnecessary, starting around the age of eleven. It decides what to trim based on what it is and is not using. This means you've got to start practicing ways to have balanced, thoughtful, rational conversations early and often so that skill gets cemented in your child's brain. Finally, we know that throughout adolescence, kids begin to pull away from their parents to begin the arduous process of forming an adult identity of their own. The few years before high school is the sweet spot before they pull too far away, when they still are willing to hear your point of view.

This places middle school as the prime time to begin having BRIEF, important, and repeated conversations about ways to make good choices in a variety of circumstances. Ready? *¡Vámos! Allons y! Challo! Auf Jetzt!*

Let's learn a new language!

2

Your New Bag of Tricks

Talking with a middle schooler is different from talking with a person of any other age. Parents are often left baffled by their kids' reactions of anger, irritation, or dismissal at even innocent attempts to ask about their day. It's not entirely your kid's fault. Tweens naturally begin pulling away at this age, and recognizing how to work with, instead of straining against, this tendency is a key part of having better communication. After fourteen years of working with kids in early adolescence, I've collected a bag of tricks that will be total game-changers in your parent/child conversations at home, and now I'm handing the bag to you. These techniques aren't specific to any topic, so you can begin practicing these in all your conversations with your tween.

Nine Ways to Improve All Conversations with Your Tween or Young Teen

1. Become an assistant manager. When kids start middle school, most parents think it's best to tighten the reins, since early adolescence exposes kids to a much bigger world of potential danger. It's true your kid will have experiences that will scare, shock, and even offend you, but resist the urge to clamp down too quickly.

It would be fantastic if your child would respond to their new environment with a sense of caution, a healthy dose of critical analysis, the right balance of curiosity and skepticism, and a clearheaded sense of self. Alas, growing up is the process of *developing* these skills. Without the opportunity to practice, kids won't ever learn how.

Your child's brain, at around age eleven, begins to make the fundamental changes it needs to become an adult brain, but it takes a good ten to fourteen years thereafter to solidify these changes. Patience is key for both of you. During this time, the prefrontal cortex—responsible for critical thinking, problem solving, reading facial expressions, and analyzing risk, among other things—takes a break. I tell kids this period is like when the manager of your favorite store takes a lunch break and goes to the back of the store to eat a sub, except this lunch break takes ten long years. The manager is still on site, but they're not paying close attention. This leaves the store vulnerable to people stealing from it, vandalizing it, or otherwise doing permanent damage to it.

When the manager (the prefrontal cortex) takes a break, the emotional center of the brain (the amygdala) jumps up and down and waves its arms, shouting "Pick me! Pick me!" at the chance to step up and be in charge. The problem here is that the amygdala is impulsive, loves trying new things, gets a huge kick out of taking risks, thrives on a range of *intense* emotions, and thinks it would be super exciting to be the decision maker for once. We've all worked for a manager like this before. Sometimes it's fun. But mostly, it's unpredictable, scary, and a little bit too close to the edge of danger to be comfortable.

What does this store need when the manager is off duty?

The answer is, a good assistant manager. Emphasis on *assistant;* it's not the assistant's job to be the boss. The assistant manager is there to support the manager, be an extra set of eyes and ears, and offer a helping pair of hands as needed. The loyal assistant is always willing to be supportive, but has no interest in taking over.

Take a moment now to close your eyes and recall the worst manager you ever had. How would you describe them? The description I get from the parents I regularly talk with goes something like this:

- too controlling
- bad communicator (inconsistent, unclear, unfocused)
- distant
- disrespectful of work-life balance, intrusive
- unable to provide a clear track for advancement
- unwilling to let employees correct their own mistakes
- overly emotional
- prone to favoritism

The hands-down most popular answer is:

- micromanager

Ask a middle schooler what rubs them the wrong way about their parents, and you'd likely end up with the same list of characteristics. In all conversations with your middle schooler, keep in mind that you are an extra set of eyes and ears and a pair of helping hands, but that your child needs to practice increased responsibility and decision making, in order to become a great manager. You will do your best to inform their decision making, values, and character, but ultimately you're . . . just an assistant. This is how you might sound in your new role:

- "How can I support you?"
- "What do you need to be successful with this?"
- "I'm here to listen while you think this through."
- "Would you like some feedback on this?"
- "Can I help you talk through your options?"

2. Put on a "Botox brow." In all my years working with parents of middle schoolers, this is the one adjustment parents tell me most often has made the biggest difference in their relationship with their child. This technique is based on research out of McLean Hospital, one of Harvard's teaching hospitals, where Dr. Deborah Yurgelun-Todd, director of neuropsychology and cognitive neuroimaging, did a small, albeit mighty, study on reading facial expressions.

First, Yurgelun-Todd put adults into an MRI and showed them pho-tos of people's faces. She then asked the participants to identify what the people in the photos were feeling, simply by looking at their faces. In her experiment, adults could correctly identify people's basic emotions by "reading their faces" 100 percent of the time. Yurgelun-Todd then repeated the experiment with teens. They could only identify emotions accurately 50 percent of the time. The difference? The MRI showed that adults use their prefrontal cortex to read facial expressions, whereas teens use their amygdala, the part of the brain that houses emotions and helps decide how to respond to them: for instance, by triggering fight, flight, or freeze responses to fear. The shift to using the prefrontal cortex to inter-pret facial expressions doesn't happen until the early to midtwenties.

Practically speaking, what does this mean?

Because tweens and teens can't accurately read facial expressions, they're forced to make assumptions about what others are feeling. Most often, they assume anger when they see a wrinkled brow. Personally speaking, I know I wrinkle my brow for a multitude of reasons when lis-tening to my kids. Sometimes it's my way of trying to show that I'm pay-ing close attention to what they're saying. Sometimes it's because they're telling me a story, and while I'm listening I'm multitasking and trying not to forget about that work e-mail I've already forgotten to send twice. Sometimes it's my way of showing empathy. Sometimes it's just my face being forty-eight years old. No matter my intention, my kids see my wrin-kled brow as anger.

Consider a scenario in which your kid comes through the back door after school, dumps their backpack on the floor, and heads to the TV room. You stop them, eager to hear about their day. "Welcome home! Hey, how did that math test go today?" (You mentally pat yourself on the back for remembering the test was today!)

"Ughhhh! We haven't even gotten our grades yet! Why are you so mad?!"

Hmm. Not the response you expected or deserved. What probably happened is this: When your child looked up, whether you realized it or not, your brow was slightly furrowed. Consider: They've just come from seven hours of sensory overload and worrying about the scrutiny of their peers, so your child is doubtless exhausted. Upon seeing your facial ex-pression, they immediately jumped to the conclusion that your question was rooted in anger or judgment. Variations of this "What the heck did I do? I just asked a question?" scenario play out daily in the families I work with across the country.

Tween emotions are complicated, but this situation is actually easy to avoid.

Begin to develop what I call a "Botox brow." Before you turn to talk with your middle schooler, and especially at that moment your kid catches you off guard with surprising or upsetting news, I advise parents: Pretend you are a celebrity on a late-night talk show who has been so overly Botoxed you can't move your forehead at all. You will feel like a robot. A Stepford Parent. If you do, you're doing it right. If you feel like a deer in the headlights, you're doing it wrong. You want to look emotionless, not shocked.

You may feel it's unkind to convey a lack of emotion, but your tween will see this as freeing—you're not judging them at all. The more you practice Botox brow, the more your tween will open up to you, knowing that you provide a safe, neutral zone for talking things out.

There are two other good reasons to adopt a neutral face when talking to your tween. The first is so they don't misinterpret any of your emotions as anger *when you aren't actually angry*. I'm not suggesting you shouldn't feel or model a full range of healthy emotions, including anger over some things, when it's appropriate. This technique is intended to help you avoid miscommunication, not rob you of your humanity. The second reason is to create an opening for your child to listen to you. When you are red-faced and ranting, your child is quick to tune you out, claiming you're "overreacting." If you can talk with a neutral face, your kid has no reason to stop listening.

3. Master the art of playing dumb. There is a post that gets circulated on social media from time to time of a fake handbill calling all teenagers to:

> *"Act now! Tired of being harassed by your stupid parents? Move out, get a job, pay your own bills while you still know everything!"*

It's funny 'cause it's true. It's also true that while teens lack our experience or knowledge, they do have some things we don't: fresh eyes, unending optimism, and faith in their abilities.

You may be put off by adolescent naïveté toward solving the global problems we adults have created. "The people running the government are so dumb. They can print more money if people don't have enough. How have you guys not thought of this?" Or by adolescent bravado that consistently overestimates their levels of ability and expertise. Tell me, do your kids think they could crush the American Ninja Warrior course? Tomorrow? With no training?

When your tween knows everything, play dumb and ask questions, rather than lawyering up and mounting evidence to prove they're wrong. Get curious. Ask probing questions: How would that work? What would that look like? Could anything go wrong? How would that feel? What's the best-case scenario? What's the worst? "How exactly would you scale that six-foot-wide gap on the Ninja obstacle course when your wingspan is only five feet? How do you propose you make up six inches on either side?"

4. Appear disinterested. You may remember when your child was little that the moment you sat down with a hot cup of coffee, picked up a book, or started chatting with a friend . . . your kid needed a snack. Middle schoolers are similarly drawn to you when you are least available. For this reason, I suggest appearing less interested when you want to talk more.

Scenario A:

Me: *Sooooo . . . [patting the space next to me on the couch] how did your project go? Tell me everything!*
Kid: *I don't feel like talking now. I'm too tired.*

Scenario B:

Me: *Oh, hey! I want to hear all about how your project went over in class, but just not now. I've got to send a few e-mails first—*
Kid: *Wait! Let me just tell you first before you do that.*

This only works some of the time, but when it does, it's thrilling, because you feel like you've run the tiniest *Ocean's Eleven* grift and gotten away with it.

5. Avoid the ambush. Tweens juggle a lot during their school day—from what assignment is due to which teacher wants what and when to where to sit at lunch that will have the least (or greatest) social ramifications. A day in the life of a middle schooler is filled with decision trees. It's no surprise that when your kid gets home they need to decompress. This is why your tween might act as if you've ambushed that plan when you ask them about their day the second they walk in the door.

To get the most out of even casual conversations, try asking your child if you can catch up with them at a later, specified time. Even better, give them a choice of times. "I'm sure you want to relax for a while now. I'd love to hear about your day and make sure you're staying on track with your work. Can we talk after dinner for ten minutes about what you have going on, or even over breakfast if you're extra tired today? Which do you prefer?"

Not only does this approach give your child the necessary time to decompress, it respects their sense of authority over their own schedule—something a tween gets little of these days—and it piggybacks onto the previous tool of appearing disinterested. The less thirsty you are for information, the less your kid will resist talking to you.

6. Take your time. Your tween's brain thrives on excitement, and when you escalate the emotions at home by yelling, crying, or pleading, they get a jolt of satisfaction (as well as a pretty convenient distraction from focusing on your point!) in that part of their brain. When you inevitably find yourself in conflict with your tween, know that one of your best tools is buying time. Unlike little kids, middle schoolers don't need an immediate response from you to be able to learn from what's happened. In fact, because they are so impulsive, teaching them how to slow down their reactions is beneficial.

For example, if your tween snaps at you for not packing the right kind of sandwich in their lunch, you might say something like, "Hmm, I'm not even sure how to respond to that. I'll get back to you in a few hours once I've had time to think." The idea that you would not snap back, and that you would go off to consider your next move, should frighten your kid right out of their selfish stupor. You may find them apologizing and pleading with you to forgive them. Depending on how often this kind of thing happens, you might decide to accept the apology right away, or still take some time to think. If you're in a situation that requires a consequence and you want to emphasize the gravity of the situation, you can add, "I'm going to give a lot of thought to the consequence. I will get back to you." Nothing is as effective at getting your child to slow down and think than a dramatic pause before delivering a verdict.

7. Multitask. Perhaps because tweens aren't great at reading facial expressions, and/or because they feel extra emotional, and therefore vulnerable, when talking about certain subjects, they seem to be more open to conversations when they can't see your face. Parents often say their best conversations happen in the car, at least before cell phones and headphones took over this space. In fact, if you haven't already established your phone rules, you might consider making the car a phone-free zone to encourage better talks. Whether riding in the car, playing video games, biking, or cooking together, kids tend to open up when they multitask. Shaking things up keeps your kid on their toes, so from time to time, you might ask your kid to sit across from you in the den, like 1950s TV dad Ward Cleaver used to do on *Leave It to Beaver*. But generally speaking, an eye-to-eye conversation will get you some head nods and one-word answers at best. Boys especially seem to respond better when they are busy with an activity, so put something in their hands or get moving when you feel like talking. There's a reason Andy Griffith had more success teaching life lessons at the fishing hole than Ward did in his study.

8. Don't talk at all. Some kids respond better to writing than listening. Perhaps they are not auditory learners. Or they feel less exposed when they can think through their answers instead of having to come up with something on the spot. Or they worry about you misinterpreting each other. Or they like to cuddle up in their beds to think about tough topics. For a multitude of valid reasons, some kids prefer texts, or letters, or journals as a way of communicating. If this is your kid, you can still have great conversations without talking. Some families I work with trade a spiral notebook back and forth with their kids where they can ask questions from "What movie do you want to see next?" to "How are things going with ___?" Others use technology to their advantage to maintain funny and informative text chats.

9. Designate a proxy. Finally, you don't have to be the one to have all these conversations with your tween. It takes a village, so start deputizing yours. Ask a couple of trusted friends if they will step in when an opportunity arises to cover important topics. Let your child know that if they ever want to talk, you're available, as well as Aunt Cathy and your best friend, Joe, who've said their doors are always open, too. One of my best friends texted both of my kids when they first got their phones: "Hey! This is Sylvie! Put my number in your phone right now and if you ever find yourself somewhere and you don't like what's going on, text me and I'll come get you—no questions asked!" This is a great way for your kid to develop that relationship, build trust, and have an added safety net.

In this chapter, I've painted with a broad brush when it comes to communicating with tweens, but I don't want to oversimplify the nuances and unique qualities of your kids. You may have a child who loves when you are effusive, wants to have formal sit-down conversations, and happily spills all the details of their day. Or one who has such lockjaw you fear the only way you'll know what's happening in their life is if it's bad enough to end up on the news. Though the study of adolescent development provides us with trends we can watch for, you know your child best. Choose and tweak the tools that best suit your kid's personality. (Even, and especially, more than those that best suit yours.) And remember, the kid you are talking with today will want and need different approaches from that same kid you'll be talking with in a month, just as one sibling will need a different approach from another. You must become a communication yogi during these years. Flexibility and open-mindedness will be key to keeping the conversation going through all these changes.

3

Conversation Crashers

In my college-level education classes, the professors drilled into us time and again that to teach a new concept the instructor must communicate both the right way and the wrong way of doing something, so that the student has guardrails on either side of their experience. You probably do this quite naturally when you're teaching your child a tactile new skill. "Hold the knife like this when you're cutting, not like this." Or "Choke up on the bat when you're waiting for the pitch. Don't hold it way down here." We instinctively give those right and wrong ways when using physical demonstrations, but we often omit this crucial step when explaining new ideas that are more cerebral, even though it's still an important part of the learning process.

In this chapter, I'll point out ways adults often derail their conversations with tweens, so that you can keep in mind not just how to have better conversations, but what makes conversations worse, too. In part 2 of this book, you can expect to find specific approaches and phrases to avoid for each topic, but for now, let's begin to train your ear to some more general, common ways to sabotage your best intentions.

Twelve Conversation Crashers That Apply to All Topics

1. Don't jump in too quickly. Most parents fret about how their kids will respond to certain topics, so they cannonball into a conversation as if jumping into a cold pool, hoping to get the hard part over with and *then* acclimate. But as soon as you make a big splash, your kid hops out and races for the snack bar. Instead of *jumping* right in, dip your toe in the water first. Give yourself and your kid time to get on the same page, or, at least, in the same mood to approach a conversation, before broaching a sensitive subject. Imagine that you're sitting side by side at the edge of the pool with your younger, nervous child and you're trying to convince them to get in. How would you do that? Laughter? Encouragement? Distraction? Support? Those same tools will serve you well here.

2. Don't make assumptions about how your kid feels, has felt, or will feel. Tweens crave autonomy and since emotions are personal and private, they take it as an affront when you presume how they feel. Saying, "You'll wish you'd done this differently when you're older" gives a kid nowhere to go other than a) to acquiesce, or b) to debate with you. Spoiler: By their early tweens, most kids are ready for a debate, so buckle up. The truth is, kids don't know how they will feel about things when they're adults. It's not entirely fair to say *you* know how they'll feel, and if there's one thing a tween can't stand (LOL there are a million), it's when adults claim to know them better than they know themselves. Instead of assuming, start with curiosity. Ask genuine questions and listen intently to their point of view.

3. Don't be vague. Tweens like specificity. For one thing, vague language is open to interpretation, which often leads to misunderstanding, and that can make anyone feel misled or foolish. For another, tweens are sensitive, but you can avoid the worry of having to tiptoe around their feelings, hoping to outmaneuver thin-skinned responses to your attempts to talk, by leaning into facts and numbers instead of opinions and emotions. To do this, you may need to dig up some data before you plunge into a topic. For example, instead of saying, "I heard vaping has become rampant in middle school and it's totally out of control. That's so scary!" you should talk in facts, not emotions. "I read the number of kids in middle school who have tried vaping has gone up by 48 percent. Does that seem accurate to you?"

Along these lines, once your kid goes to middle school, it's time to leave behind generalities when explaining anything to do with their body and its functions, including all aspects of puberty and healthy sexuality. Any attempt to ease awkwardness by being discreet about sex or anatomy will be at best, unhelpful, and at worst, unsafe. Plus, if your child doesn't see you as an accurate source of information, they'll stop coming to you. Hello Google.

4. Don't talk in absolutes. In contrast to being too vague, sometimes parents rely on absolutes, words that have no wiggle room, to convey the magnitude of a thought. We tend to speak this way when we have a deep desire to be taken seriously, but statements that contain absolutes often sound desperate. "You never listen!" is an offensive accusation, even if it's meant to convey, "I need to feel heard." Words like *everyone, only, entirely, exactly, always*, and *never* can be inflammatory because they usually aren't true. When a kid senses you're exaggerating to make a point, they lose trust this will be a conversation in which they'll be treated fairly. End of conversation.

5. Don't be indirect about what you need. So often, we hint at our needs without being direct. Perhaps we don't feel entitled to having our needs met. Or we weren't raised to advocate for ourselves. Or it somehow feels impolite or selfish to ask outright for what we want. Consider this statement: "You spend all your free time with friends and no time with the family anymore." What is your point? What do you want out of this? Again, don't leave the conversation open to interpretation. Rather than making an accusation, ask for what you want. "Can we spend some time together this week? I miss you! If you have a free hour on Saturday, I'd love to throw the ball with you outside or whatever sounds fun."

6. Don't make threats. How many times have you witnessed a desperate parent lob empty threats at an uncooperative kid? "If you don't STOP

IT, I'm going to pack up all our stuff and we are leaving the pool *immedi-ately!*" The parent's hope is that if the threat is as dramatic as possible, the kid will shape up—and fast! Meanwhile, you're eavesdropping with the clairvoyant knowledge that dragging a wet, wild, and unpredictable child away from the fun, all while balancing a cooler, beach bag, towels, and foam noodles, is never, ever going to happen.

The kid knows it, too. Empty threats teach a kid they can keep pushing your limits while ignoring your consequences. Empty threats are my pet peeve, but I'm not a fan of loaded threats either, and that's because a threat is hostile, angry, and retaliatory. A clearly stated outcome, on the other hand, is just a fact. Maybe it's a matter of personal style, but I always thought an unblinking pause, followed by a serious whisper, to be far more effective than a loud yell. [Whispers] "Listen to me. I've asked you to stop and you haven't. If you kick your brother again, you and I will sit side by side on these chairs for the next thirty minutes while I read my book and you do nothing." Not empty, not punishing the parent, and not even angry. Just serious as can be.

While I'm talking about threats, I should mention a specific threat parents tell me they sometimes pull out during desperate times that causes me great concern: the threat of therapy. "If you don't stop this be-havior, you will have to go see a therapist!" Threatening therapy is no dif-ferent from threatening your child with an annual physical or trip to the dentist. Positioning any health care as a punishment is extremely dan-gerous.

7. Don't be passive-aggressive. This one has been my personal Achilles' heel. If, like me, you sometimes struggle with feeling underap-preciated, you may find yourself, in a moment of weakness, lashing out with a passive-aggressive comment. When I'm able to reflect with clar-ity, I see that this is my way of acting like a victim, which I guess I hope will force others to become my helpers. (Boy, is that backward.) But isn't self-awareness an amazing thing? Gratitude is important to me, and when I feel my loved ones don't value my efforts, my instinct is sometimes to act hurt so they will feel guilty and *then* be moved to appreciate me. This is a terrible instinct and I've learned not to indulge it. I am far more likely to get what I need by asking for it, rather than trying to orchestrate a situation that only confuses and alienates the people who care about me.

Here are some common passive-aggressive comments we, as parents, would do well to avoid:

"Lighten up."

Or any version of this, which insinuates someone can't take a joke. If it's a good joke made with good intentions, people will laugh. If not, the onus is on the joke teller to correct their approach, not the recipient to be less sensitive.

"Fine."

As in, "Fine, do what you want." Or "No I'm FINE." Neither of these *sound* fine. People shouldn't have to guess how you feel. If you're not comfortable saying how you feel, it's okay to say, "I'm not sure how I feel right now. I need some time to think about it." You can also practice being more honest about how you feel by starting a journal or keeping a notes app on your phone to explore and track your real reactions.

"Don't overreact."

Making someone feel out of control or making them feel bad for having an emotional reaction is unfair. It's true, when measured against an adult emotional scale, tweens do overact sometimes. If you use a tween emotional scale, though, it's probably not an overreaction. Reactions are personal. If you don't want to indulge your tween's emotional responses, you might say, "It sounds like you're very upset and I'm guessing that's uncomfortable. I hate it when I feel that way, too. I recommend you take twenty minutes to (journal, cry, run, shower, be alone) and then come down, and I will have a cup of tea and a listening ear waiting."

"Whatever you want."

Caution. Tweens are quite literal. Say what you mean or prepare to be surprised! Once, my parents were so frustrated by my inability to stick to a curfew they threw their hands in the air and exclaimed, "Fine, we'll just leave it to you. You decide when is a reasonable time to come home then." They thought I'd be happy to be treated like an adult and would therefore self-correct. You know where this story is going, right? I believe I was grounded shortly after arriving home at 2:00 a.m. the following Saturday night.

"You must have missed my point."
I put this one last because it burns my biscuits. I read it from time to time on Internet threads from politics to parenting, but the kids I work with also tell me some of their teachers express a similar sentiment with "I've already explained this and I won't repeat myself." These kinds of comments assume you've made your point perfectly clear, and the listener wasn't paying close enough attention, or wasn't smart enough to catch on. The trouble is, we don't all process or comprehend information in the same way. What seems perfectly clear to you may be foggy to someone else—even if you have explained it well. Your explanation, though accurate, still may not resonate.

If it's your goal to increase comprehension, then you should strive to be as flexible as possible when explaining your rationale. Haven't we all had the miserable experience of calling customer service to have someone read from a script to "explain" something that makes no sense? Yet the service agent keeps repeating the same line?

8. Don't be afraid to set boundaries. Typically, I want you to head into these topics with an open mind as to where they might take you. Having said that, there will be times when what you say is not up for debate. Not all situations require a heartfelt exploration of motives, circumstances, and outcomes. Sometimes your words need to function like a safety gate. Use the BRIEF model when you want to talk with your child in a way that supports better decision making. But please, do not use the BRIEF model when you need to move swiftly and provide clear boundaries, expectations, or consequences. If your child is in danger emotionally or physically, it's time to be the safety gate. If that's the case, let your kid know at the outset what to expect. "This is not a conversation where we can explore this topic, although I'd like to do that later with you when I've had some time to think. Right now, I just need to give you some information to control the damage from getting worse and/or to keep you safe."

9. Don't be tricked into proving yourself. Tweens like to drag some conversations out simply for the thrill of the debate. At around age eleven, your child's brain makes a shift from thinking only in concrete ways, to beginning to entertain hypotheticals. This makes middle schoolers natural debaters, albeit pretty awful ones. When your child disagrees with you, they tend to either a) reach an illogical conclusion first and then cram a bunch of ill-fitting evidence in later to support their decision, or b) go on the attack in an attempt to make you defend your position. When you fall back on your heels, they pick up the push and you feel increasingly backed into a corner. In your desire to get your tween to *just stop badgering you*, you might keep trying to find that one piece of "proof" that will get them to believe your side of the argument. Don't fall for these tactics. Instead of trying to prove that 9:00 p.m. actually is a reasonable bedtime, you can simply say, "I understand you are frustrated and you'd like a different bedtime. I'm sorry you're upset. Bedtime is not going to be moved later. If there is anything I can do to make the hours before bedtime easier, please let me know." Case closed.

10. Don't make yourself the center of the story. Middle schoolers are notoriously self-centered, but it's for good reason. One of the key steps in a young person's journey to becoming independent (now is a good time to remind yourself that's the goal!) is figuring out who they are *apart* from their parents. The more a parent pushes to stay at the center of their child's story, the more a tween is likely to push harder to separate. Your instinct may be to pull your child closer when they start to pull away in middle school (to keep them safe! to make them value family!) but the best way to help kids grow safely and stay connected is to give them space to explore and a safe place to return. When you prioritize your role in your child's story it feels unnatural to them. For example, if your child confides in you that someone was mean to them at school and you reply, "Oh, it hurts me when people hurt you" or "I hurt when you hurt," you've made yourself the co-lead character. Your intention is to be empathetic, but kids don't like it when their parents appear in their social scene. You can express empathy by saying something like "That sounds painful. Is there anything I can do to help?" Just listening is also an excellent way to show support.

11. Don't use hyperbole. Hyperbole is an exaggeration or overstatement, and is as crucial to avoid as the bubonic plague. Hyperbole sneaks into conversations when parents want to give a point *extra* weight. Unfortunately, exaggeration has the opposite effect, making the situation seem less believable. Most often, I hear hyperbole when parents compare their children's childhoods to their own. We're all familiar with our own grandparents having to walk both ways uphill to school in the snow, yes? The modern equivalent of this is, "Well, I grew up without social media and *somehow* I survived. You will, too." If you're trying to have a serious conversation about what you may or may not allow when it comes to social media, you've just put the final nail in the conversation coffin. Of course (OF COURSE) kids can also survive without social media as their parents did. Survival, though, is a low bar for raising kids.

Sometimes parents say this kind of thing as though it will add some humor or levity to the situation, although I think that's a generous assessment. At its core, I believe comments like this are meant to be slight digs. The word *somehow* in the above example makes it sound like the kid is too dumb to realize that people can literally still live without social media. It diminishes the kid's real feelings about wanting to fit in, have fun, and communicate with peers. You may not agree social media helps with any of these things, but your kid's feelings are nonetheless true for them. Finally, it puts blame on the child for things outside of their control (the parent's childhood, or the timing of when Instagram was invented) and the whole thing lands on a self-centered "Why would you possibly need anything I didn't have?" message. Beware the backfire of hyperbole.

12. Don't drag it out. What's more important? Getting the final word, clarifying and nailing your point, or leaving a conversation when someone can stomach coming back to you if they have a question, or further thought, later? We all know that person who overexplains things and it leaves us firmly vowing to never ask them another question. Insisting on having the final word is likewise alienating to the person you hope will listen to you! If you've got just one more thing to say, you might try this approach: "I have a feeling we will both think of a few more things to say on the subject. Why don't we take a little break and enjoy some relaxation time and we can circle back in a couple days?" Then jot that thought down somewhere so you don't forget it.

This is a lot to take in, so don't expect immediate fluency. Indeed, learning how to speak a new language is inherently awkward and embarrassing, not to mention it can make you feel lost in translation when you start communicating with a native speaker. You'll get there. It just takes time and practice. As you learn to speak your adolescent's language, don't dwell on the conversations that crashed. There will be days when you try and it just doesn't work. Keep trying. Eventually, you'll find yourself speaking easily together.

PART 2

The Fourteen Conversations

Talking About Your Parent–Child Relationship

The foundation of having better conversations is earning trust and building rapport. In this chapter, you'll learn how to establish curiosity in your tween without risking the appearance of neediness, how to determine the right amount to share from your own life without crossing into oversharing, what your tween really wants to know from your perspective, and how to coax private kids into opening up more.

Remember when your toddler would climb onto your lap, softly cup your face in their pudgy hands, and peer curiously into your eyes? It's not that you want your twelve-year-old to do this still (that would be more than weird), but you're probably searching for at least a nod to the pure and tender connection you had during their early childhood. How did you get from there to here, where the sound of your laugh causes your kid to wince, or your hand resting gently on their shoulder has the immediate effect of a chemical burn? And how do you have meaningful conversations during such a tense and disconnected age?

It's not easy. But it's not impossible. With some small tweaks to how you interact with your tween, your relationship can change to accommodate their need for independence as well as your desire to stay close.

First and foremost, it's time to make that shift from manager to assistant manager that I introduced in chapter 2 (see page 17). I can't over-emphasize the importance of this change to your dynamic.

Second, now is the time to reintroduce yourself to your tween. You're a real person with interests and talents outside of being a parent, and you can use those interests and talents to create a new kind of bond between the two of you. This chapter will give you some ideas for starting conversations that will scaffold your friendly rapport before you dive into some of the meatier conversations that come later in the book.

I'm not suggesting you stop parenting and start friending your kid, but rather that you stay open to an important shift in your relationship that will allow you to get to know each other in a more grown-up way. One way you can think about this is by considering how the student-teacher relationship evolves over time. A kindergarten teacher has a very different relationship with their students than a high school teacher does with theirs. Neither should be best friends with their students, but the margins of the relationship do relax a bit. Working with older students gives teachers opportunities to share more of their personal interests, humor, humanity, and even shortcomings. In doing so, they create spaces for their students to be vulnerable and, in those spaces, the most powerful learning occurs.

The Evolving Family Democracy

Some of you had that French parenting thing down: your kids grew up listening to David Bowie and the Beatles, dined with you on delicious curries and spicy tuna rolls, politely listened to you talk with your friends about current events, and otherwise seamlessly folded into your preexisting interests. Most of us pledged some amount of allegiance to this way of life before having kids, but along the way we ended up agreeing to being held hostage instead. It probably started right after the night you finally got to try that new restaurant all your friends love, where as soon as you checked in with the host your kid complained for twenty-nine minutes about the thirty-minute wait, and then refused to eat their twenty-dollar mac 'n' cheese *because it had bread crumbs on top.* Right then, you realized it would be less painful from here on out to just acquiesce to their needs, and put yours on hold. Until one day you realized you were driving around in a minivan, covered in Goldfish dust, humming along to Kidz Bop on repeat—hours after you dropped your kids off at school.

By middle school, the age of tyranny must end. Let today begin your family's steady march toward democracy. You will find two unexpected benefits to this: First, your tween will learn to coexist respectfully with others, be a good guest, and embrace a more diverse range of experiences. Second, when your tween realizes they are not the center of your world, they will not be outraged or indignant. They will be *relieved.* When young adolescents feel that relief, they begin to open up to you even more. Let me explain.

Kids Want You to Be Curious About Them, Not Dependent on Them

Laney, a girl at my summer leadership camp for middle schoolers, confided that she believed most of the kids at her school didn't like her. We talked about her experiences with her peers and how their interactions made her feel like a loser. The past year, she'd felt lost and lonely at school. I asked Laney whether her parents had considered transferring her to another school, and she admitted she hadn't told them. When I asked her why, she said, "My mom would be so sad. She'd cry so hard. I don't want to make her feel worse." Through more conversation, I understood Laney's mom to be her biggest fan, with few friends of her own, a marriage that had ended badly, and a deep need both to make sure Laney felt adored and find happiness vicariously *through* her. At least that's how Laney saw things. And that's what matters here.

Your tween wants to know you are an independent, satisfied person with hobbies, interests, and friends to keep you busy and fulfilled. When they know this, they'll understand it's safe to share with you what's going on in their lives, without fearing the extra burden of having to shoulder your emotional reaction on top of theirs. Knowing you're strong enough to ride out whatever happens to them without getting pulled under gives your kids a strong sense of security during these tumultuous years. And not for nothing, you'll simply wear yourself out if you become emotionally invested in every one of your kid's ups and downs through early adolescence.

It's the Little Things That Matter Most

The most rewarding conversations don't always end in an epiphany or include a teachable moment. It's just as important that you take a break from making a point, and with no greater motive than fostering simple curiosity about each other, to shoot the breeze. Getting closer often comes from sharing little nuggets about your day-to-day life or your past that your kid may not know. What's the best part of your day when you're not together? What song brings back the strongest memories for you? What book had the biggest effect on you? Your tween will also benefit from getting to know your short-

> Your child is ready to learn more about the full scope of who you are and by letting your relationship evolve this way, you'll establish yourself as someone who can be trusted and relied on during the more complicated teen years ahead.

comings and weaknesses. What are your flaws? What makes you anxious? When were you last scared? I'm not suggesting you share more of yourself as a way to seem cool or as a way to have more fun with your tween, although either of those could be pleasant side effects. Your child is ready to learn more about the full scope of who you are and by letting your relationship evolve this way, you'll establish yourself as someone who can be trusted and relied on during the more complicated teen years ahead. That's the real point of this connection.

Beware the Overshare

Perhaps you're ready to open up and have more adult conversations, but you're hesitant because it's unclear what's appropriate at this stage of the game. How will you know when sharing becomes *over*sharing? I'm reminded of a trick that preschool teachers use to discourage incessant streams of tattling: They distinguish between tattling and telling by explaining to their kiddos, "If you're reporting to get someone in trouble, it's tattling. If you're reporting to keep someone from getting hurt, it's telling." Telling is helpful. Tattling is not. When it comes to building a more personal relationship with your tween, you can similarly examine motivation. If you're sharing to build a connection or to give your child neutral, clinical information that will help them make more informed decisions about their own choices, go forward. If you're sharing in an effort to use emotions to sway your tween's decisions (to impress, scare, or manipulate your child, for example), dial it way back. The following list contains more ways to recognize when you shouldn't share:

Don't share to scare. "When I was in high school, I once drank so much I blacked out and woke up on a stranger's porch in my own throw-up, so I'm telling you from experience you have to be careful. Don't make the same mistake I did." Parents who use this approach are desperate for compliance because they know firsthand the trauma that can come from bad judgment. The mistake is in thinking that kids are more likely to make safe choices if they know their parents have made bad choices, when in fact, this has either little effect or it backfires. Your teen is likely to downplay your mistakes and assess by all the other evidence they have collected about you. "Yeah, but no big deal. Your life wasn't ruined or anything." Furthermore, teens don't believe they're like their parents. They're more inclined to hear your story and think, "That would never happen to me because I'm so different from you."

Don't share to impress. "Once my friends and I threw a huge party in the woods and the cops showed up and I was grounded for a week!" See, I'm like you! I'm not just an accountant who cares about taxes. I used to be cool and probably you can tell by this story that I still am a little bit! Parents share things like this as if trying to buy their way into a private poker game. You don't need to earn your way into a conversation about tough topics by proving you know firsthand about the things teenagers do when adults aren't looking.

Don't share to manipulate. "You want to know why I'm so angry at your dad? Why don't you ask him what he did that has broken my trust? He's not exactly the saint you think he is." *Never* share something personal to make someone else look bad, just so you'll look good. You won't look good. You'll look petty.

Don't share overly personal, historical information. Drs. Melisa Holmes and Trish Hutchison, cofounders of the popular *Girlology.com* health education programs, tell parents that kids don't need to know their parents' sexual history to make informed decisions about their own intimacy. A child may ask, "What age were *you* when you first ___," but Drs. Holmes and Hutchison agree the best response is, "My job is to help you make the best decisions for yourself and your decisions shouldn't be influenced by the choices anyone else has made." I agree, and in my estimation, sharing personal information is more likely to cloud a child's thinking than clarify decision making.

So . . . What Should I Share?

Share facts about risky behavior. When it comes to keeping your kid safe, personal anecdotes about your own mistakes don't cut it. Save those for when they're adults. Data and research, as well as therapeutic recommendations, are terrific things to share. By the time your tween is ready for sixth grade, you need to be ready to serve as a reliable encyclopedia for clinical information on *all* subjects. Don't worry, you don't have to know everything, but you need to be willing to find answers and report back when you have them.

Share your personal experiences about emotional hardships, when your child wants to hear them. How will you know when they're ready? Ask. If your child is struggling with a friendship breakup, ask, "Would it help if I told you about the time I went through something similar?"

Share decision making. Consider the many ways people make good decisions and help your kid discover their favorites from among a variety of approaches, such as making pros-and-cons lists, asking for feedback, praying/meditating/quietly reflecting, researching, visualizing, journaling, even flipping a coin. Share the process, not the decision.

Share your feelings. It's helpful to let your tween know how you feel about what *you're experiencing* (not so much how you feel about what they're experiencing). Are you stressed about an upcoming family reunion? Concerned about a political issue? Jealous of a colleague? Your child is not your confidant, but you don't need to keep all your complicated emotions hidden from them. They'll benefit from seeing you navigate the scope of your emotional life and learning what helps you deal with negative feelings and embrace positive ones.

Share your values. It's not uncommon for young adolescents to question their parents' values. The more you fight them on this, the more they'll buck, but if you can share *why* your values matter to you without projecting the same significance onto your tween, you're more likely to earn their consideration when it comes to respecting your beliefs. "I know most people don't write thank-you cards anymore, but I believe gratitude is the key to happiness, and I hope my effort shows how much I appreciate other people's kindness."

Share your memories. Though I discourage sharing the raunchy or rowdy details of your own adolescence, I do think sharing stories of adolescent relationships, adventures, and experiences are a lovely way to connect. What is a good rule of thumb for discerning what memories are appropriate to share? You know how people always tell kids, "Don't post anything online you wouldn't want your grandmother or teacher to see"? In the same way, I counsel parents not to share private stories with teens that you wouldn't share with a new coworker or new acquaintance.

Share the day-to-day stuff. Isn't this how closeness is often stitched, by knowing the little things about each other that others don't? Without prattling through the minute-by-minute playbook of your day, choose a few personal moments to share with each other. What did you notice on your way into work? Did you hear a funny story on a podcast? What did you eat for lunch? Less is more, but inviting your family into a few parts of your day they don't normally get to see is important, no matter how uninteresting or inconsequential they may seem at first blush.

I'm On Board, but My Kid Jumped Ship

Many of you readers are now feeling like I'm preaching to the choir. You'd love to talk with your tween, but all you can get back is "Okay," "Fine," and "Are we done?" I've said it before and I'll say it again: this is a long game.

There is an art to appearing open and receptive without seeming needy. The more you practice, the more you'll convince your tween you're an easy person to talk with about the small stuff—and then eventually the big stuff, too. Plan on this taking *years,* in some cases. Don't freak out if your child doesn't buy in right away. Just stay the course. Consistency is key to earning trust.

In every chapter, I'll give you an overview of the topic and then a sample or two that demonstrate how a conversation on this topic might sound with your young adolescent. With this chapter, we're setting the stage for all the conversations to come, so the sample dialogue below is a little different. Never has the BRIEF acronym been more pertinent. When you show you can get in and get out quickly, it takes the pressure off your kid and they'll be more likely to open up. Let's look at how you might bring up your evolving parent-child relationship with your tween.

BEGIN peacefully

Parent: *Hey, I want to tell you about something I read today. Do you have two minutes?*
Kid: *Yeah.*

Parent: *Great! It was in that book I'm reading about parents and tweens.*
Kid: *Okay.* [Eye-roll alert]

RELATE to your kid

Parent: *I know it's not a book you have any interest in, but it's giving me some ideas that will ultimately make your life easier, so maybe that makes it a little more interesting?*
Kid: *Did it tell you to buy me a new phone?*
Parent: *Ha! No . . . not like that. But I haven't finished it yet!*

INTERVIEW to collect data

[Flexibility is key, I always say, and for this BRIEF conversation, I don't think you need to ask questions. Skip this step.]

ECHO what you hear

[And since you skipped the Interview, you don't need to Echo anything. This example is so BRIEF, it's BRF.]

FEEDBACK

Parent: *Well, the interesting thing I just read was that, starting at your age, our relationship will begin to change. You're becoming a young adult, so our conversations will become less about me telling you what to do and more about us talking through your choices together. My job is to listen and help you make decisions that are best for your health and happiness. Your job is to talk with me about what you have going on, so I can support you. Does that sound good? Less me telling you what to do and more us talking through decisions together.*
Kid: *Yes, what's the catch?*
Parent: *You're smart to ask. No catch, but there is an important distinction to be made. When it comes to your immediate safety, I'm still in charge. I have to make sure you don't make any mistakes that could put you in permanent danger. But when it comes to figuring other things out, from*

*friends to schoolwork and all the stuff in between, I'm like your support
staff . . . your assistant manager. I know that sometimes you'll make
choices that will make you proud, and sometimes you'll make choices that
will leave you with regret. That's normal. This isn't about making perfect
choices all the time. It's about you learning to make the choices that you feel
best about and I'm here to help you think through it all. Just keep me posted
so I can help in whatever way you need.*

*That's basically it. I just wanted to share so we could be on the same
page. I'm gonna do some work now, but I'll be free in thirty minutes if you
want to hang out or go to Target or something.*

With luck, your tween will want to talk more about what you've read, what
to expect, and so on, but chances are they'll sit with this for starters. This
example is a great setup for future conversations because kids want to
rise to the level of your expectations when your expectations are couched
in compliments. Saying, "Wow, you're a young adult and now we get to
talk with each other in a mature way" is far more inspirational than, "If
you want to be treated like an adult, start speaking to me like you are one."

Ways to Start Talking with Your Kid About Fun Stuff

The less micromanaging you do (ticking off to-do lists, supervising dead-
lines, arranging social outings with friends), the more space you'll free
up for your relationship with your tween to evolve. By choosing to be less
concerned with what your child needs to do and more curious about what
your kid is thinking, you can also share more about yourself than just the
demands of your daily tasks. This is how your child will become naturally
intrigued about who you are outside of a taskmaster.

What follows is a list of question/conversation prompts that you can
use to have easy, fun, quick chats with your kids. These questions are repeated at the end of the book (see page 283) in the event you want to tear
the prompts out and lay the page between you and your child—a literal

conversation starter. While most of these questions are for you to ask of your child, it's with this scene in mind that some of these questions are meant for them to ask of you. Still others can go both ways: you *or* your child can ask them of one another.

In addition to questions that are just for fun ("small talk"), I've included a section on preferences. When your kid was little, you may have been able to end their meltdowns with bear hugs or slapstick comedy routines, but try either approach now and you risk sending your tween into deep fits of rage or embarrassment. As you prepare for the changing parent-child dynamic, it will be helpful to reestablish preferences around handling conflicts, emotions, expectations, and other sources of potential volatility through adolescence.

If your tween/young teen isn't used to you trying to relate to them in this way, they may say, "This is dumb," or just clam up. If that happens, don't worry. Just say something low-pressure, like "Yeah, it is different, isn't it? I just like hearing your opinion. If you think of something later, I'll be around." Then go do something you enjoy. With any luck, you'll get a better response once the shock and suspicion have passed.

Small Talk

Parent to Child:

- Given where we live, what do you think will be your first job?
- If you were giving a tour of your school to a new student, what part of the school would impress them and what part would you just skip?
- What do your friends like about coming to our house and what do you like about going to theirs?
- Which song would most kids get hyped up for if it came blaring over the loudspeaker during lunch?

Child to Parent:

- What was your first job? What was your worst job?
- What was your best subject in high school? And/or what was your college major and why did you pick it?

- What is something cool you did before I was born?
- What is something your parents could have done better? What is something they did well?

Parent to Child and Child to Parent:
- If you could spend time with anyone outside of our family, who would it be?
- What is something that makes you laugh, but probably shouldn't?
- What are you the best at in our family?
- What do you wish your friends would do more of?
- If you suddenly had a free day tomorrow with zero responsibilities, what would you do?
- What's your least favorite chore?
- What was the most recent scary thing you saw on TV or read in a book?
- What's something about our house that maybe only you know?
- If you could redesign one thing about our town, what would you change?
- What famous person do people say you look like?
- If you won a contest and got to meet a mystery celebrity, who would you be wishing for? Who would you be hoping against?
- Think of the people you spend time with outside of our family. If you could pick one to be more like, who would it be and why?

Preferences
- When something good happens to you, do you like a lot or a little attention? Is it different depending on where it happens? (In public versus home, for example.)
- When you feel sad, do you want me to check on you or leave you alone?
- When you've had a hard day, what could I do to make it easier?
- When I appreciate something you've done, how would you like me to let you know? A hug, high five, nice text, in-person compliment, or expensive gift and lavish vacation?
- When I want to brag about you, who can I tell? Just family, certain friends, the whole world on social media?
- When we've had an argument, do you prefer to talk about it right afterward or later? How much later?

- When I need you to do something, do you want me to tell you or write it down for you?
- When we need to talk about a problem, do you want to do it in your room, in my room, in the car, or somewhere else?
- When you have friends over, how much do you want me to talk with them?

Conversation Crashers

"If you don't like me, good. That means I'm doing my job." Consider the "Mean Parent" badge of honor carefully. Good parenting doesn't equate to being at odds with your child. Sure, your tween is bound to think you're mean sometimes when you set limits. Yes, it feels good to find solidarity in laughter with other parents when this happens. Just be careful you don't buy into this Mean Parent trope to the exclusion of a happy relationship with your child. Setting limits fairly and firmly, without taking pride in being mean, is a good way to show your tween how they can do the same with their friends, employers, and romantic partners later in life.

> Setting limits fairly and firmly, without taking pride in being mean, is a good way to show your tween how they can do the same with their friends, employers, and romantic partners later in life.

"Bottom line, the lesson here is . . ." Resist the urge to teach a lesson. As you and your child begin to share more with each other, you'll be tempted to respond to their anecdotes with ways they might improve. Recently, my family attended a major sporting event uptown. Our teens drove and parked separately near the stadium, while my husband and I parked at his office five blocks away. After the event, the kids were stuck underground in a line of cars for an hour and a half waiting for the deck to clear. They felt claustrophobic and anxious. My husband, feeling bad for the kids but not knowing how to help them in their time of perceived crisis, could only offer up ways to prevent this from happening next time. "The lesson to be learned here is never to park close to the event because it's awful on the back end." Needless to say, our kids weren't happy with being taught a lesson in the midst of their struggle. Remember, experience is often the best teacher. You only need to listen and commiserate.

In a Hurry? Here's Your Crash Course

- In early adolescence, your relationship with your child should mature and will benefit from you making space for conversations that are simple and carefree, not always teachable moments. A good path toward mutual respect is prioritizing pleasant conversations.

- Your tween will be more responsive to your attempts to connect if you explain ways you can both expect your relationship to evolve.

- As your child grows up, their preferences for handling emotions, conflicts, and problem solving will change periodically. Discuss preferences with your child about how to handle these going forward.

- It's great to share, but don't overshare. Share your personal values, feelings about your own experiences (but not about theirs), hard facts about health topics, interesting memories, and some of the small parts of your daily life they never get to see. Avoid sharing if you're doing it to be impressive, scary, or manipulative. You'll know you're *over*sharing if you tell your kid personal stories about your own adolescence that you wouldn't tell a boss or new acquaintance.

- Don't expect instant gratification in this new relationship with your child. Your child will open up incrementally, over a long period of time. Stay the course. It will be worth the time and patience you invest.

5

Talking About Independence

In this chapter, you'll learn why independence doesn't look the way we think it should, at least at first, and how thoughtful conversations about becoming independent include recognizing the two primary ways kids practice autonomy, accepting that mistakes will be made, knowing how to set milestones for further independence, and saying no (at times) to too much freedom.

Remember when your toddler was learning to walk? They fell down a lot and knocked stuff over and cried and got hurt and whined—and you *cheered them on!* If you can possibly bring that same enthusiasm to your tween's attempts to walk away from you now to be independent, even rooting for them as they leave you behind and downplaying it when they fall, you will save yourself a small piece of sanity over the next ten years.

Sometimes, though, we just want compliant kids who do what we ask and stay home with us when we want, because letting a kid become independent is hard, annoying work. In our minds, we imagine independent young teens doing their own laundry, earning money at a part-time job, and making themselves dinner when we can't be there to do it. In reality, it may look more like them arguing with you over curfew, watching adult shows on Netflix, copying what their friends do, and hiding out in their room away from your critical gaze.

When parents take a realistic look at how independence shows up in a young teen's life, long before the payoff of *mature* independence, they can separate reasonable and developmentally appropriate independence from unsafe risk taking. Middle school opens up a new world of potential dangers to kids, and parents often react to the possibility of danger by instinctively clamping down on their kids' autonomy, essentially making their worlds smaller.

Unfortunately, when we don't give kids a chance to test their independence, we deny them the opportunity to practice—and practice is what leads to maturity. Kids who are incrementally exposed to more activities that require independent thinking and problem solving learn how to gauge the safety of situations, read people's intentions, listen to their gut, and even keep themselves company, instead of relying on others to make them happy. Having conversations about reasonable ways to open up a kid's world in middle school actually keeps kids safer throughout adolescence more than clamping down could ever do.

Accept That Trying Means Failing

When I was in fifth grade, my family lived in a suburb of Boston. One Saturday, my parents announced we were heading into the city for a day of sightseeing and told me to get ready. For some reason, I decided this was my day to draw a line in the sand. I put my foot down about being old enough to stay home alone. "You know we'll be gone all day, right?" they asked. I could hear the doubt in their tone, which only strengthened my resolve. I promised I would be fine, and underscored how totally *bored* I would be walking around the city. I swore I wouldn't need anything while they were gone.

About an hour after my parents had left the house, though, I was hit with a wave of fear. I can't recall if anything in particular set me off, but I felt alarmingly alone and the hours loomed impossibly long until dinner.

An hour and ten minutes after my parents had left the house, I found myself at my neighbor's front door, tearful and shaky, claiming I'd gotten an upset stomach while my parents were out of the house, though that was just my ruse to find someone to look after me. My kind neighbor, with four kids under the age of six, invited me in and added me to her brood for the day. After I composed myself, she gave me a cup of ginger ale to calm my stomach. I remember she expertly shook the ginger ale first to release the bubbles so my stomach wouldn't be irritated by the carbonation. Yes, you never forget your first foray into young adulthood, drinking flat ginger ale from a three-year-old's plastic sippy cup between bouts of nervous diarrhea in your neighbor's bathroom. (Cue sad trombone music.)

My parents were reluctant to give me another shot at being on my own for quite a while after that, because even though I'd been certain I was ready, I wasn't. I sure felt like a failure that day, but looking back on it, I can see I did what I had to do, both in asserting my independence and in looking for help when I realized I'd bitten off more than I could chew. As an adult, I can give little Michelle some credit and see that as a kind of success, but my twelve-year-old self filed it under defeat.

It's hard to know when to give more freedom. Like many parts of growing up, self-sufficiency is nonlinear. One day your tween will seem so mature you'd trust them to file your taxes, and the next they'll have an inexplicable temper tantrum over the fish you're serving for dinner. Two steps forward, one step back.

There will be many potholes on the road to independence. It's not your job to help your tween avoid them, but to teach them how to fix a busted tire if they get a flat.

Two Types of Independence

In my work, I see two primary ways kids assert their independence after elementary school: 1) by isolating themselves from their family at home, and 2) by separating from their family to explore the world. Both of these cause parents a great deal of worry.

Before I help you launch into how to talk about independence with your child, it may help to first understand a bit about isolation versus exploration, so you'll have a sense of what's normal and safe, or if you might need to be more concerned.

Independence Through Isolation

Why do tweens spend a colossal amount of time in their rooms? Why do they stop (willingly) participating in family movie or game night? Why do family dinners feel like a timed race to the finish line, so your kid can hop up and rush back to their room? You used to be close, but these days it probably feels like you're being ghosted by your kid.

Don't worry. It's not you. It's them.

Adolescents need to cocoon. Cocooning is a term coined in the early 1980s by Faith Popcorn, a social trend analyst with a bizarre and compelling name. (That's neither here nor there, but it can't go unsaid.) Popcorn describes cocooning as "the impulse to stay inside when the outside gets too tough and scary." Since its introduction to our lexicon, it has come to be used regularly to describe adolescents and their relationship to their rooms.

Tweens and teens cocoon because at a time when most things in their lives are changing—their bodies, brains, emotions, friends, and even their self-concepts—bedrooms are safe havens. There, they can think about any and all things ad nauseam, or push them aside and take a break from the mental turmoil of their busy minds.

Most kids take cocooning so seriously they will, if allowed, suddenly redecorate or rearrange their preteen rooms to reflect a new sense of self. They want to establish that this space is more theirs, and definitely not mom's or dad's. Due to financial constraints, I wasn't allowed to redecorate my room when I was a teenager, so I covered the 1775 colonial-themed wallpaper I inherited when we moved in with floor-to-ceiling black-and-white ads I collected from old magazines. This décor wouldn't have been my first choice, but it sent a clear message: this is *my* space, not yours. Eventually, kids emerge from their cocoons with a better-formed sense of self. It may feel like mindless sequestering to parents, but it serves as a safe place to grow.

When cocooning goes well, kids feel a sense of independence and autonomy right in the safety of your own home. When cocooning doesn't go well, kids become overly self-indulgent, forgetting that they are still members of a family unit and they must still do chores, engage in pleasant conversation, and balance their own needs with what's best for the group. As you talk with your tween about their cocooning habits, you'll want to keep in mind that not all isolation is bad. Seek a compromise on balancing their needs with those of the family. You'll see this in action later in this chapter.

Independence Through Exploration

In contrast to isolating at home, sometimes your tween will want to assert their independence by venturing out into the world without you. However, because of our constant exposure to news showing us how seemingly every kid is in mortal danger from guns, drugs, and sexual trafficking, parents accordingly react by limiting those freedoms. Lenore Skenazy has written an incredible book about the perils of this crack-down phenomenon: *Free-Range Kids*. If you are nervous about letting your kids explore your neighborhood, town, or city, I urge you to read it.

Exploring the world in middle school might look like doing one of these things without parental supervision: going to the mall with a friend, meeting up with classmates at a roller rink or trampoline park, riding a bike to the gas station to buy a candy bar, taking public transportation, or being dropped off at the movies or a sub shop for lunch. All of these are fairly typical middle school explorations.

In any of these scenarios there are three kinds of learning happening for tweens:

1. Learning how to navigate traffic, strangers, and public spaces safely.

2. Learning how to assert themselves by asking for directions or help (as in, "What do I do? The soda machine is broken and I already paid."), ordering for themselves, figuring out a tip, or trying not to get yelled at by grumpy people who don't like kids milling around.

3. Learning how to think for themselves, by themselves, and becoming okay with the sound of their own thoughts. It's about tuning in to that inner voice tweens may not yet be familiar with, if all they have ever heard is an adult's voice telling them what to do.

When exploration goes well, kids develop confidence in their abilities to overcome obstacles and solve their own problems. Giving kids a chance to earn this confidence actually makes them safer, because if someone is going to target your kid, whether that's a manipulative friend, bully at school, older teens at the mall, or god forbid, stranger with bad intentions, you want your child to be confident and street smart enough to speak up, get loud if necessary, and get help. People who do bad things at any level don't like an audience.

When exploration goes wrong, it can go wrong in a broad range of ways. Like me when my parents left me home alone, kids may ask for more than they can handle. An experience like this can leave a kid emotionally drained, but it's not likely to have any long-term effects (other than being useful one day when writing a book). I'd be more concerned about kids who are sent out before they're taught how to explore safely. They may run the risk of getting hit by a car, or getting seriously lost, or as mentioned above, not knowing how to speak up for themselves or get help if approached by someone with the intention of testing your kid's boundaries.

Tweens exploring their world also run the risk of making dumb decisions. Maybe they'll get kicked out of a store for being too rowdy, or get yelled at by a server for leaving a bad tip or making a mess. Maybe they'll decide to see what happens if they pocket a golf ball from the sporting goods store without paying for it. Think ahead about what choices you want your kid to make when you aren't there, and have those conversations ahead of time.

In this chapter, I'll show you some sample dialogues you can use to discuss isolation and exploration, so that you can give your tween the freedom they want and need, while still making sure you're covering safety and good citizenship as well as setting reasonable parameters.

Talking About Isolation

On any given evening, at any given house across this country, a scenario is likely playing out in which enthusiastic parents want their tween to hang out with them, and the tween isn't interested. It's not what the parents had hoped for, but on the upside, it's a great entryway into a conversation.

BEGIN peacefully

[Family is together for the first time of the day and tween automatically heads off to their bedroom instead of hanging out together.]

Parent: *Are you headed up to your room?*

Kid: *Yeah.*

Parent: *Okay. Is your room comfortable, or is there anything you need up there?*

Kid: *It's fine. I mean, can I get a TV?*

RELATE to your kid

Parent: *I used to want that, too. Unfortunately, no TVs in the bedroom. I know it sounds like fun, but it does wreck your sleep and distract you from homework. I'm happy that you love your room though. I'm glad it's a place you like to be.*

Kid: *Thanks, bye.*

Parent: *I don't want to interrupt your time to relax, but I do want to get some time to hang out with you, so after you relax can we hang out for a bit? How about after dinner for fifteen minutes?*

Kid: *Yeah, that's cool.*

INTERVIEW to collect data

[After dinner]

Parent: *Thanks for hanging out for a bit. I love hearing about you and your day.*

Kid: *Okay. What do you want me to tell you?*

Parent: *Oh, nothing specific. I was thinking about how now that you're older you enjoy spending more time in your room and less time with the family than you used to. I can remember feeling that way, too, when I was your age. I wanted to check in and share my expectations around this now that you're getting to an age where you'll want more privacy.*

Kid: *Ughhhh . . .*

Parent: *When you spend time in your room, is it because you just like it, or are we doing anything out here that you don't like?*

Kid: *Honestly? Mostly I just like texting friends and I don't want my annoying sister looking over my shoulder. And sometimes I just like watching my own shows on my laptop. Like, when I watch out here you always ask me "Who's that?" or "What's this show?" or "What's your homework today?" And it's hard to have to pause it every time you want to ask me something.*

Parent: *That makes sense to me.*

Kid: *But I don't want you to be offended by that. I'm just saying it's easier in my room. I'm not mad at anyone when I go there.*

Parent: *I get that. I'm not offended and it helps to understand.*

ECHO what you hear

Parent: *You like to have privacy sometimes and you don't want to be interrupted when you're relaxing. That sounds reasonable.*

Kid: *Thanks.*

FEEDBACK

Parent: *From my point of view, I love that you have a place in the house where you can totally be yourself, relax, and have fun. I'm happy that we can provide that for you because it's an important part of growing up.*

I also want to be sure you know how important you are to us and how much we miss you when we don't get to see you for family time. As you get older, I don't expect you to hang out in the living room with us every night. But I do think we can reach a good compromise so you get your alone time and we get our "you time."

We want to keep giving you the time you need in your room by yourself, and I ask that you give us three things in return:

Keep up good grades and extracurricular commitments. That's probably obvious!

Join us for family dinner when we serve it, and for at least one family movie night a month.

Make a ten-minute contribution every day for the "greater good" of the family. * It's understandable to want lots of "you time" at your age, but we also don't work well as a family unless everyone contributes. You can choose how you give back: walk the dog, empty the dishwasher, wipe the counters . . . just be sure you're contributing a little every day.

As long as you have these things accounted for, you are free to listen to music, text your friends, or just relax in peace to your heart's content!

As your kid begins to pull away, it's natural to feel twinges of abandonment. I remember my friend's husband telling her, "You're acting like our daughter is the most popular girl at school and you're fawning over her! You'd do anything to get her attention."

Sometimes our desire to stay connected comes across to our kids as being needy, and that's a surefire way to get snubbed. Kids are most interested in you when you are least interested in them. They choose the moment to talk when you are least available, because that means you're also least emotional. Kids have to deal with their own fickle emotions, as well as the unpredictability of their classmates, all day long. It's as exhausting for them as it would be for you. This is why they choose to open up when you seem the least emotionally invested in them: as you're leaving the room, concentrating on an e-mail, or finally settling into your favorite show. The more interested and invested you seem in what they have to say, the less willing they are to say it.

Timing is important in almost all of the fourteen conversations in this book, but particularly when approaching your kid to talk about their self-imposed isolation. Along those lines, when it comes to craving time with your kids, it may be helpful to do some soul searching around what you need from your kid versus what they need to grow up. There is a difference between *enjoying* someone's company and *needing* someone's company. I work with some parents who think they need their kids around because they no longer enjoy spending time with their spouse, or

---

* Ten minutes is my arbitrary assessment of what's reasonable. Your household structure may require kids to do more, so you should set the amount of daily chore time to what works for you, keeping in mind that if your child is overscheduled, this can be tough to fit in.

they're alone often and crave companionship, or they worry exhaustively when their kids aren't near them. Kids who are tethered to their parents despite feeling ready to separate might comply as long as they live under the same roof, but they will be the fastest to make a break for it without staying in touch when they turn eighteen. Kids whose parents respect their need for some privacy tend to have better long-term relationships with their parents. If you feel desperate for your child's attention, it may help to remind yourself that by giving them space now, you're investing in more time together in the future.

Conversation Crashers

One of the obvious difficulties of trying to convince a tween to spend more time with you is that cocooning in their room goes hand in hand with not wanting to talk. This can make for some fairly one-sided conversations. Tweens are easy to scare off at this point, so my advice is to approach important conversations with patience and a sense of sport. Think of this like fishing. Stay sensitive to what makes them skittish and what gets a nibble. Say less and be tranquil. Last but not least, try to avoid these ineffective strategies that make a big splash, but don't get results.

Forcing your agenda: If your tween doesn't want to participate in a family activity, be flexible, at least some of the time. (I'm not opposed to compulsory participation sometimes, but it helps if these events are announced in advance.) Being strict for its own sake though (as in, "This family always runs errands together on Sunday afternoon," or "You can spend time in your room some other day, but for now I want you down here with us") is going to get you nothing but sulky company and ruined fun.

Probing for pain: "Did something happen? Is something going on? Tell me what's going on." Sound familiar? If you're legitimately concerned, knock on your tween's door with a cup of tea or some dessert, ask how they're doing, and offer to listen if they want to talk about their day. But asking repeatedly on the spot sounds more like suspicion than concern. Your kid will read this as mistrust and clam up even more.

Resorting to being the victim: Sometimes, after asking, pleading, and debating, parents feel they have no choice but to escalate their tactics. You've tried kindness and logic, so why not give pity a shot? It's usually a last-ditch effort made before giving up, with a side shot of wanting to injure your kid a little for putting you through the wringer, and it sounds something like this: "I was hoping for a nice family night, but if you're just going to fight me on everything you might as well go back to your room." I can relate to the urge and admit I recognize this tactic because I've used it out of frustration. No surprise, it never, *ever* works. By early middle school, a tween practically chokes on their own emotions—and those of their peers—all day long. It's exhausting. If *you* add to the drama? You both lose. But when you reinforce that you can create a calm space for them, kids repay you by sharing more of their time and their thoughts with you, even throughout high school.

The Stigma Around Giving Your Kid More Independence

Adjusting to your child as they pull away from you means wrestling with feelings of rejection. You may overhear parents joke or commiserate about this, but it's not a milestone a parent takes pride in. Often, I see a sense of shame or embarrassment among parents when this starts to happen in their family. Because middle schoolers develop at such different rates, it can be hard to swallow why your friend's kid hugs them after the soccer game, and yours won't speak a word to you until you get in the car and roll up the windows. Don't feel bad when your kid becomes sullen, glum, or withdrawn from you in public. It means they're on track to becoming independent . . . and you want that. Remember that you want that! I wish parents could freely boast when their kids start isolating. "Hey, look whose seventh grader won't talk with any of our family friends at the middle school open house! *It's us!* We're doing something right!" To state the obvious, don't say that out loud (and certainly not in your child's presence!); just think it proudly in your head.

When your tween begins to isolate from you, especially in public, you may feel rejected or embarrassed, but nothing rivals the stigma of a parent who is labeled too permissive about their kid being unsupervised in public. "To each his own, but I'd never let *my* kid go to the mall alone. I couldn't live with myself if anything happened." This is a strange sort of brag that implies the parent who lets their kid explore public spaces independently a) doesn't understand the risks involved, b) understands the risks but willfully ignores them, or c) would somehow be *inhumanly* okay if a tragedy befell their child. I understand and relate to being afraid of what might happen when your kid starts navigating the world without you. I've had all the same horrible fantasies as the next parent. But it's not only unfair, it's also cruel to blame parents for the terrible things that can happen, at random, to anyone.

It's not hard to find evidence that can be used to back up a parent's decision to never let their kid venture out unsupervised (a viral story of a child lured away from a skating rink, a forced abduction from a park, a memory of a missing child from the parent's own elementary school days). I empathize with the feelings of horror those stories evoke. To feel this way is natural. But what do we do with those feelings? I don't think we should use them to make our safety decisions for us. I'd encourage parents to look at the data and probability of crimes involving tweens and young teens. Some will say, "Probability doesn't matter. If it happens one time, to my child, that's all that matters. It's my job to protect against the *possibility* of danger, no matter how small."

My response to that is simple: You can't even *try* to keep your child safe from random acts of tragedy. Car crashes happen. Abductions by strangers happen (ever so rarely). Cancer happens. Relieve yourself of that burden right now. Do what you can to take reasonable precautions—wear seat belts, take a self-defense class as a family, eat well—but don't let the fear of an unlikely tragedy keep you, and your child, from the normal patterns of life.

Talking About Exploration

One of the most common ways a child first asks to explore the world unsupervised is by asking to go the mall with friends. Some parents handle this rite of passage by going along and looking in other shops, giving the kids some time to explore while still being nearby in case of emergency. (Ninety percent of the time the "emergency" is that someone ran out of money and needs cash for the food court.) That's a fine first step, but the real taste of independence comes when a tween gets to experience the exhilarating and slightly scary feeling of being their own safety net.

This is how the conversation might sound when your kid asks to take a step like this toward independence:

BEGIN peacefully

Parent: *So what are your plans for this weekend?*
Kid: *Actually, some kids are going to the mall tomorrow and I wanted to go . . .*
Parent: *That sounds fun. Is anyone staying with you or do you mean just kids?*
Kid: *Maybe a parent will be there . . . I don't know what the plan is yet.* *
[Parent, resist the urge to skip ahead to data collection. Just connect here.]

RELATE to your kid

Parent: *I used to love going to the mall with my friends. Hey, speaking of the mall, did you see they're expanding the food court?*
Kid: *No, they are?*
Parent: *Yes! We can cross our fingers for something good. What do you hope they put in?*

---

* One of the more infuriating aspects of parenting a young adolescent is that they are terrible at making plans with their friends. It helps to remember that your kid is developing the ability, clunky as it may be at first, to plan for themselves, and that this pays off in the end when you don't have to be involved in every last logistical detail.

Kid: *They need a Chipotle.*

Parent: *Yeah, that would be good!*

INTERVIEW to collect data

Parent: *I know you don't have the details yet and we can talk more tomorrow morning when you do. If you're talking about having a parent there, it just depends on the timing. If you're talking about going without a parent, I'll need a little more info. Would it be helpful if I told you what info I need so you can find it out?*

Kid: *Okay.*

Parent: *I'll want to know who is going, how long you'll be at the mall, and who is driving you there and back.*

Kid: *Okay. I'll let you know. Are you going to say yes?*

Parent: *I might. Once I know more. And if you agree to talk with me about all the safety stuff you know I need to cover.*

Kid: *Definitely.*

[The next morning]

Kid: *Angel's mom is driving us to the mall and her dad is picking us up. We're going from one to four o'clock. And I think Simone is coming, too.*

Parent: *Three of you?*

Kid: *I think.*

Parent: *That sounds like the plans aren't firm yet . . .*

Kid: *We might meet some people there. But I don't know who yet. Some friends of Simone's.*

Parent: *Do you know them? Do you go to the same school?*

Kid: *Yessss, jeez, I'm not meeting strangers at the mall!*

Parent: *Okay, I'm just trying to understand, since this is all so new. Clarify who you might be meeting and let me know.*

[Later]

Kid: *It's me, Angel, Simone, and her friends Evan and Michael. I don't want you to get mad at me if that changes though. I can't control if someone comes or doesn't come.*

Parents: *But wouldn't you know who's coming because you have to make the plans?*

Kid: *It can be super last minute if someone just texts "Where are you?" and then comes over.*

ECHO what you hear

Parent: *I understand what you're saying. It sounds like some people might just show up unexpectedly. When I was your age, people couldn't do that because no one had cell phones. Plans had to be made well in advance, but it sounds like things are more last minute now that everyone is always reachable by phone.*
Kid: *Exactly!*

FEEDBACK

Parent: *I know there will be some things that are out of your control when you go without parents, like another kid might show up who you weren't expecting. So let's talk about what you can control in this situation. I think if we can agree on a few key things, we'll both be ready for you to do this.*

I want to hear from you occasionally so I won't worry. If you're at the mall for three hours, how often do you think you can text me?
Kid: *Every hour? But I don't want to have to spend all my time telling you everything we did. Can I just say I'm fine?*
Parent: *I agree to that. Once an hour. Set a reminder on your phone. **
Also, let's go over some safety stuff you probably know but I need to say. NO leaving the mall. If someone makes you feel unsafe, you can always tell a person working in a store to call a security guard. Keep your eyes up so you can be aware of what's going on around you. Don't go the wrong way on the escalator. If anyone in your group does something that makes you uncomfortable, text me "What's for dinner?" Then I'll text you an excuse why I need to come pick you up early. And last thing, remember

---

* Is this reasonable? I think so for the first time if it puts you at ease, but not all the time. If your child shows they can do this, loosen the rules. You want them to be present with their friends, paying attention to their environment, not checking out to check in with you all the time.

your manners. Don't run through the mall. Don't make a mess. Put things back where they belong. You don't want to make someone's job harder when they're already working hard. Do you agree to all of this?
Kid: *Yes.*
Parent: *Have fun!*

In this scenario, by sticking to the BRIEF method, the parent kept the conversation positive and kept the kid focused on what is reasonably within their control in a new situation.

Conversation Crashers

I know when you're put on the spot, sometimes things just come out of your mouth that aren't as "productive" as a perfectly crafted dialogue. Since your conversations will be more improv than theater, you can't memorize exactly what to say. Instead of trying to plan the whole thing out, it's helpful to just steer clear of certain showstoppers. In improv training, actors are trained to replace responding "No" (a total scene killer) with "Yes, and" because it keeps the sketch alive. Here are some phrases that might similarly kill your conversations with your tween.

"I know you're ready but I'm not ready." You're working the emotional angle here and tweens don't respond well to this. By positioning yourself as the bad guy you've opened yourself up to a debate on who should win this argument—the person *you admit* is ready to take the next step, or the one who is holding that person back for their own comfort. It's an easy choice.

"I love you too much to let you go." Do you drive your kid to school? Go sledding? Send them to summer camp? Let them play a contact sport? We put our kids at risk all the time. Couching your no as an act of love won't make it any more satisfying to them. They might even argue back. "Oh, so other parents don't love their kids. That's what you're saying?" This feels like sidestepping the issue. Instead of deflecting, offer up solid reasons why you're saying no.

"It's not you I'm worried about—it's all the other people out there." Kids sense something insincere about this nugget and they're right. Parents may feel this is a softer, kinder way to let a kid down without insulting them, or maybe that it's a way of putting a vague umbrella over the endless things that are out of your control in the world, but it's not a true statement. At some point, you presumably *will* let your offspring leave the house without you. Is this because on *that* day the world will be void of creeps, temptations, and distractions? Nope. It's because on that day you'll feel reasonably confident your kid can handle those challenges, should they bump against them. Remember, you can't protect your child against everything in the world, but you should make sure they can pass the typical and foreseeable tests independence might throw at them.

"I said no." And . . . scene! In all seriousness, there are plenty of times when you should say no. I just think there's a more productive way to say it. Let's take a look at how.

When No Is the Best Answer

As we saw with my experience staying home alone for the first time, a kid's desire to be independent isn't always proof they're ready. Your tween might be dying to do what their friends are doing, but you know full well they're too impulsive, anxious, irresponsible, or unfocused to be sent out on their own, even for a couple hours. Your tween is going to be disappointed when you say no. That's okay. Learning how to deal with disappointment is an important life skill. However, if you're too rigid when rejecting your tween's request, they might decide sneaking around is the only way to get what they want. Instead, relate to their desire for independence and share measurable milestones your child can reach in order to earn that independence.

You might start off saying something like "I know you want to go the mall with your friends and I'm sorry you're upset that I'm saying now is not the time. I want this for you, too, and I also want to be sure you're prepared. The good news is, there are things you can do to show me you're ready. Here are the things I need to know you can do before you take this next step."

Below is a list of the types of independence milestones you could communicate to your child. Of course, you'll want to modify this to your preferences and your child's needs.

In preparation for going out unsupervised, here are some things you can do to show me you're ready:

- Talk directly to a teacher when you don't understand an assignment or agree on a grade.

- Make a phone call to order food

- Ask a server, librarian, or store clerk questions in person.

- Look both ways before crossing any street!

- Exhibit good manners in public spaces; don't bump into people, yell, or cut people off.

- Reply within a reasonable time to my texts or phone calls when you are at a friend's house. What's a reasonable time? Let's discuss.

- Say no when a friend asks you to do something you don't want to do.

- Listen to me while I explain why adults never need to ask kids or teens for help.

- Practice saying, "I have to go get my dad right now," if a stranger engages you and makes you uncomfortable.

- Have my phone number memorized. With cell phones, people rarely memorize numbers anymore. This is important for when your phone dies or is lost.

You can use this list, or customize one to suit your family.* Whatever milestones you choose, make sure they aren't arbitrary and that they relate directly to readiness. You can explain your list to your tween this way: "These aren't just a bunch of random challenges I'm using to make this hard, or make it take longer for you get permission. These are a mix of tasks that show me you understand the importance of safety, you're responsible enough to communicate with me when we're not together, you can communicate clearly with adults you don't know, you're confident enough to say no to friends and strangers (because, at some point, either might ask you to do something you don't feel right about), and you demonstrate a mature level of courtesy to the people around you. Let's work together on this list to help you reach your goal."

Your kid isn't going to hug you and thank you for the opportunity, but they will understand your expectations and see the path toward more freedom.

Independence is hard for both parent and child, like growing pains. It's hard to drop your kid off at the mall and not secretly stalk them, and it's hard not to miss eating popcorn together while watching your family's favorite movies together. But there is fun to be had: watching your child develop into a new, responsible teenager who is competent and assured, and perhaps using some of that extra free time to explore your own interests outside of being a parent.

---

* This list assumes your child is not at risk for being targeted by other children, adults, security guards, or police officers for the color of their skin. Parents of black and brown children, in addition to these kinds of conversations, have "the talk" about how to best stay safe in public spaces and specifically what to do if questioned by police officers. If your family is white, you can share the responsibility for protecting those who are not as inherently safe in public by acknowledging the added security your privilege brings, and talking about being witness to, and supportive during, other people's experiences. For example, you wouldn't want your child intervening in a physical altercation, but you could let them know if they witness harassment they should call you right away and you can stay on the phone with them to figure out how they can report it and to whom, or that they can video the incident on their phone to provide documentation that would support a victim.

In a Hurry? Here's Your Crash Course

- Giving kids more independence in their tween years keeps them safer than clamping down ever could. Tweens need practice to learn what's safe and how to cope with new people, places, and situations.

- Your child will almost certainly think they're ready for more than they can handle. That's okay. Figuring out how to cope with their failures is an important life skill to start learning now.

- Adolescents seek independence in two ways: by isolating themselves from their family, and/or by exploring their community without supervision.

- Kids this age need to learn how to navigate public spaces and interact with strangers safely and with confidence.

- Parents who respect their young adolescent's need for privacy have better long-term relationships with their kids. When kids feel their parents were overly strict or needy of their companionship throughout adolescence, they can't wait to experience a normal amount of freedom. When those kids leave home, they disconnect from family for fear of being pulled back into codependency.

- You won't find a broader range in maturity and social-emotional development than among kids between ages ten and fourteen. As a result, some kids are ready for independence much sooner, or much later, than their peers. During these years, parents tend to become more judgmental of how other people parent. Resist the urge to compare your rules to others'. There will always be stricter and more permissive families. Do what's best for your family, and specifically for your child, and don't waste any emotional energy on what other people choose for theirs.

- Tweens need limits. They shouldn't feel arbitrary to your child, because that feeling can lead to unsafe rebellion. When it's time to say no, give your child reasons why and, more important, concrete ways your kid can show you they are ready for more responsibility and freedom.

Talking About Changing Friendships

In this chapter, you'll learn why talking about friendships can be especially sensitive, why you shouldn't get emotionally invested in conversations about friend drama, how to normalize changing relationships, and how to emphasize that different people can fill different needs instead of searching for perfection in one friend.

Consider the friend who calls you from the grocery store to see if you need anything, laughs extra loudly when you tell a funny story at a party, or texts you just to vent about a shared gripe. A good friendship is magical, and connecting with a true friend, however briefly, will inevitably reduce stress, lift your spirits, and brighten your day. Friendships give our lives purpose, joy, and comfort.

Yet . . . middle school.

Middle school is a weird/wonderful/*mostly terrible* time for friendships.

This is the age when your child becomes obsessed with their friends and classmates to the exclusion of logic, reason, prior commitments, curfews, family time, and geographical restrictions. Between grades six and nine, kids will do just about anything to be brought into the social fold of their peers.

Here's why: your child needs to figure out how to be successful in the world, independent of your help. You may be frustrated by your child's prioritization of friends over family, but remember that, statistically speaking, few of us can rely on our family pedigree and accompanying social connections, inheritances, or enterprises to pave our paths in life. Most of us have to look outside the family unit for ways to ensure our future happiness and livelihood. Whether it's for big stuff, like getting hired for a job or finding a loving partner, or for smaller stuff, like making friends with the neighbors so they'll pick up your mail while you're on vacation, our social connections outside the family set us up for success in adulthood. Middle schoolers intuitively understand this and begin exploring how to connect with, and be accepted by, people outside of their families in ways that may seem extreme to you, but do serve a developmental purpose.

Despite that drive, making friends isn't easy in middle school. It's a relational skill that takes time to learn through trial and error, particularly because as your kid is developing social skills at their own pace, their peers are developing theirs at different rates. Picture a bunch of mechanical gears spinning at different speeds on a board. Despite the odds, sometimes two gears latch and that part of the board operates smoothly. More often than not, though, the gears keep bumping against each other, missing their timing and fit. Eventually, kids stop changing so rapidly and they settle into themselves, making settling into each other easier. But the first few years of this gear-dance are tough to watch.

Leah was a typical seventh grader at my summer leadership camp for girls. Her mom, Jocelyn, described middle school as a period of misplaced connections and loneliness for her daughter. Leah had been best friends with a girl named Myra throughout elementary school. In middle school, they were suddenly no longer in the same classes, and when they got together, Leah used to complain. "Mom, she still plays pretend." Because they had no more daily routines together and no longer had shared interests, the friendship had run its course. Leah no longer wanted a playmate; she wanted a confidante to share crushes and pet peeves with, someone who would fall into fits of laughter with her over private jokes.

Even still, and sadly, the void left by Myra was tough to fill. The rest of middle school passed with mostly superficial interactions that were pleasant, if not deep. Jocelyn and I talked about giving Leah lots of opportunities to meet new friends, but without putting any pressure on her to find a replacement. Instead, Jocelyn reframed the years before high school as the first round of a game Leah would soon come to love. It was practice, Jocelyn told her, for the opportunities she would find once she got to high school where she would be immersed in a bigger crowd full of new kids like her who had also been practicing for when the game took off. Sometimes practice isn't as fun as a game, but it's how you learn to get good.

Normalizing Tween Friendships

It's hard to see your child pine for a close friend with no likely candidates in sight, care too much about what people think of them, or sacrifice their self-worth for the opportunity to hang with kids who mistreat them but lend social status.

In some ways, our culture sets kids up for this. We advertise good friendships as part of the Complete Teenage Experience, because good friendships make for great stories. Content creators romanticize adolescent friendships the same way Hallmark movies treat love: there is a lid for every pot, a yin for every yang, and a savior for every screwup. Turn on any Netflix original movie about teenagers or read any great YA book, and you will see that the perfect sidekick (funny! supportive! quirky! endlessly loyal!) is a fixture in each teen's life.

In reality, middle school friendships play out less like Netflix originals, and more like those toy commercials that came on during Saturday morning cartoons when we were kids. As an only child, I remember yearning to have the same fun those kids were having, begging my parents for the Barbie Jeep or Hot Wheels Track until they gave in. But soon after ripping the toy from its packaging, I came to the stark realization that it was nothing like advertised. Those kids were only pretending to have fun, the set designers made the toys seem infinitely cooler than they actually were, and more often than not, we didn't even have the right-sized batteries. What a colossal disappointment! Especially when those kids on TV looked like they were having *the time of their lives*.

So how do you reconcile your tween's idealistic vision of a best friend with the reality that young friendships are usually tumultuous and un-predictable? Begin with normalizing the ups and downs of friendships. Remind your child, while watching Netflix or reading a book by Rainbow Rowell, that friendships rarely work the way they do on TV or in books. (Important disclaimer: I love Netflix and Rainbow Rowell and John Green and Bo Burnham and a bunch of other creators of amazing YA con-tent. They not only make great entertainment, but you can use their sto-ries to talk with your kid about how fiction compares to real life.)

In reality, elementary friendships predictably dissolve in middle school, and new friendships go through ups and downs. Some kids get dumped by their best friends. Others do the dumping. Some kids don't find their missing puzzle piece until high school, or beyond. Others seem to go through a revolving door of besties. You can point out that having a soul mate in middle school would be a nice lottery to win, but the odds are small. Most of us, after all, aren't still best friends with the person who sat next to us in middle school homeroom. For the 1 percent of you whose seventh-grade friendships lasted until twelfth grade, congratulations! You really did win the lottery.

For the other 99 percent, success may not look like sharing two halves of a heart-shaped locket, or meeting outside of school to walk in together. Having a wide range of friendship experiences, including the good and the bad, helps kids learn what makes for a good friend and eventually a good partner. Remind your tween, even if they are struggling, lonely, or doubtful, that their job is to be open to new experiences and new people. Learning how to talk with lots of different people, fluidly move among friend groups, initiate invitations, respectfully say no, and recognize the things people do that make them feel good or bad, will set your child up for friendship success down the road. At the risk of sounding like a Pinterest quote, being successful at friendship in middle school is more about what the journey teaches you and less about the end result. (Excuse me now while I go get a lengthy tattoo.)

There are countless ways conversations about friends will come up for you and your child over the next few years. Below I've given you two scenarios that have emerged in most of the families who work with me. More than providing a right or wrong answer to help your kids through the highs and lows of young friendship, I hope these sample dialogues will give you a feel for the general vibe of this topic. You can then tweak the ideas and sentiments in these specific dialogues to fit the other ways you'll talk about friendship before the start of high school.

Let's begin by looking at how a conversation about friendships in a state of flux might naturally come up in your home.

BEGIN peacefully

Parent: *Hey, should we invite the Berkmeiers over for a cookout this weekend?*
Kid: *Do we have to?*
Parent: *Well, no . . . Is everything okay with you and Josh?*
Kid: *Everything's fine. I just don't want to.*
Parent: *Okay, no problem.* [Resists urge to say things like "But you and Josh are best friends!" or "We love family game night with the Berkmeiers."]

RELATE to your kid

Parent: *I may be misreading this situation, but just so you know, I used to hate it when my parents would make me hang out with our neighbors when I didn't want to. I know friendships can come and go, and if you guys are in a rut, I can hold off on scheduling things for a while.*
Kid: *Yeah, let's do that.*
Parent: *Could I get some guidance from you on my timing and how to handle this, since I'm friends with Josh's parents? Just to make sure I'm not messing this up?*
Kid: *What do you mean?*

INTERVIEW to collect data

Parent: *Well, if you feel like you need a break, I can just not ask them over for the next couple of weekends, or say we have plans if they call. But if you*

*think this is a bigger break, I can't stall forever, so we'd need to plan
for that.*

Kid: *Josh has just gotten so annoying. He waits for me at school outside
of class when I'm already planning to walk to my next class with someone
else, and then he jumps in and takes over the conversation. He acts like we
have to do everything together. He texts me every day after school. I don't
want to hang out with just him.*

Parent: *Oh, yeah, I see what you're saying. It's hard when a friend needs so
much from you. Do you think he's had a hard time making other friends?*

Kid: *I have no idea. He could make other friends if he gave me a break.*

Parent: *Is there a way to get this message to him without hurting his
feelings?*

Kid: *I'm not gonna say right to his face to leave me alone, because that's
mean. Some kids do that. Mostly, I just go out of my way to avoid him. I
don't know why he's not getting the hint.*

Parent: *Do you think he is getting the hint, but doesn't want it to be true?
Or is it going over his head?*

Kid: *He gets mad when I'm not where he expects me to be. He'll text me like
a million times "Where r u?" And I just ignore it, so he'll get the hint. But he
doesn't, so then I just text back after school that I couldn't look at my phone
earlier.*

Parent: *I get that. Was he like this with you in elementary school, or is this
new behavior?*

Kid: *Well, we didn't have phones in elementary school, so he couldn't text
me all the time. But he was more chill, too.*

ECHO what you hear

Parent: *For whatever reason, it sounds like Josh is pretty needy right now
and that's hard on you.*

Kid: *It's too much. I just want him to give me a break.*

FEEDBACK

Parent: *I respect that. Part of your job at this age is figuring out how to
set boundaries and limits with people. That's hard to learn, because when*

you have a long history with someone they sometimes think your limits shouldn't apply to them.

Kid: *He's* definitely *pushing my limits.*

Parent: *I'd like to help. I have a few ideas to share and if you could think them over and then give me some feedback later about how to proceed, that would be helpful.*

We have an unusual situation because our families have been friends for so long. I think I will arrange for me and Dad to have dinner this weekend with Josh's parents and leave the kids at home. I'll say I need a "kid break."

That will buy you a couple weeks to think about how you want to move forward, but I can't stall forever. While I would never force you to be friends with someone, I will expect you to treat him like a family friend when we are together. If you can still be kind without being as close, you have a good chance of this working itself out better for both of you.

One last thing: I think you should consider how you can communicate your limits better to Josh, because it seems that he's not getting the message you're sending when you ignore or avoid him. Since ignoring his texts doesn't work, maybe you could politely just say no? It's not mean to say no to someone. In fact, it's usually nicer than letting them wonder what's up.

Anyway, that's something to think about. Let's touch base again in a couple weeks to see how you're feeling about a family get-together.

This is a specific, although common, scenario for families dealing with friendship breakups. No matter the context, below are three of the key messages that will be universally true for all your discussions about friendship:

1. Who your kid is friends with is *their* choice, not yours. You can put restrictions on what places your kid is allowed to go and what things they're allowed to do, but not who they can speak with and especially not who they find interesting. If your child falls into a pattern of being attracted to people who make terrible choices or treat them badly, a good counselor can help them look at their relationships with more clarity.

2. Your kid doesn't need to be friends with (or friendly to) everyone, but everyone deserves to be treated with *dignity*. If you're not familiar with author Rosalind Wiseman's work with teens through her Cultures of Dignity website, check out her distinction between *dignity* and *respect*. Wiseman teaches teens that respect is earned (and let's face it—not all kids earn respect from each other), but that dignity is inherent to being human.

3. The Greek philosopher Heraclitus said it best: "The only thing that is constant is change." Emotions between friends are intense, but not permanent. When you talk with your kids about their relationships, encourage them *not* to burn bridges. After all, if things could change once, they could certainly change again. (An aside about old Heraclitus: while historical details from this era are fuzzy, I can say with certainty this was a kid who had to develop some strong coping skills in middle school to get over being born with a name like that.)

In Lieu of a Mega Friend

When my son was little, he would sometimes build a Mega Man out of Legos. Mega Man never looked the same twice, and he never looked like a man once. He was a blob of incongruous bricks mixed with wheels, windows, heads, doors, machine parts, and anything else that could be attached. The object of building Mega Man wasn't to achieve realism. It was to cram as many possibilities into one guy-like action figure as possible.

My son was onto something big. (Mega, even.)

Too often, adults expect one person to be all things for them. We search for a partner we will hold to impossible standards: *please be totally stable with a spontaneous side, contemplative yet outspoken, enjoy quiet nights of reading but also be the life of the party, and be completely transparent while leaving a little room for mystery* . . . and when we can't find this unicorn, we think we're the misfits destined to go it alone, untethered and incomplete.

Be careful not to set your child up for failure by expecting their friendships, or the friends themselves, to be perfect. Instead, discuss the value in connecting with different people to meet different needs. Best Friend doesn't have to be an exclusive title at the top of the pyramid. It can be an inner-circle level of friendship reached by those who've put in the time and built the trust to be there.

> Be careful not to set your child up for failure by expecting their friendships, or the friends themselves, to be perfect. Instead, discuss the value in connecting with different people to meet different needs.

Understanding this will serve your kid well in early adolescence as they long for a bestie, and later in high school when romantic relationships evolve. For now, your kid likely will not find another middle schooler who loves listening to musicals, learning sign language, eating fried okra, and practicing taekwondo. But maybe they have a friend at Scouts who knows all the words to the *Hamilton* soundtrack, and a school friend who cracks them up and doesn't mind okra, and a neighborhood friend who'd be up to try taekwondo this summer. If the perfect one true friend is nowhere to be found, kids can piece together a rich experience with a variety of people, creating an amalgamation of a Mega Friend from several different people. (Windows, wheels, and extra heads sold separately.)

Let's look at how you might have a conversation about this new take on friendships with your middle schooler.

BEGIN peacefully

Parent: [Watching TV with kid] *This show makes me wonder something. Should I pause it or do you want me to talk after?*
Kid: *You can pause it.*

RELATE to your kid

Parent: [Pressing pause] *Seeing how this show handles the main character and his best friend . . . it doesn't seem realistic to me.*

Kid: *How?*

Parent: *They had that big fight, but then joked it off and got over it quickly. That wasn't my experience when I was your age. I had friends, but not this kind of perfect, unbreakable friendship you see on TV.*

INTERVIEW to collect data

Parent: *Does it seem realistic to you?*

Kid: *It's just TV, so I don't think it has to be realistic. A lot of people get over stuff easily with friends. But some kids are more sensitive. And some kids love drama. They can't put every type of person in a TV show.*

Parent: *True. Maybe I'm just more sensitive. Do you feel like you fit in well with your friend group, or do you wish anything were different?*

Kid: *The kids in my group are good, but yeah, I wish I had a friend who was more into all the same stuff as me. I used to do everything with Lizzie, but now that we're at different schools I don't have one person who's great, just a group of people who are pretty good.*

ECHO what you hear

Parent: *What you're saying sounds like how I remember it. I think most people, when they get to middle school, experience a shift in friendships and feel a little less connected than they did in elementary school.*

Kid: *Yeah, I like my group, but I'm still kind of waiting to find my best friend in middle school.*

FEEDBACK

Parent: *That's totally normal for this time of your life. Did you know only 1 percent of people stay close with their middle school best friends through high school? So you're right on track if you don't find your person until later.*

Kid: *Is that true? That's kind of depressing.*

Parent: *It's true, but I think it's liberating. It takes the pressure off of you to make the perfect connection. Instead of looking for one person to be the perfect friend, you can just practice being in a group and connecting with* *lots of different people. You might have one friend who makes you laugh the most, one who you like studying with, one who matches your soccer skills. That's why I brought this up. TV shows like this make it seem like you should have a perfect best friend, but in reality that is more of a high school thing. For now, you're right where you should be.*

Should I press play on the show again?

The idea that everyone else has a best friend is a falsehood and when you reframe your kid's expectations, you help them feel more comfortable in their skin. And what's better for making new friends than being comfortable with yourself? This will likely become a self-fulfilling prophecy: care less about finding a close friend and you're likely to find one sooner.

Conversation Crashers

One of the biggest obstacles to having a nice conversation with your middle schooler about friendship is that they are actively trying not to care what you think about their friends. The more judgmental you seem toward people (in general, but especially toward people their age), the more likely they will be to write off your opinions. Stay neutral and open to their interpretations of friends. Show them what it means to be a good listener more than a teacher. Above all else, avoid the following conversation crashers that are sure to stop a good talk cold.

"I don't like you being friends with so-and-so." By the time your kid starts middle school, you can't control who they're friends with. You could establish rules about who they can hang out with outside of school hours, but it's impossible to police who they spend time with during the school day, or run into in public. Maybe you have a bad impression of someone, but maybe you're wrong. When someone controls who their partner is friends with, it's a red flag for power abuse in a relationship. You don't want your future teen to think this is normal because they heard it from you first. Instead of banning a person, you can restrict certain activities with someone.

"It might be for the best. I never liked them." When your child is hurt by a former friend, you might be tempted to smack talk the other person as a way to make your kid feel better. Remember, your kid is hurt because they liked that person, and may still. They'll hear this as an indictment on their judgment. Also, *ouch*, it's hard to hear something is for the best when it hurts.

"I wish people could see you the way I do." Barf, is what your kid will be thinking. No kid wants the other kids at school to see them the way their forty-five-year-old parent does.

"You'll find your person eventually." Maybe not. Perhaps it will be equally fulfilling to have lots of people in your life you can rely on for different things, instead of just one you count on for most everything.

"Just remember to be kind to everyone." Your child is going to hear this and think it smacks of kindergarten. "Be nice to the bully who pushes me into the wrong bathroom? Smile at the frenemy who tells the others at the table not to talk with me at lunch?" The middle school social world is too complex for such a simple approach. Instead, acknowledge the nuances of social dynamics and brainstorm responses that fit what the situation calls for.

"But [that person] is so nice!" Have we learned nothing from Eddie Haskell, Nellie Oleson, Draco Malfoy, or Regina George? Your child's perception of another child is true for them. In the same way that the doctor trusts your perception of your pain on a scale of 1 to 10, you have to take your kid's word for it on how others make them feel. Instead of asking for a more accurate evaluation of someone's character, pay attention to how your child self-reports their feelings. Then focus your energy on helping your child deal with those feelings, instead of correcting their interpretations.

"A real friend wouldn't treat you this way." It's tempting to use our kid's bad interactions with peers to teach them what a good friend would or wouldn't do, but it also feels confusing to a kid who hears this

and simultaneously thinks, "But they *are* my friend, and they *did* do that."
When you think your kid is being mistreated by a friend, try asking them
to imagine someone else in their situation. "Does that seem okay to you?
If this same thing happened between your sister and a friend, what advice would you give her?"

Look to the Future

Early adolescence is just the beginning of learning how to make new
friends, independent of a parent's or teacher's influence and matchmak-
ing. Middle schoolers need you to normalize the bumpiness of the road
at the beginning, so they can relax from the pressure to be well-liked and
ease into the comfort of getting to know themselves and what they can
expect from friends. Kids this age often feel like they're floating and un-
attached, but if you can frame that sensation as practice for the more en-
during relationships they'll form in high school, it will give this period a
sense of purpose.

Further, now is a good time to ask your child to consider what kind of
friend they want (and hope to be). The qualities they choose will serve as
a guidepost to future connections, first friendly and then romantic. This
doesn't need to be an actual list written on paper, but could be a topic of casual conversation. Resist the temptation to generate the list of the qualities your child should look for in a friend. Your list would likely sound like
a generic character education word bank: nice, supportive, fair, funny, reliable, and so on. Plus, you'd be listing the attributes that matter most to
you. Maybe stability is high on your list, and adventure-seeking is high on
your child's. It's time for your child to develop their emotional vocabulary and you can support this by asking your child how certain people, or
certain interactions, make them feel. This is a great starter step to them
identifying what to look for in a friend, as you can begin to recognize patterns like "I notice you seem happiest with friends who are introverted/
extroverted/creative/curious/well-mannered/spontaneous. Does that
seem true to you?"

As you think about your child making new friends over the next few
years, picture an amusement park. Can you see that parent waiting on a

bench next to the roller coaster, holding everyone's coats and bags? That person is you now. Don't get on the ride with your kid to experience all the emotional ups and downs of friendships at this age. You're there to encourage them to take some risks and have as much fun as possible, be a comfort when they're nervous or unhappy, and provide all the cold drinks, snacks, and chauffeur service you can reasonably tolerate.

In a Hurry? Here's Your Crash Course

- Becoming an independent adult involves a shift from being pleasing to your parents to being successful among your peers. This creates new pressure to be accepted by friends and classmates, and makes it harder for kids to cope with the changes that friendships naturally go through during adolescence.

- Only 1 percent of friendships formed in seventh grade last until twelfth grade. Remind tweens that learning how to talk with new people and being open to new experiences will benefit them more down the road than finding a soul mate at age twelve.

- Pop culture romanticizes teen friendships, increasing the pressure kids feel to find a best friend. Parents should normalize an honest portrayal of adolescent friendship. It's not ideal, but it is perfectly normal, to feel like a misfit, or long for better friendships, or mourn lost friendships.

- When kids don't want to maintain old friendships, teach them how to treat people with dignity, even if they aren't going to stay close.

- Help kids see that they may not have *one* friend who is all things to them. Having different friends who fill different needs can be just as satisfying.

- Kids get defensive when you comment on their friends. Use other people's experiences, in real life or in books/on TV, to talk about how good friends treat each other.

CHAPTER

7

Talking About Creativity

In this chapter, you'll discover why creativity is critical to future happiness and success, how to foster creativity during an age when it appears to disappear, what usually replaces play in adolescence, how technology pairs surprisingly well with creativity at this age, and ways to introduce more conversations about creativity with simple household fun.

Why Creativity Matters

Fast-forward to ten years from now: your twelve-year-old is now twenty-two, and starting their first entry-level job at a major national bank. You feel as though your work here is done, and you're ready to celebrate. And you should. Getting kids out of the house and able to pay their own bills is the dream, and yours has come true.

Now imagine your newly minted adult in a staff meeting at the bank with a boss who is panicked over a problem no one seems able to solve. Boss Person is anxiously pacing the floor, demanding "We need to fix this! Why can't anyone figure out what's going on here?" Creativity isn't just the domain of artists. Creativity is a vital part of all jobs, whether you design clothes for a living or work at a bank.

A 2010 survey of 1,500 CEOs from sixty countries identified creativity as the "most crucial factor for future success." The boss in the opening scenario doesn't need someone to decoupage the desks to make the office prettier. She needs someone who can solve problems, and that requires creative, flexible thinking. Young adults who haven't practiced creative thinking will get stuck at work, and in life. They're used to accepting the status quo. Leaders, in work and elsewhere, must be creative enough to question things, see things differently, and execute new ideas in clever ways.

It's not just future employers who need creative thinkers, either. What happens when your kid can't make rent? Or when they're asked to be in a wedding they can't afford? You don't want them coming to you for a sofa to sleep on or a handout whenever a problem presents itself. How can we expect young adults to solve problems they've never experienced before, unless they're used to brainstorming and thinking creatively?

Which brings me to resilience, that enviable ability to bounce back from tough situations. Creativity and flexibility go hand in hand, while rigidity is the enemy of mental health. Your child will fail and feel pain often throughout life, but the more they learn to tap into creative ways to get past that, the more resilient they will become.

Last but not least, creativity is fun, and what is life without plenty of fun? I'm someone for whom putting words on paper is the most fun creative outlet I know. I have friends who would rather sew a dress or make a clay pot. I'm not good with my hands in that way, but whatever the outlet, creativity leads to a *product*. Most of us work hard every day, but don't get to see or touch the results of our hard work. It can be depressing to feel the cumulative effect of constant, daily effort with nothing to point at and say, "Look, I did that!"

I live in the second largest banking city in the United States, and most of the bankers I know tell me they are happiest after they've planted a garden, painted a room, or cooked a good meal. They like their jobs, usually, but their daily work doesn't give them *joy* the way making something tangible does. Keeping this sense of joy and pride alive in adolescence so it can buoy your future adult through later life is as important as anything I can think of when raising a teen.

Having conversations that speak to the value of creativity may not seem like a top priority in middle school, but take a moment to imagine the many possible challenges a kid in high school may face: unreasonable teachers, pushy romantic partners, persuasive friends, and demanding schedules. Any of these could cause a young adolescent to give in against their gut, but a person who is used to approaching problems creatively, and has an outlet for stress, stands a better chance of staying true to themselves, despite the challenges they are sure to face.

What Happens to Creativity During Adolescence?

Little kids are naturally, abundantly creative. This has two major upsides: one, it keeps kids busy on impossibly long days and two, it helps them communicate how they're feeling to you. Kids will offer up chunky beaded necklaces or crayon masterpieces to express their gratitude and love. Or on rough days, like adorable little psychopaths, they'll slide an unflattering I Hate You! portrait under your door. At least you know where they stand.

These days, you're mostly in the dark. Imaginative expressions of your child's emotions drop off as kids age out of elementary school, and it's not just because so many arts programs are cut at that age. Do middle schoolers stop creating things for you because they no longer want to show you gratitude? Does their general expressiveness go mute? Or does the well of creativity just dry up in adolescence?

Let's look at gratitude first, because so many parents struggle with their kids' lack thereof. We all know tweens long to feel more grown-up. Appreciation toward a parent can seem childish to them, and can even feel (incorrectly) like it's the same thing as dependency. You say, "I tidied up your room for you while you were at school!" and, instead of a hug, you get, "I didn't ask you to." Ouch. Your tween is thinking, "I can do that for myself, the way I like, on my own schedule. I'm not a baby." So yes, gratitude wanes somewhat during these years. But creativity . . . where does that go?

Between the afternoon-long battles over your son wanting to play Fortnite, your daughter bingeing all ten seasons of *Friends* on Netflix, or your oldest scrolling endlessly through Snapchat, screens *seem* to be a big culprit. No doubt, it's easy to lose track of time on screens, though adults are probably as guilty as the rest of the population when it comes to vacuous consumption of social media or TV. I'm just not convinced technology is the only guilty party here in sapping our kids' creativity.

What seems to be a disappearance of their imagination may actually be more of a temporary relocation. Just as kids transition from concrete to hypothetical thinking in middle school, their creative projects also become less concrete, less visible, and less tangible. Rather than creating fun new games, art projects, forts, or baked goods, your middle schooler's current creative drive is probably directed toward building something much bigger: themselves. Young adolescents are almost always working on their new personal brand. I remember a lot of my own energy in adolescence was spent figuring out how to achieve bangs that were simultaneously spiky *and* cascading. It took hours of observation and practice, and in the end, I had little to show for my creative efforts, other than limp, overgelled hair. Had there been such a wondrous thing as YouTube hair tutorials in the 1980s, I can say with certainty I would have increased my Time Spent on Bangs by at least a multiple of ten.

Likewise, your child may not have a lot to show for their efforts at this age, but they are probably spending a lot of creative energy on both contemplating and practicing who they want to be and how they want others to perceive them. Still . . . you'd like for your tween to recognize the value of contribution over consumption, because it's not fun to live with someone who always seems distracted, zoned out, or self-absorbed. So how do you have a conversation that inspires your tween to be creative in a way that isn't merely self-serving, but also contributes to their friends, family, and community?

How to Talk About Creativity

Because creativity is all around us, there are lots of natural ways to segue into this topic. One easy way I've found to encourage creativity is to latch on to a tween's almost universal desire to start a business and make money. Early entrepreneurial endeavors often replace "play" for kids in middle school. This is when kids begin babysitting, offering pet care or lawn services, or selling wonky, homemade pot holders/cookies/brace-lets/tie-dyes/bookmarks.

At a parenting talk I gave in Boston, a woman in the audience asked me to explain my reasoning behind letting kids start their own businesses when so much of the burden falls to the parents to get supplies, clean up, deliver to customers, and so on. Her (correct) assessment was that kids this age are all idea and little follow-through. In other words, they aren't ready. True! But I'm not suggesting your kid start a *successful* endeavor. That's a highly unlikely endgame, although, more power to the kids I read about in the paper who start city-wide clothing drives for the homeless, or sell record numbers of cookies to cure cancer, or mow enough lawns to take their family on vacation. Perhaps you've read these articles, too, and shown them to your kids as examples of what they could achieve with the right amount of perseverance. For a middle schooler, this is probably the equivalent of showing them an article about Steph Curry and saying, "You, too, could be in the NBA one day!" Sure, maybe! But also, almost definitely not.

Don't let the creative superstars trick you into thinking that coming up incredibly short isn't the real goal.

> Don't let the creative superstars trick you into thinking that coming up incredibly short isn't the real goal.

My answer to the mom at my parenting talk was not to get involved in a kid's business endeavor. Aside, perhaps, from helping pro-cure supplies, kids *should* flounder here. When they do, that's when they get creative. The purpose of saying yes isn't to back a successful plan. It's to acknowledge the importance of staying creative, curious, and engaged. It's about keeping kids' brains fired up. Yes, even if half of the pot holders never make it to their customers. (Right there, for example, is an oppor-tunity to learn how to send a creative follow-up e-mail about refunds.)

Let's look at how you might have a conversation about creativity around a small business using the BRIEF conversation model.

BEGIN peacefully

Kid: *Mom, Jamie and I are going to make tie-dye socks and sell them at school.*

Parent: *Oh, cool! How are you getting supplies?*

Kid: *I don't know. Would you . . .*

RELATE to your kid

Parent: *I'm glad you've thought of a creative way to make some income. Are you asking me to get the supplies? Are you asking me to pay for them, too?*

Kid: *Well, we don't have any money, which is kind of why we're doing the business.*

Parent: *I see. As a business owner myself, I respect that you might need a small investment.*

INTERVIEW to collect data

Parent: *Can you go on Amazon and find a good price for plain white socks and a tie-dye kit and get back to me?*

Kid: *Yes! How much are you giving us?*

Parents: *Oh, I'm not sure I am yet. I need to see some figures first. Do the research and come back to me. Then I can give you an answer.*

[Five minutes later]

Kid: *Okay! We need thirty dollars for socks and fifteen dollars for tie-dye. Unless you want to get the bigger kit with more colors. That's thirty dollars.*

Parent: *You need forty-five to sixty dollars to make socks? How many socks will that buy?*

Kid: *We can get twenty white socks for thirty dollars.*

Parent: *And how much are you selling them for after you tie-dye them?*

[It's key to keep your voice neutral. Don't give feedback yet—through words or tone—no matter how absurd the idea may seem. Just collect data.]

Kid: *Um, I don't know. Fifteen dollars each?*

Parent: *You sound uncertain. Is that what you guys agree on for the price?*

Kid: *I don't know. It could be more or less. What do you think? We just want to make as much money as possible.*

ECHO what you hear

Parent: *Got it. Sounds like you want to have the most profit and the smallest expense. That's good business sense. And you also need some way to purchase your starting supplies. Am I right so far?*
Kid: *Yes!*

FEEDBACK

Parent: *What I'm thinking is that first of all, this is a cool idea. In terms of the cost of supplies, forty-five to sixty dollars is a lot of money for me. Here is what I'd be willing to do: I'll contribute fifteen dollars toward the first sock purchase. You can make up the rest with your savings. Once you sell your first batch, you can repay me my fifteen dollars. For the tie-dye, I'm willing to buy the smaller kit for fifteen dollars and instead of repaying me from your sales, I'll accept payment in fifteen dollars' worth of favors and chores.*

It's up to you how you price the socks. Fifteen dollars sounds high to me for kids your age, but you could do something called "market research" and ask your friends what they would pay. You can also take orders ahead of time. That part is totally up to you. If you don't sell enough to pay me back for the initial socks, we'll take it out of your allowance. But if you hustle and work hard, you can make enough to order more supplies and make more money! Oh, and it goes without saying, only do the tie-dye outside and let me check your setup before you start.

Sound good?

Who's to say if this hypothetical business venture will ever make money, or even get past the planning phase? But time spent planning, dreaming, and executing—even if that phase is short-lived—is time well spent.

This conversation could have gone in a totally different direction if the parent had started off with skepticism for the plan and criticism for past messes made. The kid's creative spark might have been squelched at the outset, or because they overheard their parent complaining to a friend that all their kid does is watch YouTube videos of other people doing things.

Social Media and Creativity: A Match Made in Cyber Heaven

Another easy space to bring up the value of creativity is around the topic of social media. Because it's such a visual medium, it's easy to spot creativity, or a lack thereof, in how a tween posts. Yes, I know, some families don't allow phones or apps until well after middle school. I do not advocate for or against social media use at any given age. I hope the format of the conversation still helps even if the topic is not on your radar yet. (Though I would add, even if your child doesn't have a phone or social media account yet, many kids around them do, and it's still meaningful to talk about creative content as a way to lay a foundation for their future use. You might show your own feed or a celebrity account to make your point.)

When I look at a tween's Instagram account, I always *hope* to see a variety of photos, but if I were a betting woman, my money would be on a string of selfies with a spattering of group friend shots. It's about as fun to scroll through as it is to read one endless, boring run-on sentence.

This then becomes a great opportunity for you to talk about creativity on Instagram, or yes, even Finsta (your child's fake Instagram account under a pseudonym). Most kids who have Finstas keep them hidden from their parents. While you can't address what you don't see, you can mention you know they exist, you don't know whether your child has one, and you hope if they are doing *anything* online, whether it feels private or not, it should contribute to their well-being and not make them, or anyone else, feel bad.

Speaking of feeling bad, creative social media use is more likely to make you feel good, while passive social media use has a negative effect. A 2017 study titled "Do Social Network Sites Enhance or Undermine Subjective Well-Being? A Critical Review" found that "passive use of social media (so-called lurking without engaging) is negatively associated with well-being, but active use of social media (posting, commenting, sharing) is positively associated with well-being." This is a great case for engaging with social media in a creative way, rather than mindlessly scrolling through.

Here's how a conversation around social media and creativity might go following the BRIEF model. Instagram is the topic here, but social media apps come and go in terms of popularity. The advice applies to any social media.

BEGIN peacefully

Parent: *Hey, that was a cute pic you posted today.*
Kid: *Had to show my new earrings!*
Parent: *Yep, they're cute! Do you want to get a snack? I want to chat for a few minutes about social media. Nothing's wrong! Just a check-in.*
Kid: *Am I in trouble?*

RELATE to your kid

Parent: *Not at all. I was just thinking this morning about how I spent ten minutes over breakfast scrolling through Facebook, and then realized none of it was even interesting. I don't know if that ever happens with your Instagram feed, too.*
Kid: *I mean, sometimes. But I like it. Sometimes it's boring, but mostly it's fun.*

INTERVIEW to collect data

Parent: *It seems like most people you know usually post selfies, with an occasional group pic. Would you say that's true, or do you see people being more creative than that?*
Kid: *Well, it might be true, but it's not a big deal.*
Parents: *I agree—not a big deal. I'm just curious about how the app is used differently by different people. Do you follow any accounts that aren't your friends?*
Kid: *No, you told me not to follow anyone who I'm not friends with.*
Parent: *True! But you can follow some bigger verified accounts, if you want. National Geographic posts amazing photos. We Rate Dogs is hilarious. I follow some comedians I like. It's a nice way to get some*

diversity in your feed if you wanted to. If you're going to use the app, might as well get more out of it.

Kid: *Okay, awesome.*

Parent: *Which kinds of posts do you think are most boring or annoying?*

Kid: *Ugh, I hate it when someone posts something like "I look really ugly today," and you know they're just fishing for compliments!*

Parent: *That does sound annoying. Do guys ever do that, or just girls?*

Kid: *Mostly girls. But when guys do mirror selfies to show their abs, that's really weird.*

Parent: *I mean, could you imagine if I did that?*

Kid: *Gross. Never. Don't you dare.*

Parent: *Ha—I never would! But really, what if I did post a selfie every day on Facebook? If someone only posts the same kind of pics every day: whether it's selfies, or ab pics, or pics of their dinner, they're just being what's called "one-note." Imagine if a song has only one note in it. Most boring song in the world. When it comes to your account, I'd encourage you to give some thought to being more creative than that.*

Kid: *Yeah, I get it. I just don't think Instagram is the place for me to change that.*

Parent: *Why not?*

Kid: *'Cause literally all my friends post tons of selfies. I don't think you realize this is just normal.*

ECHO what you hear

Parent: *I get that. It definitely seems like that's how other people use the app. It can feel weird to be the first to do something differently.*

FEEDBACK

Parent: *So here is my thought on this, and then we don't have to dwell on it. Your account is like a window into your personal brand. And if your account is 90 percent selfies, it runs the risk of sounding like a one-note song. You do a ton of cool things people don't see if you only post selfies. You volunteer at the barn, have a cute dog, take amazing pics of the beach. I just think those would be cool photography subjects for you.*

Check out five or six certified accounts—the ones with the blue check marks to show they are official—on a range of topics or from a range of people. Get an idea for how people outside your friend bubble are posting. Then maybe also download an editing app for your photos. There are some cool things you could be doing with adding graphic design elements to nature pics. Play around a little with it. You don't have to post what you edit, but learning the tools could be fun. And if you decide you want to start photographing a broader variety of things, we can even look into photography lessons this summer. Sound good?

It's important to note that these conversations can take any number of twists and turns, as you discover more and more important things you need to tell your kid about these big topics. Stay focused and narrow. This conversation could have easily branched off into a myriad of issues: Internet safety, good digital citizenship, commenting etiquette, and not overposting, to name just some. All important. But never beat yourself up for not touching on everything at one time. Remember to stay brief and focused (here, for example, on creativity alone) or your kid will tune you out.

Conversation Crashers

A lengthy conversation isn't the only thing that will make your kid stop listening. Here are some other ways you might inadvertently thwart your kid's receptiveness to talking about this with you:

"I can't handle another mess!": Creativity is inherently sloppy, so I understand and relate to the instinct to say no when it comes to one more mess to clean in an already chaotic day. The mess will be less when it's contained to a screen (so there's another check in the pros column for kids using technology), but there's something unique about the creativity that comes from digging your hands into something; it's worth saying yes when you can. You can, and should, say no to some ideas without worrying it will squelch your kid's creativity as long as you sometimes say yes to others. When you want to say no, try the yes-no-yes approach to balance their enthusiasm with your need for peace and quiet. "Yes, that sounds like a great idea. No, we can't do it today because [fill in the blank: I am exhausted and this might require my help, our chores need some attention, we don't have the supplies]. Yes, this weekend would be the perfect time for that fun idea."

"I don't get it.": Guilty. Sometimes I'm not sure how to show enthusiasm for a project, especially when I don't understand it, or in my head am thinking, "This couldn't have turned out the way they wanted." My go-to in that position is to interview about the process. "Oh . . . neat. What, uh, what's this part? What did you do? Did you mean for this thing to be over here?" It's nice to ask someone about their process if you're genuinely curious, but if you're substituting a lackluster reaction with logistical questions, your tween can read that. It will sound like you're digging for flaws in the process. If you don't have a positive reaction, instead try asking one or two questions about their experience. "Was it fun or hard or both? Were you surprised by anything? What's your plan for this creation?"

"What could you do better next time?": We can be so focused on results with our kids, we jump right to evaluation without realizing it. You focus on how much money they raised, or how many awards they won, or the praise their teacher heaped on them. Certainly, working hard for results and learning to evaluate success is a skill you want your child to develop. This chapter is focused on creativity for its own sake, so for these conversations, try reacting and relating to their experience, instead of talking about what worked and what didn't, or how to improve next time.

"Now, can you apply that to something meaningful?": Sometimes we inadvertently devalue the types of creation our kids enjoy, especially when talking about our kids to our adult friends. "She's so funny, I just wish she'd use that talent for something other than making memes—ha ha!" "He's a good writer and his teachers say he's got a gift, but he's obsessed with making manga comics and they have about ten words a page. We don't want him to waste his gift." "She used to be such a good painter. If only we could get her to care about something other than her nail polish now." The way your kid expresses creativity in middle school will likely not be how they did in elementary school or how they will in high school and beyond. These years are for remembering the joy of being creative and exploring new ways to be expressive.

"This is so cool. Here's what I'd do to make it better." If you are someone who loves being creative, or if your kid is naturally talented, you probably delight in their projects and how much potential they have. You love watching them work and maybe you even have ideas for "making it better!" I have to check myself here, because creativity excites me. When my kids have to write *anything,* I bite my tongue so hard it hurts. When they post a funny caption on social media, I send a quick text saying it cracked me up and I resist the urge to correct grammar or suggest a funny follow-up. (I don't always resist. This is hard.) But the moment I remember my mother suggesting a tweak to any of my endeavors, I know what *not* to do. Nothing kills momentum like a suggestion, even a good one.

Everyday Creativity Gets a Boost from Brainstorms

Outside of specific conversations about creative projects or outlets, another way to keep your child engaged with their creative mind is to brainstorm often in your home. It's as simple as floating a bunch of ideas about where to have dinner, how to teach the dog a new trick, what to pack for a road trip, how to respond to someone's mean comment, or the best way to organize the chore chart. We're all too busy to do this for every little thing, but now and again, engage your child in coming up with solutions to common family tasks or challenges.

The key to encouraging creativity when brainstorming is to accept all ideas initially, even the dumb ones. Most of us think spontaneously and our worst ideas come before our best. If you shut down an early idea your kid suggests, even if it's ridiculous ("The new chore chart should not include any chores that take more than two minutes!"), your kid will stop contributing. Write down all ideas, and after you get a full list, in a range from excellent to terrible, only then go back and scratch the ones that aren't feasible.

Our brains are skilled at shooting down creative ideas. Most of us operate in risk-assessment mode: "That is too hard, or might be embarrassing. I'm not ready yet." We're pretty adept at blocking our creative ideas before we even get a chance to try them. Getting your kid comfortable with creative thinking through brainstorming teaches them how to push back on the voice that says "you can't" and listen to the possibility of "maybe. . . ."

Other Ways to Bring This Topic Home

I've shared two sample conversations on creativity, but if neither of these specific scenarios comes up naturally with your kid, you can bring this up organically by looking for ways to encourage your child in something they're already doing. A common complaint I hear from parents of middle school boys is "All he wants to do is play video games." How do you find the creativity in *that*? Well, you extrapolate. Maybe he'd like to take a coding class at the community college to begin learning how video game designers make the magic happen. Maybe he'd like to host a gaming club at your house on Saturdays. (And maybe you say yes, if he agrees to design the flyers or cook the snacks.) Since he's so busy playing video games, you'll likely have to start this conversation yourself, instead of waiting for him to come to you with a request.

Family dinners or car rides are great times to casually bring up new topics. You could cite the statistic I mentioned in the beginning of this chapter about CEOs. "I heard something interesting today. A survey of CEOs found they rank creativity as the most important factor in business success. I don't think most people equate being creative with being a business person. Does that surprise you, too?" Playing naïve helps gets these conversations started, because it shifts the normal dynamic, positioning your child to feel more worldly or insightful. Then, once you're "convinced," let your kid know you agree about the importance of creativity. Say you'd like to support them by looking into fun things they could do in the areas of interest. Make it clear you aren't looking to replace what they already love, but to supplement it with more cool stuff.

You can also try a straightforward, inquisitive approach. "Remember when you used to build Lego kits for hours? Do you ever miss having a project like that to work on?" Some kids think it's time to stop playing in middle school, but with your permission, would love to indulge. Google "architectural Legos" if you think your tween would respond to a more mature theme. Offer to build with them to show playing isn't just for kids. "You'd be doing me a favor, because I've been looking for something to do as a family other than just watching movies."

Finally, be patient. Take baby steps for the win. You'd love it if your tween pored over your cookbooks and made a beautiful dinner for the family, but maybe the best you can get is them dumping in the premeasured ingredients for their favorite cookies, as they briskly pass through the kitchen en route to their room. Later, when you're sitting around eating the cookies, your tween will surely take credit, though. "I helped make these!" Resist the urge to counter with facts. ("Yeah, hardly! I had to twist your arm to get you to stop and dump in the flour.") Praise the tiny wins in hopes of reeling your kid back in. "Yep! Thank you for helping. Let me know if you ever want to cook with me again. Or I can buy ingredients if you want to make something with a friend."

Unlike some of the heavier topics you'll need to cover with your young teen, this one is all about fun. The more positive and accepting you are of their creative choices, the more likely they will be to share them with you now and in the future.

Ten More Ways to Encourage Creativity

The ways to encourage your child to stay tuned in to their creativity are endless, but here are ten simple things you can do or make available to your tween that may spark their creative energy.

1. A bin of art supplies (usually most appealing after it's been freshly organized and looks in need of messing up).

2. A gift card to a print shop to make business cards and flyers.

3. Blank journals, colorful pens, stickers.

4. Access to technology: graphic design apps, private YouTube channels, online lessons for a new hobby, and so on.

5. A subscription to a (cooking, nature, science, and so on) magazine with inspiring photos.

6. Photography lessons.

7. A cheap instrument bought off Craigslist.

8. Permission to decorate their room. The less you do for them and the less you finance, the more creative they'll have to be.

9. Toiletries, cosmetics, hair dye (temporary or permanent), and other drug store items for experimentation.

10. Boredom. Lots and lots of time to stare at the ceiling.

While you're encouraging creativity in your child, don't forget to treat *yourself* to some time to sit quietly and daydream, make something with your hands, or indulge your senses. When your child heads off to high school, you'll find yourself with a lot more time on your hands as they will soon be driving themselves places, hanging out with friends more, and needing your help and supervision less. If you can reconnect with a hobby you once loved, or discover a new one to explore, you'll find that time less lonely and more rewarding. As a bonus, you'll be practicing what you preach and setting a great example for your kids.

In a Hurry? Here's Your Crash Course

- Creativity is a crucial aspect of successful life and not just for artsy types. Business leaders cite creativity as the biggest factor in success.

- Encouraging creativity in—get this—creative ways, will help build your teen's resilience during the challenges of adolescence.

- Creativity changes in two important ways during early adolescence. First, tweens often turn their creativity inward, working on new ways to present themselves to the world. Second, creative play is often replaced with entrepreneurship. Encourage both.

- Technology isn't just a mind-numbing void. It can be a creative outlet for kids to express themselves.

- One of the best ways to encourage creative thinking at home is to engage your tween in brainstorming as often as possible. They need to learn their best ideas are often hiding behind their worst.

- Look for ways to encourage creativity by extrapolating from what your child already enjoys. Yes, even if that's video games.

Talking About Taking Care of Yourself

Conversations around the varied components of self-care are rooted in developing coping skills. In this chapter, you'll learn why it's important to remain neutral and nonjudgmental about all aspects of personal health, from hygiene to weight to self-harm. Your conversations should shift from telling your little kid what to do and when, to transferring responsibility to your adolescent by helping them notice what strategies work best *for them* in taking care of their minds, bodies, and hearts.

I call middle school one of the stickiest times of life, because what happens to you in middle school sticks with you for a long time. You probably still vividly remember the person who made fun of your clothes, or laughed when you gave the wrong answer in class. In general, people remember negative experiences more distinctly than positive ones, usually because sad or painful experiences require more rumination. We need to remember bad, scary, dangerous, and uncomfortable events so we can avoid repeating them. We don't need to remember the mundane, or even happy, moments of our lives because they don't serve the same purpose in our brain's survival tool kit.

In middle school, embarrassment triggers our brains as though it's actual danger. As adults, most of us can shake off being embarrassed because we have a pretty strong sense of self. When we were twelve, though, any little scratch to our delicate egos could become a scar we'd carry into adulthood.

If the bad news is that people tend to carry adolescent pain forward, the good news is that the coping skills and strategies your kid learns in adolescence *also* stick with them. This is why learning about self-care at a young age is important. If your tween practices new coping skills now, they will be firmly cemented for recall later in life, potentially when your older teen or young adult needs them even more—when facing a job loss, at the end of a relationship, or as the general stress of daily living and responsibility increases.

Self-care is a bit of a buzz term these days, but its growing trendiness shouldn't dull its necessity. Kids and parents alike need to learn how to do this well. By showing your kids what self-care looks like for you, you're teaching your kid how to take care of themselves. Note: don't confuse self-care with materialism or pampering. It's more complex and personal than spending a day at the spa or buying a new shirt. Self-care is the building of habits that protect your wellness in body, mind, and spirit. In practice, it's different for everyone. Many parents I know put others' needs before theirs. If this is you, keep in mind you're being a bit of a martyr when you refuse to make time for yourself. Don't be afraid to say no, especially to your kids, if you need time to recharge your batteries. As the writer Anne Lamott so nicely put it, "Almost everything will work again if you unplug it for a few minutes, including you." Show your tween how it's done from time to time.

In this chapter, we'll talk about self-care from the most basic sense (hygiene) to the most complex (suicidal thoughts). Much of what we say to kids throughout early adolescence about their health issues is either *directive,* as in "For the love of God, please put on deodorant!," or it's *reactive,* as when your child asks you about a celebrity suicide and you need to answer their questions. But families need to talk with their kids in a more preventative way, too, about keeping themselves healthy. Let's take a look at how you can position your child for long-term health through talking about early self-care.

What Smells? Talking to Your Kid About Hygiene Without Upsetting Them

Susan, mom to a sixth-grade boy, confided in me about an embarrassing problem she had with her son, Jack. "He stinks and I don't know what to do. I tell him to wear deodorant, and when I ask him if he has put on deodorant he says 'yes' . . . but I know he hasn't."

If I had a dollar for each parent who asked me how to get their kid to wear deodorant, I'd be on the beach in Turks and Caicos right now sipping an overpriced gin and tonic. While we can all agree that BO is an embarrassing issue, it's also not a unique one. Still, kids need to learn that smelling rotten isn't polite, so how do you convince your kid to care?

Actually, trying to convince them might be the problem. Often, parents conflate not caring about hygiene with poor character. They worry that their child isn't wearing deodorant because they are lazy, unwholesome, or they lack normal self-awareness. They worry that this will be a hindrance to their offspring as they try to fit in socially, make friends, get a job, be happy, and develop into a functioning adult. Thus, they pressure and cajole and even shame their kids in hopes of sparing them future failures.

Hygiene is one of those health issues that requires less talk and more strategy. Kids become incredibly defensive when parents bring up body odor. I remember when I was twelve, my mom, after doing the ironing, came to me—shirt clenched in hand—and said, "Your shirts smell awful, and you need to wear deodorant. When the iron hits them, the smell is unbearable."

I can think of no better example of a conversation crasher. I don't think I spoke to her for a week.

Remembering my own mortification, I suggested to Susan with the stinky child that she buy six fresh deodorants and leave five strategically around the house, plus one in her car. That way, when her son was heading out and was too lazy to run back upstairs to get deodorant, he could grab the one off the desk by the back door. If he failed to get the one by the desk, he could get the one in the center console of her car. You get the idea. At some point, almost all teens begin using deodorant. Putting deodorant around the house is a great way to start forming a habit when kids are reluctant.

If you approach the hygiene conversation as an opportunity to discuss having self-respect, living in a community, and taking care of your body, your tween will tune out. It is probably more effective to say something relatable, like "It can be a real pain to take care of your body sometimes. Let's make it as easy on you as possible by stashing these deodorants all around so you don't have to think about it."

Coping Takes Practice

When my daughter was in the second grade, she developed severe anxiety, to the point that she cried from the beginning of school to the end on most days. She begged me to homeschool her. Because that is my worst nightmare, I refused. Being around your kid 100 percent of the time is taxing. Being around your emotionally anxious kid 100 percent of the time is a deal breaker, and would not have helped either of us. I feared my home-school curriculum might quickly devolve into home bartending school.

But I did bend over backward to help her develop coping skills. For weeks, I sat in the school office all day, every day, and she was allowed to check in with me every twenty to thirty minutes. Supportive staff at her school helped her with this process. Eventually, we weaned off that approach and I sat outside the school. Then, we whittled down the amount of time I was there. While these strategies helped her cope in the short term (and kept me out of homeschooling), it wasn't until we found her a terrific cognitive behavioral therapist that she learned the skills to soothe herself, rather than relying on seeing me to get her through the day. Now, as a young adult, my daughter is both independent and accomplished. And, humble brag, she's also a *very* successful deodorant wearer.

I was lucky enough to be self-employed when we were going through the high-anxiety days, and I know I was incredibly lucky to have that kind of flexibility. Each parent does what they can within their set of circumstances. Regardless, when facing a crisis, parents can be supportive in making the problem manageable, but they shouldn't feel the burden of responsibility to eradicate the problem. When we clear problems out of our kid's way, they learn that's how problems are solved—by someone else. They don't get to practice coping.

The Try This First Approach

Most tweens get overwhelmed by their emotions and regularly ask their parents to fix things, even when they can't articulate why or how or what needs fixing. Here's something you can do to mitigate this behavior in your home. When your tween is happy and relaxed, ask them to make a list of things that help them feel better when they are anxious or upset. You might say, for example, "Hey, I read about this idea in a book and I wanted to try it with you. When something is upsetting, it helps to have a list of easy-to-access and relatively simple things you can do on your own that make you feel better. What are ten things that usually make you feel better when you're upset?"

I call this activity "Try This First." By way of example, a Try This First list might include: shooting baskets, reading, watching a TV show, baking, doing yoga, taking a bath, turning off screens, meditating, watching YouTube videos of puppies, drawing, listening to music, running, and so on. Resist the urge to edit your kid's list. You may hate YouTube, but if twenty minutes of watching videos helps them regulate, it can't be all bad.

Your child's vague despair can render you impotent to help. Try This First gives you something to do and say. For example, imagine your child comes home in tears after a rough day. You ask what's wrong, but they can't, or won't, articulate. Of course, you want to make them feel better, but you don't know what to do. Rather than shouldering the burden of having to uncover this mystery and then figuring out what might actually make it better, you could say, "I'm sorry you are having a tough time. Why don't you look at your list and choose one thing to do for the next twenty minutes?" (Note: if you're feeling generous, you could even offer to make a snack while they're looking at their list.) "Come find me when you're done and I'll be here to talk."

The key to this approach is to offer support, while at the same time conveying confidence that your child can figure out how to feel better.

This will help them develop a belief that they aren't actually helpless, even though they feel overwhelmed. Want to empower your tween even more? Ask them to help you create a Try This First list of your own. This is a nice way to subtly reveal your humanity to your child and give them an opportunity to think of someone's needs outside of their own (a practice all adolescents benefit from, whenever possible). Your kid's involvement helping with your list also encourages their buy-in for when you need time in the future for your own self-care.

Nutrition and Growing Bodies

Linda is a successful businessperson with degrees from two Ivy League colleges and three daughters in first through sixth grade. Her middle daughter, Mary, told me Linda loves for them to be healthy. There are plenty of household rules dedicated to the pursuit of health, including requirements to be active for a set time each day, no sugar allowed in the home, and all meals must include something green on the plate. When friends come over after school, Linda makes all the kids get out of the car two blocks from the house and run home in order to get in some activity and earn their after-school snacks. All food is carefully purchased, low-calorie and nutrient-rich, with the earnest intention of raising strong, healthy girls.

Linda's approach to health matches her approach to business: disciplined and results-oriented. Her control and caution, however, are likely to backfire with her girls. When it comes to food and movement, the healthiest thing we can do for our kids is teach them how to find joy in their bodies, self-regulate, and eat intuitively. Having lots of food rules doesn't allow kids to learn how to trust their feelings, and sends signals to kids that can damage self-esteem and migrate into unhealthy relationships with food.

During early adolescence, your child starts building the three primary things they need to become an adult: an adult body, an adult brain, and an adult identity. I call this trio the "Middle School Construction Project" and it is a lot for your kid to handle at once. Brain and identity development happen behind the scenes, but body development, that's up for everyone's scrutiny.

Because puberty hits over the span of many years, a kid in middle school can scan the cafeteria and see classmates who still look like third graders, while others could pass for high schoolers. This can plant a seed of self-doubt in your child's mind as they wonder, on a daily basis, "Am I normal?" It's hard to figure out what is normal when everyone around you is so vastly different! As a parent, you probably have your own ideas about what's "normal" for your child. Because we carry our own body baggage, and are inundated with abnormal beauty messages (often wrongly disguised as health messages), I can say with confidence that most of the parents I work with have an incorrect understanding of normal body development during adolescence.

I host several mother-daughter conferences a year. At each, there is a breakout where girls leave the room and moms can ask me anything they want. More often than not, I field questions about girls' body weight and lack of physical activity. Moms tend to worry, *a lot*, about their kids' weight, especially in early adolescence when kids naturally start gaining at what can feel like a startling rate.

Before concluding that your child is unhealthy, you need to know how kids grow. On average, boys do most of their growing between the ages of twelve and sixteen. During those four years, they might grow an entire foot and gain as much as fifty to sixty pounds. Girls have their biggest growth spurt between the ages of ten and fourteen. On average, they can gain ten inches in height and forty to fifty pounds during that time. That was not a typo. Tweens gain a surprising amount of weight during middle school. This is not a cause for alarm. When you notice your child gaining a lot of weight during this period, the best thing you can do is . . . *nothing*. You don't want criticism about their body to lodge itself in that "sticky part" of their developing brain. "But I would never criticize my child's body or weight! I simply stress the importance of making healthy choices," you counter. Your child knows full well when *healthy* is code for *attractive*. Tread carefully around this word as a catchall.

It is helpful to explain statistical norms, and useful for your child to know healthy weight-gain numbers during puberty, but stats and numbers aren't much comfort when your kid is worried about their appearance, especially in the eyes of their peers. One of my favorite things to say to the kids I work with (and to myself when I'm having a crisis of confidence), comes from my friend and fellow author Rosie Molinary, in her book *Beautiful You: A Daily Guide to Radical Self-Acceptance.* "You are here on purpose. You have a unique gift to give this world—one that it desperately needs for its own healing—and it has nothing to do with how your body looks."

From the adult perspective, it's one thing to accept weight fluctuations on an intellectual level, but on an emotional level many parents still question: "Will my kid's weight cause social consequences for them?" And "Is my kid's weight a reflection of their bad health (and if I'm being honest, a reflection of my parenting, too)?"

If your worries are motivated by a concern that your child's weight will cause them to be teased or embarrassed by their peers, consider this: What is worse? To have your confidence undermined by kids at school or your parent? A parent's job is to love their kid unconditionally—despite their achievements and failures, changes in appearance, and moments of self-doubt. It is important for your kids to know, no matter how they feel about themselves or what other people say to them, you find them pleasing without any strings attached to how they look.

If your concerns are motivated by health, consider this: the healthiest thing your child can do is learn to self-regulate when it comes to their own body. If you control or restrict their food in an attempt to make them healthy, you risk ruining their ability to manage their relationship with food themselves. To learn more about helping kids maintain a healthy relationship with food, read Ellyn Satter's *Child of Mine: Feeding with Love and Good Sense.*

> Until your child is done growing, which might not be until after high school, you are working with a moving target. Better to build up resilience than to trigger self-doubt.

Your job is not to agonize over your child's shape—but that doesn't mean *they* won't. Your young adolescent will want to look good, fit in, and feel confident in their clothes. How can you help? Your child's body will morph a lot quite naturally throughout adolescence. Something you *can* do is help your child present themselves in a way that gives them confidence. When my kids had trouble finding clothes that fit well, I would always say, "It's not your body's fault, it's the clothes' fault." And then I would get things tailored to be more flattering. Until your child is done growing, which might not be until after high school, you are working with a moving target. Better to build up resilience than to trigger self-doubt.

Conversation Crashers for Nutrition

Keep your emotions entirely out of your conversations regarding food with your child. Here are some ways you might unintentionally bring emotions into your conversations:

"I just want you to be healthy." *Healthy* sounds so vague it might be code for *thin, attractive,* or *disciplined,* none of which equate to health. Your child will be healthy when they can self-regulate. Instead say, "It's your body. Notice how certain foods make you feel and listen to what your body tells you about what it needs more or less of."

"You're so pretty/handsome, and I think it would help your confidence if you got to a healthier weight." What your child heard is that they aren't pretty or handsome enough *yet.* Talk with your kid about what foods and activities they enjoy most and why, instead of suggesting where they fall short.

"You will feel so much better when you eat better." This is an attempt to make healthy eating about feeling good and not looking good, which is a step in the right direction, but how food makes us feel is personal and inconsistent. Instead of assuming, suggest your tween journal how they feel after meals and then they can track which foods make them feel good or bad.

"But I worked so hard on this meal." Have you ever been invited to someone's house for dinner only to feel a little scared when a yuck plate of food was put in front of you? Could you be persuaded to crave that food if the host told you how hard they had worked preparing it? Guilt doesn't usually make food taste better. We all want recognition for our efforts, but that won't convince anyone to be a less picky eater.

"Food is fuel." I've said not to be emotional when talking to your child about food or bodies, but that doesn't mean eating is emotionless. While it's true food provides the energy your body needs to function, that's only part of its purpose in our modern society. If food were just fuel, we could all happily survive on protein goo alone. But food is community. It's why we eat our meals together. Food is joy. It's why we like things that taste good to us. Food is culture. It's what connects us to each other. If you rob your child of the inherent connection and happiness that food can bring, they may end up chasing those feelings by sneaking or hiding food. Also, sharing food and going out to eat are some of the earliest social activities that kids can do together. Eating together can be a fun, communal, safe activity. Understand that this will comprise the bulk of your child's early adolescent social life and that you won't be there to regulate their eating, so they need to develop self-regulation early.

Sleep Matters

The average teenager in America gets seven hours of sleep a night, but experts suggest most need at least nine hours. Talking with your child about the importance of sleep can feel futile, especially when you have an early start school schedule working against you. In adolescence, kids experience a shift in their circadian rhythms and they don't naturally get sleepy until about two hours later at night, making it harder for them to wake up early.

Practically speaking, there are a few things parents can do to help with this. Removing electronics is ideal, both because the screen light suppresses melatonin, our natural sleep hormone, and because the temptation to check in with screens (and friends) is hard to resist. The earlier you start this habit, the easier it will be to maintain. Cooling bedrooms to a crisp 65–68°F also helps trigger a hibernation effect. Finally, a weighted blanket can help adolescents fall asleep and stay asleep.

Keep in mind, though, you aren't only battling against circadian rhythms when it comes to your child's poor sleep habits, but their social drive as well. In early adolescence, kids need to connect with each other. It's how they practice being adults. But heavily scheduled kids might not get the chance to do this amid after-school activities, then family dinner, then hours of homework. Kids might only be able to check in with each other well past bedtime.

How you speak to your kids about this is important. If you downplay their need to connect with their friends, they'll think you're out of touch with what matters to them, especially if you're asking them to sacrifice friend time for what matters to you—tutoring, chores, piano practice, or family time. Ultimately, you can't make a person sleep, so instead you'll have to aim for helping them understand why you hope they'll choose to prioritize a good night's slumber. Here's how a sensitive conversation about sleep might sound:

BEGIN peacefully

Parent: *Hey, kiddo, it's about time to turn the TV off and get ready for bed.*
Kid: *Can I please just finish this movie? I'm in sixth grade now. No one goes to bed this early.*
Parent: *Well, we can certainly have a discussion about bedtimes, if you want. The thing is, I'm about to go to bed, so I may be too tired to think it through tonight. Since I get cranky when I'm tired, let's talk about this tomorrow before dinner.*
Kid: *Fine, but can I stay up later tonight? I'm not tired at all.*

RELATE to your kid

Parent: *I understand you're not tired right now. I'll allow you to finish the movie tonight if you keep the volume low and promise to shut it off before* *bed. This doesn't mean that's the new rule. It's a special exception until we talk through this again tomorrow.*

Kid: *Okay, thank you so much! I'll be quiet.*

Parent: *Do you understand and agree? Following the rules is a good way to show responsibility going into the talk you want to have tomorrow.*

Kid: *Yes!*

Parent: *Okay, good night! Love you!*

INTERVIEW to collect data

[The next day before dinner]

Parent: *Okay, do you still want to talk about bedtime?*

Kid: *Yes! I think I should not have a bedtime anymore now that I'm in middle school, because I have a ton of homework and I'm not tired, so I just lie there doing nothing when I could be doing something better with my time.*

Parent: *What kind of things would you do instead of lying in bed?*

Kid: *Literally anything would be better. I could work on homework, watch TV, draw, have a snack, do push-ups and sit-ups, do research online. . . . Anything would be better than just staring at my ceiling, which is what I do now.*

Parent: *And when you say no one goes to bed when you do, how do you know? What time do you think they go to bed?*

Kid: *Most kids don't have a bedtime. They probably go to sleep at eleven or twelve o'clock.*

Parent: *And wake up at 6:00 a.m. for school?*

Kid: *Yes, it's not a big deal.*

Parent: *What about how you feel in the morning. . . . Would you say you have a lot of energy when you wake up for school or are you sluggish?*

Kid: *Yes, fine, I knew you were going to say that. I start off sluggish, but by the time I get to school I'm wide awake and not sleepy at all. I promise.*

ECHO what you hear

Parent: *Tell me if I'm understanding this so far. You're frustrated by lying in bed awake at night and think that's a waste of your time. You think*

you're old enough not to have a bedtime and you are tired in the morning,
but not for long. Did I get it all?
Kid: *Basically, yeah.*

FEEDBACK

Parent: *Well, there are a couple ways to look at this. On the one hand,*
you are getting older and I can appreciate that it's harder to fall asleep at
the same time. On the other hand, I know it can seem like rest and sleep
are a waste of time because it feels like nothing is happening then, but
actually what you may not realize is that when our bodies sleep, that's
when brain development happens. To get smarter, have faster reflexes at
sports, improve your memory skills, and so on, you have to sleep for about
nine hours a night. When you get less, your brain doesn't fully recharge.
It would be like only recharging your phone to 50 percent each time you
plugged it in. If we care enough about our phones to fully recharge them,
we should at least care that much about our brains to put them back to
100 percent overnight. Even if you don't feel *sleepy, your brain still*
needs a full charge. Bedtime isn't just something arbitrary we enforce
to flex our power over you kids. It has an important purpose in how
you grow.

I hope you can see then why having no bedtime isn't an option for us.
But I'm willing to be flexible on a trial basis and see what happens. For
example, we could start with giving you a one hour increase in bedtime
two nights a week. Let's start with Wednesdays and Thursdays. If you go a
month without us noticing any negative effects, we will talk about adding
another night on. Negative effects would be: if your grades suffer, if you
become grumpy or hard to talk with throughout the day, if you become
more forgetful or have trouble focusing, or if you can't get up easily. We can
start this week!

Like most conversations about good health, the best you can do is educate
your child, set reasonable and clear expectations, and stay calm so your
child will remain open to further discussions.

Risky Substances

Picture a party in high school. Do you conjure up a scene from a John Hughes–esque movie? Parents out of town, kids of all shapes, sizes, and social stratospheres channeling liquid courage, finding unexpected love, and (finally!) offering acceptance to the school nerds, all for the small price of a completely destroyed home. If you were a teen in the 1980s like me, you learned that drinking was everyone's rite of passage in high school.

Drinking in middle school is much less brazen. According to a 2010 study out of Reed College in Oregon, the most common scenario is a small gathering of three to four friends inside someone's home. Less wild party, more sneaky experiment. Still, you can picture it. Where this territory gets even harder to talk about is when we don't know what to picture. Enter vaping.

If you're not familiar with the vape and Juul epidemic among early teens right now, tell me where you live—because I want to move there! Someone is doing something right in your local health-care community or school administration and we need it as a national model.

Our kids are facing a health crisis that feels hard to stop. While we were enjoying good news about newly published research showing a decline in U.S. high school students having sex, having sex without contraception, and even a twenty-year low in teenage alcohol and marijuana use, vaping was sneaking in the side door with a new temptation.

There has been a tremendous rise in nicotine use among teens due to the popularity of vaping, and of the brand Juul. Juul is marketed as a tool to help smokers quit smoking, but it is incredibly popular with middle and high school students as first-time nicotine users. A 2016 study reported five hundred thousand middle schoolers admitted to vaping in the previous thirty days. It's likely gained in popularity for three main reasons: 1) though many flavors have now been banned, it was initially marketed in fruity flavors that appealed to younger users, 2) the buzz of nicotine is a new and fun feeling for some kids, 3) and probably most compelling, it's *sneaky*. Kids in early adolescence look for ways to rebel, and Juuling provides an easy one. The vapor has no smell and quickly dissipates, so vaping even during class can go virtually unnoticed. The tiny cartridges can be concealed in a sweatshirt sleeve and the vapor blown right back into the sweatshirt. Because the cartridge looks like a flash drive, it's easy to be a rebel right under the eye of a teacher or parent.

With something as prolific as vaping, it's important to have ongoing conversations. Several short talks will be more effective than one long lecture, because kids are only willing to listen for so long before they get restless and tune you out. (In chapter 2, I covered tips that are useful in talking with teens no matter what the subject. This is a good time to point out that having a "Botox brow" is crucial here, and to suggest you revisit that section if you need a refresher.)

Since one of the main appeals of vaping is that it is an act of risk and rebellion, it's important you don't come into the conversation as a contrarian, because that will position your kid to take the opposite stance. Rather than saying, "I know vaping is popular, but it's disgusting and it's terrible for you and if you do it, you'll be in a world of trouble," try a more inquisitive approach. Mention that you've been hearing a lot about it and you're wondering how prevalent it is at your kid's school. If your child is willing to talk with you about this, listen openly. At this point, it might help to employ a technique I find useful when talking about sensitive issues with my own kids. It helps me if I pretend that I'm talking with someone else's child instead of my own. When I imagine myself more removed from the situation, I become less concerned about my kid's future, and naturally slip into a more curious, less condemning tone. I find it creates a better rapport for conversation. I learn more and my kids seem more open to what I have to say as well.

Lots of parents try to scare their kids with the threat of future health crises, like the fear of developing "popcorn lung," a condition that damages the lungs' airways, but that's not been entirely proven. Whenever I'm uncertain if an "Internet fact" is true, I go to *Snopes.com* and type in the major details of the story I've heard. Searching on Snopes for "vape popcorn lung" shows that a December 2015 Harvard study did research to see whether vaping leads to popcorn lung. The study found . . . it might. And that more research is needed. Parents Googling *vape* and *popcorn lung* will likely see that many clickbait websites capitalized on this possibility by posting side-by-side images of a man who they claimed had been hospitalized for popcorn lung from vaping. In fact, it was a falsely used photo of a man whose e-cigarette blew up in his face.

It may feel like I'm splitting hairs. A blown-off lip is surely something we want our kids to avoid, so what's the harm in showing them the photo as a deterrent? Well, if your kids are proficient at Googling (they are), they can easily find articles refuting popcorn lung ties to vaping, especially from online "news sources" like *Vaping360.com*. Your kid might not know enough to realize that a website called *Vaping360.com* isn't exactly a great source for unbiased health and wellness news. But the point is, accuracy matters when talking to your kids about health. Do your research on reputable sites with data-driven studies and, definitely, refresh your research often. I first wrote this chapter with no data on vape-related deaths, and in just the few months since my first draft, as of September 2019, the CDC has announced 12 deaths and 805 confirmed cases of lung illness related to vaping. By the time this book is published, these statistics will have changed drastically. When something moves this quickly, you need to stay on top of accurate information or your tween will have reason to discredit your knowledge and then your opinion.

Here's how a conversation about vaping (or any experimentation with substances) might go.

BEGIN peacefully

Parent: *I was at work today and someone brought up vaping. They said it's big in middle schools now.*
Kid: *I don't think it's really big.*
Parent: *Do you mean it's not a big deal, or not a lot of people are doing it?*
Kid: *Kind of both.*

RELATE to your kid

Parent: *That's interesting. Do you think this is one of those things adults have a tendency to overreact to?*
Kid: *Kind of.*
Parent: *I get that. I know sometimes adults, myself included, have a big reaction to stuff like this because we worry about health issues. I don't want that to keep us from talking about it, though.*
Kid: *Sure.*

INTERVIEW to collect data

Parent: *When you say it's not a big deal, how many kids at school would you guess have tried it?*

Kid: *I dunno. Maybe twenty?*

Parents: *Okay. And do you feel like you have an understanding of what vaping is and what it does?*

Kid: *What the heck? I'm not going to vape! You don't need to worry.*

Parent: *Okay, we can still talk about it, even if you aren't going to do it. It's good for both of us to be educated about it. I just want to talk, not because I'm suspicious of you. Can we agree that we're just talking about this in a general way?*

Kid: *Yeah, sure.*

Parent: *Have you heard anything about what it does? Either how it feels or what it does to you?*

Kid: *Not really. I just think it's like smoking. And I have seen some people do it in the bathroom, so I don't think it makes you act crazy because they go to class after.*

Parent: *Wow, in the bathroom. That's a bold choice.*

Kid: *I know there's no smoke, so they can't get caught.*

Parent: *How often do you see it?*

Kid: *Maybe just a few times a week.*

ECHO what you hear

Parent: *Well, it sounds like it's something kids and adults need to learn more about. My coworker made it sound like everyone is doing it, but from what you're saying some people are but not everyone.*

Kid: *Yeah.*

FEEDBACK

Parent: *I was curious, so I did Google a little. They have found undeniable evidence that there are harmful chemicals in vape that can actually alter your DNA. It's the same stuff they use to embalm dead bodies! They don't know yet that this means it will lead to cancer in people who vaped, because it takes a long time for the government to study. We will have to wait decades probably to know for sure.*

So a lot is unknown about it. That's partly why I'm so curious. I understand that kids are curious about it, too. The bottom line is, you're the person who gets to decide what to put in your body. No parent wants their kids to use harmful substances, but sometimes it still happens—you've seen that at school. I know you've said you're not doing it, and I believe you, but I still want you to be informed about it since it happens around you.

If, at some point, you have friends who do this, and they end up asking you to try, what I'd like you to remember is that you've always been good at thinking for yourself. I hope you'll continue to research the health effects of this and I hope you'll decide this is a risk you don't want to take with your own health.

And one final thought I want to leave you with: As you get older, kids around you will experiment with more and more things. If you ever want to talk with me about that, even if you need to say, "I made a mistake and I need some help figuring this out," I will be a good listener. It's more important to me to help you solve problems than to lose my cool, so know that you can come to me.

Suicide and Self-Harm

Here we reach the hardest conversations about health. A significant number of kids begin experimenting with self-injury around the ages of twelve to fourteen as an outlet for their feelings of sadness, distress, anxiety, or confusion. Research has found that one-third to one-half of American teens have self-injured. Adults need to know that self-harm is not correlated directly with suicide, but it does indicate a need for intervention. Let me say again, if you discover a child you care about is self-harming (cutting, bruising, or otherwise hurting themselves with the intention of feeling pain), it does not mean they are suicidal. It *does* mean they need help coping with their emotions.

Should you discover that your child is hurting themselves, your reaction matters. If you are horrified, disgusted, or afraid, your child may shut down and keep from you the emotions they're having trouble processing.

On the flip side of overreacting, some parents think cutting is so common now that kids try it for attention, to fit in, or to experiment, and that it will naturally just work itself out. Self-harm habits may go away temporarily, but they usually resurface if kids aren't given the proper coping skills. This often requires dialectical behavior therapy (DBT), a highly effective way of teaching kids to handle emotions that can otherwise be overwhelming or unbearable.

Even if you believe your child wouldn't self-harm, you should still introduce the topic to them because they may be worried about other kids at school who are doing this or talking about it. As with other sensitive topics, this one benefits from referring to an example outside the family. Kids become defensive if they think you're bringing a topic up because you're suspicious of them. Use a character in a book or show, a celebrity who discusses this openly, or a general news story about self-harm, as a neutral entryway into this topic. Then, ask your kids to explain their understanding of the issue to you. This can make your child feel helpful to you, and not as if they are having to defend themselves or their friends.

Talk of suicide is another big part of kids' lives today. In 2016, suicide was the second leading cause of death for people ages ten to twenty-four. In their media-saturated lives, kids are aware right away when a celebrity dies by suicide, and they're also tuned in when friends hint online about suicide or self-harm. In fact, kids are often connected to friends of friends online, so that news travels fast when there is a tragedy. In short, middle schoolers absorb a lot more information about mental health than we did at their age. Before your child leaves elementary school, it would be a good idea to have frank and open discussions about mental health, self-harm, and suicide.

Important note: Watching a fictional character on TV attempt suicide can increase suicide ideation in some kids, so avoid watching programs that dramatize suicide; however, research shows that *talking* to your child about suicide does not have the same effect. Studies show no statistical increase in suicidal ideation from asking about suicidal thoughts. In fact, talking openly about suicide with kids actually improves their thoughts. In other words, you can and should talk with your child early about suicide. The same is true for self-harm. Make these topics part of your family conversations.

Conversation Crashers Specific to Self-Harm and Suicide

How you talk with your child about suicide and self-harm is incredibly important. For conversation crashers on the topics of self-harm and suicide, I spoke with an expert, Dr. Amanda McGough, a clinical psychologist who specializes in suicide prevention and postvention and serves as president of the American Foundation for Suicide Prevention's North Carolina chapter. She suggests these tips:

Don't ask "Why are you doing this??" Your child probably doesn't know, and asking a question that doesn't have an answer can be a quick conversation ender. Hug your child, be supportive, and let them know they don't have to bear the burden of their feelings by themselves. You are there to listen and find someone who can help them.

Don't express worry. Remain calm. Children who have thoughts about suicide often feel they are a burden to others, thinking, "You'd be happier if I weren't here and you didn't have to worry about me." Expressing your fear or worry may contribute to the feeling that your child is a burden to you. Instead, emphasize there are always options other than suicide, and that you can get them support.

Don't call it "crazy." McGough's teen patients tell her when their parents say things like "You're not thinking of doing something crazy like killing yourself, are you?" they were less likely to report their feelings to their parents. They opened up when parents asked direct questions, such as "What kinds of thoughts are you having about your life?"

Beware how we stigmatize mental health to our kids. When speaking of a celebrity suicide, never say things like "I just don't understand how someone could do that," or "That's so selfish." These statements send a signal to your child to keep suicidal thoughts to themselves. Even the term *committing suicide* carries a stigma, because we usually use the verb *commit* with sin, murder, or crime. McGough recommends asking about "suicidal thoughts" rather than "committing suicide." She encourages being compassionate toward your child's emotions, even when they feel scary to you.

Don't say "I just want you to be you again." It's hard to see our kids change, especially when that change brings sadness. During the bumpy parts of growing up, you may long for the ease and joy of the past. But as Theodore Roosevelt said, "Comparison is the thief of joy," and this doesn't just apply to comparing our own happiness to others'. Don't rob yourself of today by yearning too hard for yesterday. If your child is hurting, they want to feel better, too. It doesn't help to imply they aren't being themselves when they are sad or angry. Instead, just acknowledge the pain and let them know it's not permanent.

Don't assume you can handle this yourself. Always connect your child to a trained therapist if they express feelings of being a burden, or convey suicidal thoughts. If your child shows imminent risk, take them to the emergency room. Imminent risk may be indicated by your child researching online ways to end their life, or expressing a personal plan for how to end their life. Never assume suicidal talk is attention seeking. Let a professional evaluate for that.

Children as young as third grade are aware of the concept of suicide, and it's okay to discuss it with your kids, even if they are this young. If your child demonstrates sadness, anxiety, or confusion to the point of talking about suicide or by self-harming, talking with your child is important, but doesn't equate to treatment. Be sure to seek out a professional for help. Please also make sure your child knows that if a friend expresses similar thoughts, or if your child sees that a friend is self-harming, not to keep these things secret. Let them know they can safely tell you and you will help them figure out the best way to get their friend the support they need. Finally, program the National Suicide Prevention Lifeline number into your child's cell phone, for their own use or for them to use to help someone else: 1–800–273–8255. Let your child know any call to the hotline is confidential, does not trigger the police or an ambulance, and that most people who call reported it helped them feel better.

In a Hurry? Here's Your Crash Course

- Gentle reminders in the form of questions, such as "Are you feeling worn out?" or "Is there anything you need from me to help reset?" can serve as pause buttons in a busy day. Help your tween take time to check in with their feelings, but don't pressure them to share with you.

- Demonstrate to your family the importance of self-care by taking time to recharge your own batteries.

- Fret less about your kid not wearing deodorant but leave a lot of it around the house and in the car. Eventually, almost all kids figure this one out.

- Encourage your tween to develop strong coping skills by making a Try This First list and helping you make one for yourself, too.

- Between ages twelve and sixteen boys gain fifty to sixty pounds on average. Between the ages of ten and fourteen girls gain forty to fifty pounds on average.

- When it comes to food, the healthiest thing your child can do is learn how to self-regulate and eat intuitively.

- Young adolescents need at least nine hours of sleep at night. You can't make a person sleep when you want them to, so the best you can do is create the most conducive environment for sleep and educate them about why sleep matters.

- When talking to your kids about substances like alcohol or vape, don't preach, exaggerate, or spread urban legends. Instead, share clear facts and your expectations.

- Self-harm is not correlated directly with suicide, but it does require therapy.

- How you talk about suicide and self-harm matters a great deal. I can't "crash course" this, so revisit that section as needed.

- Talk about suicide and self-harm in your home. Studies show no statistical increase in suicidal ideation from asking about suicidal thoughts. In fact, talking openly about suicide with kids actually improves their thoughts.

9

Talking About Fairness

How an adolescent perceives fairness changes over time, and that can affect your conversations about what's "unfair." In this chapter, you'll hone your definition of fairness to help you and your tween communicate more easily on the subject, learn how to introduce reason to a kid who feels mistreated, and discover how to inspire your kid to (incrementally) speak up for others who've been treated unfairly. Bonus: you'll learn things you can say (and should avoid saying) that will increase your chances of being perceived as a fair parent by your adolescent.

There is a version of this chapter that goes like this:

Fair? Life isn't fair. That's all there is to it.
The sooner you accept this, the happier your life will be.

The End

I could leave it there. I'm tempted. But I have some nagging questions poking around in my brain. Like . . . how? *How* do you get over feeling unfairly treated? Or . . . what if? *What if* you see someone else being treated unfairly? Do you just ignore it and move along with your life, or do you try to figure out how to make things more equitable?

This concept of fairness comes up regularly for tweens as they navigate early adolescence, first, dwelling on all the ways they are mistreated, and eventually, maturing into a concern for how others are treated in the world. Talking about this topic early and thoughtfully will help you empower your kid to think critically about what upsets them and what reasonable action they can take on a wider scale.

Perception of Fairness Evolves over Time

Have you noticed that *unfair* is a highly contagious word? (If no, congratulations on having avoided Twitter this long.) The proverb "Misery loves company" is as true online as in a middle school. For example, a child who complains that the teacher gave her a bad grade for no reason will quickly attract flocks of sympathizers. For some, it feels good and right to comfort a victim. For others, it alleviates anxiety and provides a sort of comfort to have dodged a bullet, knowing someone else took the hit. For others still, it is simply nice to be part of a group, even if that group's common thread is commiserating. Being outraged together bonds people. For frenemies, commiserating provides a socially acceptable, albeit emotionally manipulative, way to wield power. A frenemy will press on someone's bruise, just to keep the conversation on that person's pain. (Side note: I tell the young adolescents I work with they can easily root out a frenemy by paying attention to who regularly blows off their happy news, but churns up drama around bad news. A frenemy will say, "Oh, you made the soccer team? Cool, but I heard everyone made it this year." Or say, "You didn't make the team?! This is the worst thing ever. Tell me *everything!*")

Whatever the reason, tweens are prone to catch Unfair Fever. Interestingly, how a young person takes the temperature on fairness evolves throughout adolescence. A 2017 study out of Dartmouth College examined how people age nine to twenty-three perceive fairness, and found that our perception changes throughout adolescence in correspondence with developmental changes in the brain. Specifically, younger adolescents believe what is most fair is that which is most equal, while older high schoolers and college students are more flexible, as they begin to consider a person's intentions and emotions when evaluating what's fair. In other words, older adolescents learn that things don't have to be equal to be fair, they just have to *feel fair*. Kind of like when Supreme Court Justice Potter Stewart famously said he couldn't define pornography ("I know it when I see it"), as teens mature, they develop a feel for fairness even if they can't measure it. Understanding this arc in your child's perception will help inform your conversations.

When I read this Dartmouth study, it told me two things: 1) not to worry too much about the "not fair!" outcry of young tweens, because it is clearly developmentally appropriate, and 2) paving the path toward a better understanding of fairness should happen in small, incremental ways, in accordance with brain development. One of the easiest ways a parent can do this is by talking about fairness perception in a neutral and curious way. Ask kids what they think is fair and why, and begin to gently suggest they consider motivation and intent as a way to sharpen their focus toward a more mature perspective. Also, in my experience, kids like being told how their brains work. There is no need to keep brain biology a mystery from tweens and teens. Discuss this research with your kid and begin to point out differences in how people talk about fairness at different ages and stages.

The Fight for Others

Another evolution in fairness is the shift from focusing on what's fair to me to what's fair to others. Open conversations about how others may be unfairly treated and tap into the famous teen mission to prove adults wrong. Adolescents are driven to solve the problems adults created and they have the unsullied confidence to believe they can. They're natural activists. Whether it's school shootings, climate change, sexual abuse, or racial injustice, today's teens are marching, tweeting, striking, publishing, litigating, and organizing their way toward a more fair and safe future for each other. This makes me immensely proud and hopeful.

I started working with middle schoolers in 2004, and I often think back to one of the first stories about teens I saw go viral. In 2008, a ninth-grade boy in Nova Scotia showed up to the first day of school wearing a pink polo shirt; he was publicly mocked by a school bully for his "gay" shirt. When two seniors heard the rumors, they went to a discount store after school and bought fifty pink shirts. The next day, the school was awash in a sea of pink. When the news caught hold of the story, Pink Shirt Day became a movement across the country.

This kind of activism is admirable, but it comes with maturity. Remember, the arc of moral justice is long, and so, too, is the arc of adolescence. In early adolescence, your kid may need to practice on smaller, more personal issues before they're ready to take a huge social risk on someone else's behalf. Don't worry that your child isn't organizing the whole school against bullying. Now is the time to foster your child's *curiosity* about fair treatment. Gently, slowly, you can begin to direct their focus outward, turning their thoughts from "making sure I'm getting a fair deal" to "making sure others aren't taken advantage of, too." Your child won't throw off the yoke of social pressure immediately to go fight the good fight. It's enough to plant a seed.

You can start your child thinking this way by:

- Letting them see you speak up for others.
- Having discussions about issues of unfair treatment as they come up, and asking, "Is there anything we can do?"
- Pointing out how small behavioral changes make a big difference, and brainstorming ways to start small.

Take Your Focus Off Sameness

In my experience, the biggest issues with fairness seem to stem from a misunderstanding of the term. Let's clear that up.

There is a popular graphic, created by Craig Froehle, often used to explain fair and equitable treatment in society. Google it later if you can, because it's lovely, but also because people have made some excellent iterations to the graphic to make it even more inclusive. For now, the gist is this: In the first frame, we see three people of descending heights trying to watch a baseball game, but there is a fence around the field obstructing two people's views. Each person is given the same-sized crate to help them see. One guy is tall and he can see over the fence fine, but to be equal, each person stands on the same-sized crate. When they stand on the crates, the fence comes to the first person's waist, the second person's neck so they can still see the field, but the third and shortest person's view is still completely blocked.

This is an illustration of fair treatment, where everyone is given the exact same resource, even though it is too much for one person and not enough for another. In the next frame, the tallest person has passed his crate to the shortest person who, standing on both crates, can now watch the game. This is an example of equitable treatment, in which the intent has shifted from everyone getting equal things to everyone getting specifically what they need to be successful. We see this kind of misuse of the term "fairness" often in race debates here in America. All Lives Matter, while seemingly an innocuous and inclusive phrase, and one I guess would have been warmly embraced fifty

> Fair treatment is when everyone is given the exact same resource, even though it might be too much for one person and not enough for another. Equitable treatment means that everyone gets specifically what they need to be successful.

years ago, now unleashes a firestorm of emotion and debate. It's not that the three words "all" and "lives" and "matter" don't make a "fair" and accurate statement when strung together. Of course, all lives do matter. It becomes contentious when the phrase All Lives Matter is used as a criticism of the phrase Black Lives Matter, which is being used in very specific response to black deaths by police officers. So, what seems fair as a stand-alone phrase, actually becomes unfair as a response to another person's pain. Fairness, then, as a concept cannot exist in a vacuum. When talking to your children about fairness in society, they must understand that context is everything.

Within a family structure, when parents confuse being fair with being equal, they often end up giving one person more than they need and another less. If one of your kids needs math tutoring, for example, you won't make the other kid sign up, too, just to keep things equal. Parents should worry less about giving all kids the same thing, and more about giving each kid what they need to be successful. Young adolescents appreciate when this is explained to them.

At home, when your kid complains "That's not fair!" what they usually mean is "I want that, too." It happens all the time with siblings. Whose happy family celebration *hasn't* devolved into tears over which kid got the bigger slice of cake? It's annoying when two kids want the same thing, but not hard to mediate. For shared food, you can use the old one-kid-cuts-and-the-other-chooses-first technique. For shared toys, many parents rely on timers and schedules. And for petty, every-ten-minute complaints, there is nothing wrong with using good old-fashioned ignoring to solve it.

Complaining about what's not fair is what kids do, but the issue becomes more complex, and deserves a bit more thought, when one child feels they don't receive the same trust, help, or attention as their sibling. It happens in every family. One kid may be more responsible than their sibling, so they get a later curfew. One kid may have anxiety, so they get more attention. The scale is rarely balanced.

In middle school, one of my kids was the type who would work on a project for days, and at 80 percent completion, rip it up and start over because it looked "kinda messy." The other would set an alarm for 5:00 a.m. the morning the project was due and work at the kitchen table for two hours until announcing it was "good enough!" before racing out the door to school. I tried to bend each kid toward the middle. Could I get the anxious child to accept that the hours spent on their project really were sufficient for (and would probably surpass) the teacher's expectations? Could I get the carefree child to plan ahead and do a little work every day, instead of cramming it all into one early morning? I tried until I was blue in the face. I thought I was helping them each be better, but really, I was just asking them each to be closer to the same. Equal. I wanted them to stand on the same-sized crate and be the same height.

My children did not need the same approach or the same rules. One needed to be told to take more risks. At one point, I suggested my young teen sneak into a rated-R movie with a friend, in hopes of breaking the spell of anxiety that caused an almost debilitating fear of coloring outside the lines. My other child . . . did not have this problem. Extreme levels of FOMO, though, led my second child to an obsessive need to be with friends constantly in middle school, often to the detriment of sleep, family, and common sense. Both kids are very different, always have been, and always will be, and both turned out to be the most enjoyable, responsible, caring, and fun young adults I could dream of, not to mention good friends to each other. I'm proud beyond measure of them: equally.

Be Your Own Public Relations Specialist

During their tween years, though, my kids cried foul. One was always getting more of something than the other. The problem, early on, was with perception. Each kid saw the other as working the system to get more attention, or resources, or acceptance, or help, or compassion, or freedom. They evaluated and catalogued every yes or no I gave, how quickly I gave it, and under what circumstances. "But she—!" and "But he—!" were common refrains.

It's impossible to sidestep sibling rivalry altogether, but talking with my kids about my approach to raising two very different types of kids would have helped. Let's look at how a BRIEF conversation about what's fair between siblings might sound like in your home, so you can get ahead of comparisons. I assume this conversation begins with one kid calling the parent out on "unfair" treatment, making the Begin (peacefully) step a challenge. It can still be done, though. We've all seen a movie where a negotiator talks someone off a ledge. Start by channeling that kind of energy. I know, I know: it would be straightforward, and less pandering, to order your tween to snap out of this ridiculousness and do as you say. But whether you're a parent or a negotiator, you have to be able to read the room. On less sensitive issues, you may be able to bring a conflict to a close with "because I said so." When your child thinks they're being treated unfairly, though, they lose faith in the system and behave like a person on a ledge, and people on ledges do and think unreasonable things. Then there's you. I want *you* to get what you want here, too, and my guess is that's a kid who calms down, keeps an open mind, and cooperates.

BEGIN peacefully

Kid: *That's so not fair! You're letting him go to his friend's after school, but you always say I have to do my homework first before I can have fun!*

Parent: *Hey, hang on. Let's talk about this. I want to hear what you think and I want to stay open-minded to your observations and ideas, but that's hard to do when you're yelling at me. If we can both talk about this calmly, we can figure this out. Do you want to talk now, or do you want to take a few minutes to collect your thoughts?*

Kid: *I'M CALM! Why do you let him get away with anything he wants but you're so strict with me?*

RELATE to your kid

Parent: *I see how it looks that way to you. That must make you feel bad. I can remember feeling this way when I was your age and my parents not getting it. I'll try to do better.*

Kid: *Okay. Thanks. But why can't you just try to be more equal? It's not fair when you make different rules for us.*

INTERVIEW to collect data

Parent: *Hmm . . . okay. Let me be sure I get it. Are you saying you think everything should be exactly equal between you two?*

Kid: *If you want it to be fair!*

Parent: *So . . . if one of you studies for a test for an hour, but the other studies for thirty minutes and understands it all, I should make you both sit there and study for the full hour? Because that would be exactly equal.*

Kid: *No, that's not the same. I'm talking about you being easier on him by letting him make his own choices, and stricter on me by saying I have to get my homework done first.*

Parent: *Okay, but before we talk about that specific thing, I want to see if we both think fair means the same thing. Do you think fair means equal?*

Kid: *That* is *what it means.*

Parent: *I think* fair *means you getting what you need to do your best, and him getting what he needs to do his best. Because I want you both to be successful. And I think you are different people who need different things.*

Kid: *Well, how come you think what he needs is more time for fun, and what I need is you being mean?*

Parent: *Hmm. When it comes to homework, I've noticed that if you don't do your work right away, you put if off until bedtime, and then you get worked up about how much you have to do. Sometimes you get upset or angry or you cry because it feels too overwhelming. And with your brother, he can wait and do his homework after dinner without getting worked up. I'm just trying to put rules in place that help you avoid that meltdown. Is there a better way I could help you get your homework done before it gets to that point?*

Kid: *I want to have time to play after school, too. But you can make me start after an hour break. That's fair.*

ECHO what you hear

Parent: *I get it. It's important for you to have some downtime right after school and you think an hour of play time is fair before starting homework. Is that right?*

Kid: *Yeah.*

Parent: *I'm glad you told me what you need.*

FEEDBACK

Parent: *And I'm willing to give that a try. Remember in the past, it's been hard for you to stop your game or to come inside after an hour. We've argued over that and I'm trying to avoid the arguments going forward. Can we agree that if we try this approach, we will set a timer for an hour so I don't have to be the bad guy and argue with you when it's time to start homework?*

Kid: *Yeah.*

Parent: *Sounds good. It's important to me that you know I am trying to be fair to both of you by recognizing that you are two different people who need different things. When you feel you're not getting what you need to do your best, please tell me so we can talk about it. Sound good?*

I know what you're thinking: "This conversation worked well because it's fiction. In an unscripted event, my kid wouldn't compromise as conveniently." True. Though, in my experience, when your tween has a series of experiences with you in which you take a collaborative and cooperative approach to negotiating, they become much more flexible. But that comes with time. How do you move forward in the early stages of adolescence if your tween's demands aren't as reasonable as "an hour to play before starting homework," and instead they insist on no bedtime so they can stay up late finishing work, dinner served in their room so they stay on task, and caffeine to avoid getting sleepy for late-night cramming?

I find parenting inspiration in unlikely places. Since I've been dancing around this metaphor of you as crisis negotiator, I did a little research into the tactics the FBI uses and found the Behavioral Influence Stairway Model (BISM). It looks like a perfect fit for parenting a tween to me, and is reflective of the BRIEF conversation model I use. Below are the steps you can take if your tween's demands are the adolescent equivalent of "and a helicopter to take me to the Cayman Islands with a million dollars in unmarked bills."

1. Active listening: *"Tell me more about that." Spend the most time on this first step. Listen for as long as your kid is willing to talk.*

2. Empathy: *"I see how you would feel upset about that." Or "I see why that sounds like a good idea right now."*

3. Rapport: *"I think we have the same goal, maybe just different ideas on how to get there. Can we work together on this?"*

4. Influence: *"I have some experience with this and I want us both to be happy, so would you trust me to make a recommendation?"*

5. Behavioral change: *"Let's give this new plan a try for a week, and then we can talk about whether it worked and if we need to make more changes."*

In other words, earn trust first, then work together toward a better solution. As with most things, skipping steps does not get you good results.

Increase Your Chances of Being Perceived as Fair

Your adolescent won't always think you're being fair and that's okay, but if you'd like to increase your odds, try the pointers below.

Define terms. Make sure you're agreeing to, or arguing about, the same thing before letting an issue escalate. Remember, *fair* may mean something different to your child than to you.

Be open to communication around conflicts. Listen with real interest and curiosity before insisting you're right.

Clearly establish expectations and consequences in advance. You can't anticipate every infraction that will come up when you're raising an adolescent, so don't bend over backward trying. I suggest playing good cop on the first offense and giving your kid a freebie. This has a double benefit of dismissing any burden to predict the future, and positioning you as a decent human in the eyes of your kid. (Reminder, kids are more likely to work hard for someone they respect.)

Let's say your kid *promised* they would clean their room by dinner and—*surprise!*—they did not. Instead of immediately punishing them, you could say, "You were supposed to clean your room today, but you didn't. I'll give you this one as a freebie and we can reset." Follow up your generosity with clear expectations and consequences for next time, because the second time this happens it won't be an ambush. "I expect your room cleaned by dinner tomorrow. From now on, if you tell me you will do a household task and you miss the deadline, the punishment will be you have to do the chore right away and you stay in the following weekend."

Set reasonable, related, and private consequences. A reasonable punishment causes enough discomfort to be memorable and meaningful, but not so much pain that it creates panic. For an unclean room, missing a weekend get-together with friends is painful. Missing two months of fun would be excessively harsh, and many tweens might resort to sneaky behavior to bypass the unfair ruling. The most meaningful punishments are not just reasonable, but related. Let's take, for example, the uncleaned room scenario. Perhaps instead of missing a weekend of fun, the punishment is adding another cleaning chore. "This one is a freebie, but if you don't clean your room by tomorrow night, you'll have to clean your room right away and stay in Saturday to organize the garage." Often parents reflexively take away the phone as punishment, but I'd rather see a kid working and contributing to the family than staring at a wall. Finally, punishments aren't for public display. Posting pictures of sullen kids doing chores, making kids wear signs that advertise their transgressions, or joking to friends about the punishment while your kid stands nearby . . . these things only add resentment. They never make kids behave better.

Give clear, measurable ways to improve. Your kids want to make you proud. They want to achieve more independence and responsibility. Make it clear to them how they can do that. Promising freedom "when I can trust you" or "when you do better" is vague. Spend time thinking through what growth would look like and then communicate that to your kid. "When you check in with me regularly when you change locations with friends," or "When you regularly attend tutoring to bring up your grades," or "When you put in __ minutes of effort toward practice," and so on. The metrics will be different for each kid and each family, but the more specific you can be, and the more you can tie your reasonable expectations to your kid earning more privileges, the "fairer" things will feel, and the more your kid will put in the work.

Create a team mentality. No one likes to feel they're working in a vacuum. Talk about how everyone in the family matters and all contributions help. Sometimes, not all the time, get in there with them and work side by side, either pitching in to help with their chores, or taking care of your own to-do list nearby.

Conversation Crashers

"Get over it." I understand the urge to shush a complainer, but have you ever been told to stop feeling emotional about something that bothers you? This phrase isn't the fix you're looking for. If your kid is worked up, hear them out, then ask questions so they can begin to come up with a solution. If they're verging on being out of control with emotion, no amount of reason or logic will calm them down. Encourage them to take a shower, exercise, or watch a show for thirty minutes, with the promise that you'll talk it out after. You'll have a better shot at a reasonable conversation once they've been (or you've been) distracted from their (or your!) mounting frenzy.

"Never settle for an outcome you don't want." This is one I've heard in the context of parents who have a win at all costs mentality, relying sometimes on manipulating the system or playing dirty to get a win. A fighting spirit is commendable in lots of situations, but a relentless denial of outcomes is just blind entitlement. Sometimes you can't force things to your favor. When the election is over and the votes are counted, what can you do? Sometimes losing with grace is your best move. Having said that, there's always next time. Learning to be a graceful loser is an important part of being seen as fair, and picking yourself up and trying again after a loss is certainly a sign of strength and integrity.

"When you see an injustice, it's your responsibility to make it better." Yes, but. Consider the age of your audience. This ask may be an impossibly big one for a kid this age. Instead of saying, "Climb this mountain!" which could freak a person out and give them an excuse to quit before getting started, you may get better results if you say, "You may not be able to fix this entirely, but how could you take a few steps in the right direction?"

In a Hurry? Here's Your Crash Course

- Make sure you and your child share an understanding of the term *fair*. Many kids think fair treatment is equal treatment, while adults think fair treatment is when each kid gets what they personally need to be successful. You cannot evaluate fairness out of context.

- When a kid complains something isn't fair, they usually mean they aren't getting something they want or need. This might be valid and parents should investigate, but it often has little to do with what is actually fair.

- If you treat your kids equally, you may be treating them unfairly, because you're not parenting to their differences. Many siblings are not alike and need different things from their parents.

- Kids will balk less at you treating them differently if you explain why and remain open to their feedback.

- To increase the odds your kids will perceive you as fair, be a clear communicator, especially with regards to punishments and rewards. When kids feel ambushed, they do not see you as fair, and when things feel unfair, kids feel right in fighting back.

- Older teens are more likely than younger teens to keep an open mind about fairness, considering other people's intent and motivation in addition to their own perspective.

- It's not easy for young teens to stick up for other people being treated unfairly. Be patient and recognize that taking small steps in the right direction is progress.

10

Talking About Technology

Since the subject of technology and teens tends to spark heated debate, both intergenerationally and among adults, this chapter asks you to begin by recognizing the value technology can provide (we'll get to the dangers, too), remember the joy technology brought you as a teen, and carry that feeling into your talks now. You'll learn how to pull your conversations out of the ever-changing, mystifying details of technology, and to focus on helping your child develop a philosophy about their relationship with technology, treating it with the same values as their off-screen lives.

Middle school and Silicon Valley have one big thing in common: both contend with the daily ups and downs of fleeting popularity and capricious friends or followers. Like your tween or teen, technology itself is in a constant race to be seen as more relevant, more connected, and more popular day after day. There are lots of fickle mistresses, from fame to fashion to fortune, but middle schoolers and tech developers know fickle better than anyone.

Adults bristle at the idea of middle schoolers and technology comingling. We tend to be a bit fickle ourselves, recasting technology as a villain at the start of our kids' adolescence, despite having developed positive, long-term relationships with technology in the home. Consider the pacifying iPad, the educational websites, the wisdom of Siri (bless her for never tiring of the relentless questions), or countless other conveniences that made life with kids a tiny bit easier. I suppose, all that early tech felt like it was within our control, or at least, a reflection of our choices. Ultimately, it's not social media or texting or smartphones that freak parents out, but the intersection of those things with tweenaged free will and, more pointedly, the loss of control that comes with the territory.

Tweens are drawn to technology like moths to a flame—a backlit, blue light, glowing, and rechargeable flame. There are lots of reasons for this, but here are the three I believe most relevant to this particular stage of adolescent development: For one, it's a socially acceptable way to play. Plastic dolls and action figures may be tossed to the back of the closet, but older kids are still drawn to make-believe, and technology enables make-believe in ways that still feel magical and limitless. For another, technology is a reliable way to connect with friends, and without a doubt forging friendships is a top priority for the vast majority of kids this age. And finally, technology gives kids a place to guard their privacy where adults can't easily intrude.

Technology Moves Quickly but You Don't Have To

The fast pace of technology paired with the unpredictable, shifting loyalty of tween consumers is exactly why you should spend zero time freaking out about which apps are on the latest alarming listicle in your Facebook feed. *Most Dangerous Social Media Sites Your Kids Love!* Or *How Your Kid Can Outsmart You with These Tricks Online!* Or *If Your Kid Has These Apps, You're Basically a Very Bad Parent!* Lists keep coming out because apps keep being developed or rebranded. Don't let this overwhelm you. More important than staying on top of which apps people are freaking out about today is understanding trends in functionality and deciding what's off-limits. For example, you may choose not to allow any apps that share your child's location with other users, ask users to anonymously rate or give feedback on other users, don't have a reliable reporting feature to block people who misuse the app, or connect everyone on the platform instead of allowing users to curate their own list of who to follow. This isn't a comprehensive list, but it gives you an idea of how to train your brain toward the kinds of themes to which you should pay attention.

If you feel like you're in the dark, always behind, struggling to keep up with the latest online threats to your family, you're focusing *way* too much on defense, and not enough on building a strong offense. You can't stay on top of everything that happens online and that's okay. I fear, when it comes to talking about technology use and tweens, we lose sight of the forest for the trees. If you can zoom out, away from the fine details of apps, and instead encourage a more broad and analytical discussion around how we can and should interact with technology, your kid will be better able to manage their online life through all the shifts and changes every new update brings.

Don't Forget That This Is Fun

When I was eleven years old, my parents bought an Atari 2600 with a cartridge for Donkey Kong. They hooked it up to a fourteen-inch tube TV that sat atop a tall dresser in our guest room—I mean, cool game room! I would stand, lock-kneed for hours, playing Donkey Kong. As I write this, I am just now returning from an Internet rabbit hole where I found the music that accompanied the earliest version of the game and my ears now hate me. How did those frantic, tinny beeps and electronic starburst noises not drive me insane? What sounds like torture now, felt at the time like sophisticated, modern fun. I loved getting lost in that pixelated world of wonder.

One evening, as our family was headed out, my mom sent me upstairs to see what was taking my dad so long. I found him standing in front of the game TV with a joystick in his hand, his tie not yet even tied, my mom yelling from the bottom of the stairs that it was time to go. "Okay, okay," he said to me in a moment of rare levity. "Just one more level."

You probably also have an early memory of the first time you were genuinely excited by technology. Was it the first e-mail you sent? The day your parents bought a VCR? The first time you watched high-definition television, or held an iPhone, or downloaded music? If you can reconnect with the awe you felt when technology made your world a little bit bigger or smaller, or more exciting or malleable, that feeling should serve as an anchor for understanding your child's emotional reaction to the technology they use and enjoy. I asked my son, who is seventeen years old at the time I'm writing this, if he remembers ever being wowed by technology, or if it was just always a given in his life. He knew his answer right away. "It was fifth grade when I first played Black Ops. That was it. I wish I could go back to that kind of fun. I'd get up early before school to shoot baskets and after school I'd play Black Ops with friends." Even among digital natives, there is nostalgia for the first time technology captured their imaginations.

While my middle school friends and I were having our minds blown by the likes of microwave ovens and caller ID, your kids are probably "obsessed" with their phones, apps, video games, and streaming services like YouTube or Netflix. As parents, we tend to blow off how much these things mean to kids. We worry that their love of technology will lead to stranger danger, a loss of social skills, vague and nefarious mistakes that might ruin their futures, and narcissism. Incidentally, these are the same things parents of teenagers have fretted over since long before *technology* became a household word. It so happens that at the same time your tween naturally starts copping a bad attitude, withdrawing from family life, and obsessing on what people think of them, they also become super interested in technology. As always, though, correlation doesn't mean causation. A sudden deep dive into their technology isn't a sign that your kid is addicted to ones and zeros, it's just that the ones and zeros make it easier to connect to the people, conversations, and things they suddenly find fascinating.

Tech Family Meeting

It may feel daunting, but keep in mind that teaching your child to use technology isn't *much different* from teaching them how to use other tools, like scissors, a stove, or a car. No matter what we teach, instruction usually follows a basic methodology, where you model how a new thing is done, assist at first, then observe without helping, give feedback, and eventually, just back off.

There is, however, one difference that you probably feel highly tuned into: unlike the many things you've taught your child so far, this one is still foreign to you and in addition to your own lack of proficiency, your child has gotten a running start with technology that leaves you feeling like the train has left the station and you're waving from the platform as your kid disappears down the track.

It would be a relief if you knew at a certain age you would send your tween to Tech Boot Camp, and much like signing them up for driver's education at a state-specified age with a trained instructor and curriculum, they would come home with the basics covered. And bonus, you wouldn't have to suffer through those first, terrifying merges onto the cyber highway. No such thing exists for technology. Sure, many apps come with a minimum age requirement of thirteen, but unlike driver's ed class, you can still participate before the recommended age. (By the way, it's important you know that the age minimum on apps has nothing to do with whether the developer thinks the content or experience is appropriate for kids. The age requirement is there because developers want to collect information on their users, and the Children's Online Privacy Protection Act [COPPA] makes it illegal for them to collect info on anyone younger than thirteen. To get around this, apps ask users to verify their age, so they can continue to mine the data they want.) The point is, I recognize that teaching your child to have

> Forget about the tech and focus on basic human behaviors you want your child to follow, whether in real life or on a screen.

a positive relationship with technology may feel unnatural to you. Don't worry about it. Forget about the tech and focus on basic human behaviors you want your child to follow, whether in real life or on a screen.

Unless you can define these basic behaviors, you'll find it impossible to keep up with the many tangential conversations about technology that will come up during early adolescence, and you will often feel like you're playing catch-up with the latest trend. It's key to determine a tech philosophy from the outset so you can set general ground rules for how your family will interact with, relate to, and enjoy technology. I recommend a family meeting format for this, so that you can establish rules and guide points together, ensuring better buy-in from your kids. Then, the smaller conversations that come up later around "Can I get this app?" and "Why do I have to put my phone away?" and "Why am I getting in trouble for posting that?" will have a foundation to rest on.

My Tips for a Tech Family Meeting

- **Be positive.** Remember, technology—like all tools—can be used for things good, bad, or indifferent. If you start the meeting with a tone of fear or an emphasis on safety from danger, your kid will think you're out of touch and probably not going to be open-minded or collaborative during the meeting.

- **Keep an open mind.** Some forms of technology are easy to embrace. The home alarm system makes Mom feel safe, the app that monitors little brother's blood sugar is a lifesaver, and Venmo sure has made it convenient to pay for services. But Snapchat? You might not be able to think of anything redeeming about this app, but I bet your tween can help explain the appeal. Listen with an open mind to how others perceive value before declaring something entirely worthless.

- **Set a goal for the meeting.** For example: "The purpose of our discussion is to create a philosophy about what role we want technology to play in the family."

- **Ask all members to contribute ideas.** Even the youngest members of your family will have thoughts on how to use technology the right and the wrong way. When everyone contributes, you're more likely to get a balanced resolution.

- **Don't predetermine the outcome.** Go in with an open mind. If your kid senses the family meeting is a ruse to fool everyone into agreeing to your rules, they won't participate.

- **Be flexible.** As much as possible, be willing to compromise. It's hard to make everyone entirely happy, but everyone should feel they've won a small concession. Also, remind your kids that nothing is permanent. Explain that it's easier for you to be flexible when you know that if you try something and it doesn't work, you can reconvene and reevaluate.

Tech Family Meeting Starter Questions

- What are ways technology is useful or helpful for our family?

- What are some ways technology might distract or derail us?

- How will we know if our technology use has moved from fun or helpful to disruptive?

- Is there anything we can be doing to make better use of technology? Are we missing anything fun or useful that could benefit us?

- What are some tech-free things we enjoy doing that can balance us out? Are we missing out on anything fun or useful outside the tech category that could benefit us?

Tech Personal Statement

Time, space, and relationships have a way of getting blurry in the online world. It's key to remind your tween that the online world is actually real and the same rules apply to both. Writing a personal statement is a nice way to ground yourself. Have family members list five to ten things they want people to believe about them. For example, I might write: I want people to believe I am creative, kind, funny, trustworthy, and fair. This list becomes a guide for how I interact online. Before I post a comment, or ignore when someone is being teased online, I ask myself: does what I'm doing now online show people what I want them to believe about me?

Do I Have To?

You absolutely do not have to be a techy family! Each family will decide for themselves when and how they will allow their kids access to various forms of technology, whether that's watching shows on PBS or playing World of Warcraft. Maybe you don't own a TV and your kids read Thoreau in their downtime. (I want your life.) No matter, you absolutely still have to *talk* about technology.

Even if you maintain tight control over what tech your child is allowed to use at home, and assuming your child abides by your rules when they're at school or a friend's house, you will *still* need to teach kids how to have a good relationship with technology in the future, and teaching works best when it happens early and often. Just as it's good practice to have many, small sex talks with your kid long before you think they're active, it's a smart idea to have incremental tech talks starting before your child is active online. And remember, though your child may not have social media now, for example, they will still be affected by their peers' use of social media right now. Along these lines, I recommend you begin talking about online pornography as soon as your young child starts using an iPad without you present. Simply let them know that if they see photos online of people with their private areas uncovered, to tell you and you won't be mad. (More on pornography in chapter 14: Talking About Sexuality.)

When I talk with parents and kids about social media, I open with a slide picturing these four items: a tea kettle on a gas flame, a hammer, a kitchen knife, and a jug of bleach. I ask the kids what the items have in common, and they always give me the same answer. "They're dangerous!"

It takes five or six repeated variations of the same answer—"They can hurt you" or "You have to be careful"—until one kid tentatively raises a hand to go against the grain with "They can help you?"

Yes. Of course. Nothing that is useful is not also harmful.

The *Journal of Emergency Medicine* found that knives cause more injuries than any other hand tool, resulting in an average 1190 visits *every day* to the emergency room. Yet, most of us beg our tweens to be more self-reliant in the kitchen. Similarly, car accidents are the leading cause of death among teens, and yet most parents encourage their kids to take driver's education as soon as they're eligible. Daily, parents allow, even encourage, their kids to engage in risky behavior—to get into a car, ride the bus or subway, swim in the ocean, play football, or cut their own apple for a snack. Why do we willfully allow our kids to do certain things with statistically high risks of injury, and not others?

I think we are willing to suspend our disbelief of danger for a few key reasons. First, we believe the reward merits the risk. Let's take cars, for example. In order to let our kids get behind the wheel for the first time, we must ignore the risk and believe having a driver will be worth it. Sure, we hear about car accidents nightly on the evening news, but . . . we can't think about it *too* much because logistically we can't drive our demanding teens with their busy schedules around town into their adulthood. Second, we don't let the *potential* consequence feel *personal*. It's fairly easy to numb out to car accidents until you or a loved one has been in a bad one. Plus, if you are in an accident, who would dare blame or shame you for exposing your kid to the danger of driving, even though we all know there are bad and careless people out there sharing the same roads as our kids, putting others directly in the path of harm. Third, we overlook the risks because it feels *socially important* to drive. Driver's ed is seen as a rite of passage. We proudly post photos of our kids with their permits, then licenses, once they get them. Of course, you want to keep your kid safe all the time, but . . . it would be *weird* if your teen were the only one not driving, right?

Substitute technology for driving, and parents do three things differently. First, we don't even entertain the notion that the rewards outweigh the risks. We view our kids' technology as entertainment, a waste of time, or an escape, but rarely as a tool, and because we fail to weigh the pros with the cons, we inaccurately position tech as an inherent danger to avoid, not a skill to be learned. When we do that, we actually create more danger by not teaching them proper use. Second, unlike other tragedies, when a tragedy hinges on technology, we take it to heart immediately. We have learned to let the stream of car crash reports wash over us, but when we hear of a kid who met up with a stranger from a chat room or another who died by suicide after being cyberbullied, we immediately cast ourselves in a "what if this were *my* family?" fantasy. Third, we parents don't extend the same empathy to the victims of online tragedies as we do to car crash victims, because we think the victim of an online tragedy should have known better, and if not the child, *at least the parents* should have been more cautious. Our minds jump right away to diagnosing what the family should have done differently, and victim blaming has become a kind of intangible talisman we hope will protect us from a similar fate.

Technology as Part of a Healthy, Happy Life

If you feel the encroachment of technology into your young adolescent's life, at some point you will have to address balance. The following is a BRIEF conversation about screen time, but please note, I'm decidedly *not* brief here. This is one of the longer conversations modeled in this book, because technology feels highly personal to kids and can, therefore, be a hot-button topic. I spend quite a bit of lead time easing into the point, so the kid doesn't get angry and disengage.

BEGIN peacefully

Parent: *Hey, how was your day?*

Kid: [Staring at phone] *Fine.*

Parent: *That's good. Are you decompressing for a minute?*

Kid: *Yeah.*

Parent: *I'm so glad. You need to take time to recharge. I don't want to interrupt, so when will you reach a stopping point?*

Kid: *What's wrong?*

Parent: *Nothing at all! I don't want to interrupt, but I want to find time to catch up. Want to talk in thirty minutes?*
Kid: *Sure.*

RELATE to your kid

Parent: [Thirty-five minutes later] *Hey. It's time. Let's talk.*
Kid: *What's up?*
Parent: *I was just thinking this morning that you have a lot more going on now and I'm not always on top of how you spend your time like I was when you were younger. Which is nice for me! But I thought I should check in and make sure nothing is falling through the cracks.*
Kid: *Nothing is.*

INTERVIEW to collect data

Parent: *Okay, good. Can I just go through a quick checklist to be sure?*
Kid: *I guess.*
Parent: *Thanks! Part of this is because I don't want you to burn out. You have a lot of demands on you, whether it's school, sports, friends, or us at home. So I want to respect that and make sure you're getting time to recharge in addition to doing all the stuff you have to do.*
Kid: *Okay, good.*
Parent: *So . . . checklist. You just stop me if there is something you feel you need help with. Homework: Everything turned in and good there? Any projects coming up in any of your classes I need to buy poster board for?*
Kid: *Wait, yes . . . I have to do a science project. Can you get some poster board and some of those fuzzy balls to make a cell?*
Parent: *Sure. I can do that tomorrow. Thanks for telling me. Now, sports: You have regular practice this week but you've actually got two games this Saturday. Good on that? [Kid nods.] House stuff: You still haven't cleaned your room and we talked about that . . .*
Kid: *I'll do it today.*
Parent: *Okay, I'll take you at your word. Have it clean by dinner. If not, we need to talk about a consequence. And friends: Are you making any plans I need to know about to drive you places, have people over, or anything?*

Kid: *I really don't know yet.*

Parent: *Okay, no problem. But you'll give me enough notice if you do? A day ahead is ideal.*

Kid: *Yeah.*

Parent: *Then the last thing on my list is downtime: I want to be sure you have enough to feel refreshed but not so much that you get lost in time and lose track of other stuff you need to do.*

Kid: *Okay, just tell me how much time I get.*

Parent: *Well, I am not sure it makes sense to set a number to it. Is it fair to say your favorite way to spend downtime is on your phone?*

Kid: *I don't know . . . I do other stuff, too!* [Kid may be sensing a trap and afraid to admit the phone is key because you might take it away.]

Parent: *Of course you do. For sure. Do you feel like you can put a number on how much time I should give you on your phone though?*

Kid: *I don't know why it matters, if I do all the other stuff you ask.*

ECHO what you hear

Parent: *You know, I agree. Which is why I wasn't keen on putting a number on it myself.*

Kid: *Oh, yay!*

Parent: *It sounds like we both think that balancing your downtime (or phone time) with the other important parts of your life is what matters most. Do you agree?*

Kid: *Definitely.*

FEEDBACK

Parent: *Great! So, as far as I'm concerned, these are the things you need to do every day to maintain that balance:*

- *Stay on top of all your schoolwork. If you don't have anything that's due, I'd like to see you reading for thirty minutes minimum at home.*

- *Move your body. That's easy on days you have practice. But when you don't, you should get forty-five minutes of activity any way you want—walk the dog, ride your bike, play outside, anything.*

- *Help around the house. We count on your contribution, so every day do something to help out. We can talk more about how this could look.*

- *Spend time with friends in real life. I know you are with friends on your phone, but there is no substitution for hanging out face-to-face. I am happy to make that happen in some way, on the weekends. Kids can come here or I can drive you somewhere.*

- *Tech-free time. I'm not a phone hater, but certain times are so much nicer without them and this rule applies to me, too! No phones at the table, during car rides, and during special family activities makes it so much easier to enjoy each other. Plus, no phone thirty minutes before bedtime so you can wind down.*

- *If you can check off all these things, then you're living a balanced life, and I see no reason to put a time limit on the phone use. If not, we will need to be stricter about how you use the phone. I'll use balance as the scale to measure your success.*

Tech time is a battleground issue for parents of tweens, but not all time spent online is equal. Let's also look at another conversation that might come up about just what your kid is *doing* when they stare at their screen for so long.

BEGIN peacefully

Kid: *Hey, can you approve my app request?*
Parent: *Bring me my phone and I'll take a look. What's the app?*
Kid: *It's called* [insert name of the very latest fad]. *It's just for taking pictures and then making memes out of them.*

RELATE to your kid

Parent: *That sounds like fun. Will you send me a meme?*

Kid: *Uh, weird. Do you really want me to?*

Parent: *I do!*

Kid: *Okay, yeah.*

INTERVIEW to collect data

Parent: *Before I approve this, a couple things. Have you looked up the rating for this app?*

Kid: *Yes, it's ages ten and up.*

Parent: *That's good. And when you make the meme, what do you do with it?*

Kid: *Just send it to friends.*

Parent: *Through the app? Or does it save to your phone and then you text it?*

Kid: *I don't know.*

Parent: *Well, find out. Can you Google it and let me know?*

Kid: *Does it matter? Like, will you say yes to one way and not if it works another way?*

Parent: *Honestly, I don't know yet. But, I think you should always know more about the technology you want to use before you get involved with it. Make sure if you make a meme with your photo in it, for instance, they don't claim the right to use it for marketing purposes.*

[Kid comes back later, having done research, and explains how it works.]

ECHO what you hear

Parent: *Awesome job researching this! I'm impressed. Sounds like you found out good info on the privacy issue.*

Kid: *Thank you. I didn't think they would make a bad app for ten-year-olds. Can we just make a rule that if it's for a certain age I don't need to ask you?*

Parent: *I'm glad you're thinking about how the apps you use are rated and that you care enough about my rules to do the research into how they work. And I understand why it makes sense to you to say any app for a certain age should be fine, but let's talk for a second about your question.*

FEEDBACK

Parent: *What you were saying about companies not making a bad app for certain ages is sort of true . . . except that people can use basic apps in bad ways. Just like a hammer isn't a bad thing—I use it to hang pictures on the wall, which is good. But I could also use it to smash a window. I'm first concerned with how the app is designed to be used, but I also want to think about how it can be misused by other people out there. Does that make sense to you, the way I'm thinking?*

Kid: *Yes. You're just being careful.*

Parent: *Right! Just trying to be smart about it. So you know as well as anyone that technology is always changing. It changes when the developers make changes to how it works, and it changes when the people with the app find new ways to use it. When I say yes to a new technology, it's not the same as when I say, "Yes, I'll buy you this football or this Lego kit." I want to make sure the technology doesn't become something different from when it started. I'm saying yes to this today, but for a while I want to keep an eye on it and make sure a) it's what they promised it would be, and b) you and the other people who use it are doing it right. Using technology can be like swimming in the ocean. We both know the ocean is fun and also dangerous. I don't want to keep you from having fun, but as your parent I need to make sure you're safe. Think of yourself as attached to a life preserver. You can still go out in the ocean, but if I see you getting in over your head, I can pull you back in a little bit. We'll operate this way for a while until I see you're staying safe out there and then, as you get older, of course you'll start swimming on your own. The key to getting there will be you staying open to honest conversations like we're having right now. Okay! Ready for me to approve the app?*

One final, important tip for parents about technology: this may feel completely foreign to you, but don't forget you're a good teacher. You can teach this, too, if you don't get lost in the equipment and instead focus mostly on the human side of things. Plus, you're a good student! Anything you're curious about, your kid can probably teach you better than anyone else.

Conversation Crashers

"Too much screen time is bad for you." Aside from being too vague for kids to act on (how much is too much?), this one has other problems. The American Academy of Pediatrics recently revised its statement on screen time, removing recommendations on time, and instead urging parents to focus on quality over quantity. All screen time is not equal. Rather than vilify screen time, make your conversations about balance. Screen time is fine if it's not at the expense of other healthy habits.

"You're going to get addicted." This a pretty scary threat, and at the same time a fairly generic, empty one. It reminds me of when parents would tell kids that if they sat too close to the TV, their eyes would permanently cross. I do not want to dismiss parents whose kids have suffered from addiction issues of any nature. Addiction is complicated, scary, and when it comes to technology, not well defined. Common Sense Media has published thorough research on the subject of technology addiction. Before you worry yourself too much, and certainly before you diagnose your child, I suggest reading their report. In the meantime, know that technology, alcohol, drugs, gambling, and gaming are not interchangeable in a sentence about addiction. They are unique and require a full understanding before diagnosis.

"I don't want you to make a mistake that will follow you around your whole life." How could we *not* worry about this one? We hear so many examples of kids who've suffered irreversible damage from online mistakes. Best case? Their college admission gets revoked. Worst case? Every parent's worst nightmare. All teens will make mistakes and have to live with them. It's awful when those mistakes keep resurfacing online. The trouble with saying something like this to tweens is, it's meaningless to them. We know young adolescents live in the moment. They are in a suspended state of denial that what happens today will matter in the least to their distant twenty-five-year-old self. You know what they *do* care about? What their friends think right now. Don't waste time trying to strike fear in them with talk of the future. Instead, talk about the cost of a mistake on their happiness today. Talk about the social isolation kids feel when that happens. Talk about making choices to preserve their good standing now when it matters to them most.

In a Hurry? Here's Your Crash Course

- Worry less about keeping up with tech trends and more about establishing a living, breathing philosophy around how your family will relate to technology.

- Don't forget the joy and excitement technology has brought to your life. Remember the first technology that blew your mind? How did it make you feel? This is probably how your kid feels. Try to enjoy some of the same fun they're having.

- Kids don't love technology for its own sake, but rather for what it connects them to: people, conversations, and things they find fascinating.

- Have a Tech Family Meeting as a way to establish common ground, guidelines, and personal statements you can use to guide online behavior.

- Tools that are helpful are inevitably also harmful. Stay balanced when talking about technology. It's neither all good nor all bad.

- Be kind to people who make mistakes online, just as you would someone who got into a car accident. We're all human. We're all still learning.

- Technology can be a happy, healthy part of a happy, healthy life. The key is balance.

- Not all screen time is equal. Encourage creative, connected use of technology.

- Technology is a hot-button topic for tweens, especially when they fear you'll take it away at the drop of a hat. Ease gently into conversations and stay open to the pros and cons. When in doubt, ask your kid to teach you about what they know and love.

11

Talking About Criticism

To help you have better conversations about dealing with criticism, in this chapter you'll gain an understanding of why kids become more sensitive to feedback during adolescence, the importance of teaching your child the difference between constructive and destructive criticism, how adults can send mixed messages about caring what others think, and why couching feedback in your child's strengths is more effective than pointing out their flaws.

One breezy spring day when my daughter was eight, we went to the playground with her new friend, Paige, and her friend's mom, Diane. We moms were enjoying that side perk of orchestrating playdates when you genuinely click with the other parent. As Diane and I chatted on a bench, Paige sidled up to her mom with a hurt look on her face. "What happened?" Diane asked her gently. She listened to Paige whisper the details into her ear, while I grew antsy and embarrassed, imagining what my daughter might have done, wondering if this might be both the first and last time my new friend and I would chat like this. "Sounds like you got some feedback," Diane said when Paige wrapped up. "What do you want to do with that?"

I tucked that memory away because it was a lovely example of good parenting, not to mention social grace. Kids tattle all the time and it puts parents on the spot, especially when the other child's parent is there. "Do I investigate? Should I give a consequence? Who's at fault? I was just sitting here and now this gets dumped in my lap and my next move is going to make or break this entire playdate."

Instead of cloying scrambling for a way to defuse the conflict, or rushing to appear diplomatic, Diane gracefully positioned what my daughter said (whatever it was, I still don't know) with neutrality, as nothing more than an opportunity for her daughter to assess. What a beautiful way to empower her daughter after she felt hurt.

If you like this approach, you will get plenty of opportunities to practice. Tweens may be the most critiqued people on the planet. They deal with a rolling commentary on a daily basis—from their outfits ("You're not going out in that!?"), to their homework ("More effort please!"), to their choice of friends (eye rolls). By middle school, kids get constant feedback not only from you, but from more than a handful of teachers, coaches, and administrators, all with differing expectations and preferences, as well as a school full of kids with no end to their opinions about all of your kid's choices. The floodgates to critique open up in early adolescence, and from then on criticism remains a fairly constant companion in life; therefore, learning how to deal with feedback is crucial.

Critiques are necessary for growth, but they can come at a price, especially for those of us who are sensitive. I reluctantly carry around a catalogue of memories from times I was embarrassed or hurt by people's reaction to me. From the classmate who laughed at my off-brand jeans, to the troll on Facebook who hammered me for my political view, to the dear friend who meant to help but I was too prickly that day to hear her advice in a loving way, I hang on tight to critiques in all forms.

In retrospect, I can sometimes see the message itself wasn't bad, but I wasn't in a good place to receive it. Other times, it was unfounded, but my armor wasn't heavy enough to deflect. Often, the feedback wasn't even *about* me. I'm just overly tuned in to the slight ways in which people let you know what they're thinking: the sigh, the quick glance away, the inattentiveness, the one-second delay in laughter. I wish I had thicker skin, were breezier, and generally gave fewer Fs about what people think. But one of the many upsides to being sensitive is it helps me do my job well, because to be a good teacher, I need to regularly imagine myself in other people's shoes. If your child is like me in this way, and you can show them the upside to their sensitivity, it may help ease the burdensome nature of being sensitive.

Whether your kid is consistently fragile or self-assured (or all the permutations in between), the way *you* feel about feedback will affect how you help your kids process the responses they're receiving on a daily basis. If your little apple hasn't fallen far from your hypersensitive tree, it may be hard for you to listen to their stories without having a strong emotional reaction yourself. Try hard to be aware of this and temper your response. On the other hand, one of the ironies of parenting is that you often get blessed with a child who is not at all like you. If you're thick-skinned, you may not understand why your kid cares at all what other people think. If you're sensitive, you might fret your child is burying their feelings, even though they're being honest when they tell you nothing's wrong. Start tuning in to how you perceive feedback, so you can untangle your reaction from your child's.

The Paradox of Caring About What People Think

As your child enters adolescence, they will begin to view the world with a *touch of narcissism*. (Your child is probably not a true narcissist, don't worry.) However, this part of a child's development centers on untucking themselves from under your wing and setting out to discover their individuality, including a wide array of personal preferences, limits, beliefs, dreams, capabilities, and so on. While this sounds reasonable and appropriate on paper, it can feel like your child only cares about how the world revolves around them.

To a tween, establishing an identity apart from parents or caregivers is as invigorating as it is lonely. Separation brings feelings of solitude, and that's what pushes kids to yearn for acceptance by their wider group of peers, and makes the feedback they get from peers feel so high stakes. A compliment from a well-liked classmate can feel like winning the lottery, but an insult can feel like fumbling the game-winning pass at the Super Bowl. Naked. Then replayed in slow motion on the Jumbotron.

Suddenly, what other kids think about your child is of paramount importance to them. If you could listen to your tween's thoughts, this is what you'd probably hear: "I don't want to be a little kid anymore who needs my parents, but I also don't want to be out here all alone. I need people to like me! I'll do anything to be liked."

They will not always be liked. You could try wrapping your child in metaphorical Bubble Wrap to keep them from getting bruised by criticism. Some parents try to do this by not allowing their kids to hang out with "bad influences," by suiting them up in the trendiest clothes and accessories, by telling them not to be weak, by instructing them to report all injuries—physical or emotional—up the proper chain of command at school, or by stepping into the role of friend. None of these will spare your kid from the pain of rejection, embarrassment, or isolation that comes with the territory of adolescence.

One of my favorite sayings is "It's not my business what other people think of me." This is a helpful mantra for someone with my level of sensitivity, but the broader truth is that humans are communal by nature, so what other people think *does* matter, at least to a degree. Most parents seem to want their kids to be totally independent, think for themselves, challenge the status quo, and disrupt outdated notions, *while at the same time* be obedient of social norms, respectful of tradition, polite to authority, and receptive to other people's needs. A paradox, right?

We have to accept the yin with the yang when it comes to raising good humans. On one hand, it would be simpler if we could just tell our kids not to care what other people think. On the other hand, that kind of isolated thinking doesn't work well when you live in a community. We all have neighbors, bosses, friends, and families who give us input, and though we don't want our kids to become conditioned into blindly pleasing others, we do want them to become adults who can balance being an individual with being part of a group. And being part of a group means learning how to cope with feedback.

Types of Criticism

Not all criticism is created equal. When I work with young adolescents at my leadership camps, I first make sure they understand the difference between constructive and destructive criticism.

- Constructive criticism is intended to help you improve.
- Destructive criticism is intended to make you feel bad.

I suggest you explain the difference between constructive and destructive criticism. A natural way to bring this up is to discuss examples from sitcoms, movies, books, Twitter, or real-world social dynamics (outside your child's immediate sphere). As you clarify types of criticism and begin to show your child examples of both, they'll become better at distinguishing between the difference. Then, when they talk with you about a personal experience, you'll be able to gently ask them what kind of criticism they received. Once they determine if it's meant to help or hurt, they can think about next steps.

Feedback in Action: A Coach's Decision

Let's consider a scenario that often comes up in middle school: your kid gets cut from a team, audition, or activity. I'll use the BRIEF conversation model to show you how this conversation might play out.

BEGIN peacefully

Kid: *They posted who made the basketball team today. I didn't make it. I can't believe it.*
Parent: *Oh, I'm so sorry to hear this. Can you tell me more?*
Kid: *I just thought I would make it. I'm better than some of the kids who made it. Like, definitely better. I knew the coach didn't like me. This is so unfair! And now people are going to think I suck worse than the bad players who made it. Some kids were saying they couldn't believe I didn't make it either. This is just so unfair.* [Kid starts to cry a little.]

RELATE to your kid

Parent: *Something like this happened to me in middle school, too, and it's really hard. Is there anything I can do for you right now? I'm happy to sit with you and talk about it, or just sit with you and watch TV if you want me to. Or if you need some time alone to feel what you're feeling, that's okay, too. This is a hard thing to go through—I'm here for you in whatever way you want.*

Kid: *I don't even know what I want. I'm so upset.*

Parent: *I understand. You have a right to feel upset. Can I ask you a few questions?*

Kid: *Sure.* [Or maybe kid says *not now.* In that case, ask again at bedtime if you can talk about it now. Then move on to the Interview step.]

INTERVIEW to collect data

Parent: *Do you know how many kids got cut?*

Kid: *No, but twelve kids made the team. And some of them suck at basketball! I'm not being a jerk—a lot of them deserved it and are better than me, but some of them I've seen at recess and they miss so many shots. I have no idea why they made it.*

Parents: *Sometimes this happens. Kids with less obvious abilities end up making a team, or getting cast in the lead role. Or in my case at work, sometimes a person who is worse at their job gets promoted and I have no idea why. Let me ask you a couple more questions: Did the coach give you any feedback at tryouts or after? And did any of your friends also get cut?*

Kid: *No feedback. Nothing. And Tyler and Marcus also got cut. And they're good, too. And obviously a bunch of kids got cut who aren't good.*

Parent: *Okay, this helps me have a bigger picture. What are Tyler and Marcus going to do this season? Do you know if they're going to join a team outside of school?*

Kid: *I have no idea.*

ECHO what you hear

Parent: *It sounds like a lot of kids tried out and a lot got cut. It also sounds like it's not obvious how the coach made his decision. I'm sure this is a* *lot of players' first experience with being cut without explanation. It's frustrating and embarrassing, and might even make some kids angry. I get that.*

FEEDBACK

Parent: *It's hard to face disappointment, but I want you to know I'm proud of you for trying. First, I think it's important to remember that not making the team is one instance of feedback, from one person. Your whole life, you'll have to remember that just because someone decided something about you, doesn't make it true. This coach's decision doesn't mean you shouldn't play basketball again. It just means you won't get to play for him this year. Second, it's time to think about where you go from here. The coach's decision is only the beginning of this story. What you do next is the most important part. You could think about joining a rec league outside of school. You could e-mail the coach and ask what he's looking for from players and what you could work on before tryouts next year. You could turn your attention to a different activity this winter. It's up to you and you don't have to decide right away. Give it some thought. But where you go from here says so much more about you than whether or not you made the team this year.*

In this scenario, your child has to learn how to cope when things don't go their way. When your child tells you they got cut, you may have one of two common reactions: you understand why, or you are just as shocked as your kid.

Let's say you had a sense this would happen. You know your kid has great aim but no hustle. Or that they have an inflated perception of their skills. Or that their desire to be on the team is not matched by their desire to practice. Or that the coach *does* pick favorites based on who the kid's parents are. Whatever you know to be true, keep it to yourself. Your child doesn't have a shot at developing the skills to cope with disappointment if you're three steps ahead of them in evaluating what went wrong. Even if you understand the outcome, ask questions that could broaden your understanding of your child's perspective. The less omniscient you are, the more your kid will have to soul-search for answers.

On the other hand, maybe you are as baffled and surprised by this outcome as your kid. Being cut from the team might feel like a real injustice to you, too. Reserve your emotions about being wronged for another time—when you're with your friends or partner. Your tween needs to process what happened without the added pressure of navigating how *you* feel. Since you're trying to help a twelve-year-old learn how to cope and strategize, outrage will only slow down the learning process.

Kids, like adults, won't always get what they want, or even what they work hard for, and while negative feedback on effort is frustrating, comments on a kid's personality or appearance are a *much* more sensitive issue, as seen in the next dialogue.

Feedback in Action: When a Classmate Insults You

Another common scenario we can all remember too well, is finding out someone at school has said something bad about you behind your back. Let's look at how this conversation might play out at home. Since you likely won't know about this unless your child tells you, assume this conversation starts with them debriefing you.

BEGIN peacefully

Kid: *Can I tell you something?*
Parent: *Of course.*
Kid: *I had the worst lunch today. Carly heard a rumor that these guys said I was ugly and then she called them over to the table to ask them if they said it. It was so embarrassing.*

RELATE to your kid

Parent: *Oh, wow. That's an incredibly rude thing for someone to say and do. I'm so sorry this happened to you. I want to say first: it's absolutely not true. I don't know whether you believe me right now, but I have to tell you*

*that as the truth. Also, I know that doesn't make it hurt any less. Insults
hurt and I'm here for you. I'm glad you told me, so we can talk about it.*

INTERVIEW to collect data

Parent: *So tell me, what happened next?*

Kid: *I wanted to cry when she told me, but we were in the cafeteria, so I
had to just laugh. The good thing is, the guys didn't stick around, but they
laughed when she asked them.*

Parent: *Okay. Do you think maybe they laughed the same way you
laughed? Because it's one of those situations where you don't know what
else to do?*

Kid: *Maybe.*

Parent: *I'm wondering if Carly was telling the truth about what she heard.
Do you think there is a chance she misheard or got it wrong? Maybe they
did say it, but not about you? You don't have the answer to that, but I'm just
thinking out loud.*

Kid: *Carly said she would tell them to stop talking about me and then she
kept checking on me.*

Parent: *Did it feel to you like Carly was enjoying being in that role?
Getting to go between you and the guys like a messenger and getting to
take care of you?*

Kid: *Yeah, I think she likes being a messenger, like you said. It gave her a
chance to talk with those guys a lot.*

Parent: *Okay. Well, we probably won't know why she did that or what
really happened, although if it seemed like Carly was enjoying the drama,
that's worth noting. What are you feeling now?*

Kid: *I'm irritated that she told me, because I'd rather not know. And I don't
want to see those guys tomorrow.*

ECHO what you hear

Parent: *Believe me, that is understandable. Most of us want to avoid people
who are rude or mean. It sounds like a very bad day. It also sounds like
Carly made it worse, so you might consider telling her you'd rather not talk*

about it if she continues to bring it up in the future, and make a bigger deal out of it the next time she wants to do something like that.

FEEDBACK

Parent: *We could spend our time trying to figure out whether those guys did or didn't say something, and why Carly got involved, but I'm not sure we'll ever understand what really happened. This is just people being rude for no reason, so now you have to figure out how to handle it. You can ignore it. You can speak up for yourself. You can look for nicer people to spend time with. You've always been mature, and I hope you will think about this situation with the same maturity, by understanding that their bad behavior says more about them than you, and asking yourself if the people you love and respect would agree with those boys. Hint: We wouldn't! Now, I love you, and if you want to keep talking about this, we can. If you'd rather do something else to get your mind off it, we can do whatever you feel like.*

When a kid gets feedback in the form of insult, it's easy for them to hunker down into their feelings of sadness. What helps most is when kids learn early to self-soothe with your support. By encouraging them to do something for themselves, you break the cycle of bad thoughts, and when they take some kind of action (no matter how small), they are able to retain a sense of control over their circumstances and avoid wallowing in helplessness. (If you're reading out of order, for more on how to help kids cope with hard feelings refer back to chapter 8: Talking About Taking Care of Yourself on health, specifically the Try This First section.)

The concepts are simple, but when tweens feel affronted, they don't pause to reflect on the intention of the messenger. Doing this as a first step can be liberating. In eighth grade, I heard that a former friend had said something mean about my performance in a school production. That night, as I ruminated over what to do, my dad asked me a simple question: "Do you care what this person thinks? Do you like and respect this person? If you do, you should consider their opinion. If you don't, don't think any more about it." It was an epiphany to have it put so simply. I felt relieved at being unburdened by this simple litmus test.

In other words, and these aren't *my* words, but this is an aphorism I've come to love: "Don't accept criticism from someone you wouldn't ever go to for advice."

The Calls Are Coming from Inside the House . . .

Do you remember that classic horror movie when the babysitter calls the police to report a series of scary calls she's been receiving, only to be told that the calls are coming from someone close to her? Someone *inside* the house.

It's one thing to deal with criticism from a coach, friend, bully, great aunt, or nosy neighbor. There will be plenty of times, though, when the criticism is coming from inside the house, and then you have to deal with all your kid's anger, entitlement, and denial coming back at you. Be afraid. Be very afraid.

Is there a way to make giving critiques to your kid less scary? For starters, in answering this, I took a step back to ask the question: *should* critiques be coming from inside the house? The answer I've come to is yes, but it's a yes-with-a-giant-asterisk (or two). The first footnote is that how you give a critique makes all the difference in whether your kids are able to use it or whether they'll have a meltdown of horrific proportions. The second is that you probably need to critique your kid a lot less than you think.

Here is my argument: Traditional feedback is not as helpful as we think. Pointing out someone's flaws or "areas for growth" (code for "flaws") is not an effective way to help them improve. A 2017 study out of the Harvard Business School confirms that feedback that focuses on correcting deficits actually stunts learning. Here's why: The human brain grows by developing new neurons and synapses. We see the most growth in the human brain when a person feels confident and competent. You've probably noticed you are most successful when you enjoy a task and also experience a high level of proficiency at that task. I know I learn the most about the stuff I love the most. Conversely, when you feel like you're already not good at something, you're slower to pick up tips and tricks for improvement, even when they are carefully explained.

When you talk with a child about their strengths, new neurons and connections bloom in abundance. When you focus your feedback on what went wrong, the brain processes that criticism as a threat and shuts down new growth. Put simply, focusing on weakness causes learning to freeze.

I fear you're cringing now. I'm not suggesting you fill your kids with an inflated sense of importance or aptitude, or that you never tell them when they need to do better. Definitely, continue to give instructions about how to do better. "Please don't interrupt when I'm in the middle of talking to a friend" is a valuable critique. "You're someone who has a hard time letting people finish their thoughts before you interrupt" is not helpful. The latter will send a signal to your kid's brain to protect itself from criticism. The former will ignite your child's learning, especially if you pair it with a strength. Ideally, you might say something like: "You have many good ideas. Remember not to interrupt me when I'm talking with friends, but I hope you'll jot down your ideas in this notebook so you can tell me all about them when I'm done."

Whatever analogy you like for kids—they're plants that need watering, sponges that need soaking, or buckets that need filling—it's our job as parents to give kids the instructions they need, to learn the skills they need, to become adults. If you're still unsure how to give feedback to your tween, think of yourself as a helpful instruction manual, and not so much an op-ed section.

Your job is to teach your kid the right way to do tasks safely and, to a lesser degree, effectively. Efficacy, after all, is subjective. As an illustration, let's look at teaching tweens how to clean a bathroom—a topic that comes up surprisingly often in my parenting group. Lots of you have middle schoolers with a Walgreens' worth of personal products—from hair dye to shaving cream and makeup to body spray—and even more of you seem to have tweens with bad toilet aim. (Gross, but normal.) In short, there are a lot of kids out there who need to learn how to clean up after themselves.

When you teach this task, there will be certain hygienic elements you'll cover, as well as some cleaning product dos and don'ts. Then, beyond the absolute no-nos of this task, you'll probably feel inclined to impart lots of *opinions* on best practices, from how often it should be done, to time of day it needs to be completed, to order of operations, to how long it should take. Resist this urge. If you stand over your kid, offering feedback along the way about how they could do it better, faster, more like Grandma taught you, this will drive your child crazy. Their resistance to your advice will likewise drive you crazy. In some twisted version of Murphy's Law of Middle School, the more feedback you give, the worse your child will actually become at performing the task.

You might assume pointing out "you missed a spot" would improve your child's performance next time. It doesn't. Whenever you're giving feedback to your middle schooler, try as often as possible to make it instructional and to couch it in their strengths. "Hey, you did a great job on your bathroom. The mirror was spotless. Don't forget to throw your towel in the wash . . . but otherwise it looked great." When it comes to driving successful behavior changes, flattery will get you everywhere.

One of the more successful forms of encouragement my husband and I stumbled upon when our kids were little was the "I caught you doing a good job!" game. When we noticed our kids sharing with each other, being patient, being kind, or otherwise naturally exhibiting the opposite of the behaviors we were prone to punish them for, we excitedly called out, "Hey, I just caught you doing something good!" Then we'd dole out high fives. It sounds corny, but once we started this, our kids began showing us more and more good behaviors. Adolescents, though they're pulling away from you, still secretly enjoy and need your praise. Catch them doing a good job and let them know they've done well. (Don't give them high fives. They will look at you like you are an adult who gives teenagers high fives.)

Tuning into the Right Voice

Remember, your child gets feedback *all day long* from friends, teachers, coaches, the media, even strangers. The world is at work almost every waking second, whispering in your kid's ear: "*This* is how you should look and *that* is how you should not. *This* is what you should weigh and *that* is definitely not. *This* is what it's cool to be interested in and *that* is not. *This* is who you should be in public and *that* is not, despite what you feel in private."

How do you teach your tween to find and listen to their own conscience over the din? Adolescents learn when to tune out those pervasive and invasive messages, if they are allowed to develop confidence in their ability to think for themselves. That requires you to regularly give your kids opportunities to make decisions for themselves, and to praise their competence, even when they choose differently from you, and especially when they make mistakes and your own confidence is shaken. Like a coach at halftime when the team is down, you need to get them to believe in their own potential, and that comes from practice and pep talks. This is how your child will start resisting peer pressure and learn to trust their gut—exactly what we all want kids to be good at by the time they head into high school.

The point is, kids want to be successful. If they struggle to keep their footing after getting some tough feedback, remember to couch your response in their assets. Not sure what assets might relate to a particular problem your child is experiencing? Let your kid tell you. You might ask:

1. What are you best at?

2. How could your strengths help you out of this situation?

3. If something could actually solve this problem, what would it be?

4. What has worked for you before in a situation like this?

Conversation Crashers

"You need to care less what they think." Sure, we all feel like saying this from time to time, or *from minute to minute* if your kid is particularly sensitive to what others think. But even if you know your child would be happier if they could do this, it's not helpful. In fact, it is akin to someone telling you not to overreact when you're upset. An emotional response is never squelched by being told to be less emotional. Instead, try saying, "It's hard to care deeply about what others think. When you feel sensitive about people's comments, is there anything that makes you feel better?"

"That person is as dumb as a bucket of rocks." Bashing the person who gave your child tough feedback is tempting, but not advisable. We all want our kids to recover quickly from the sting of rejection. And sure, if the feedback falls under the category of insanely rude or judgmental, or if it pertains to something your child can't and shouldn't change, like their identity (race, ethnicity, sexual orientation, gender, or physicality), it's fine to say, "That person is an idiot. Ignore them." But generally, kids need to learn to evaluate feedback and criticism for themselves. If you develop the knee-jerk habit of dismissing coaches, teachers, or classmates who have critical opinions of your child's skills or behavior, you set up your adolescent to blame others for their failures, which is a highly annoying trait in any adult. Instead, prompt your child to consider the source, and think through the feedback.

"I'll tell you how to fix this . . ." When your kids were little, you would often fix things for them. It was both practical problem solving and an expression of love. By the time your kid is in middle school, they need to fix things for themselves. At least, they need the opportunity to practice fixing things for themselves. When you tell a kid explicitly how to do this, you shortchange their experience. Even if you give vague advice, like "Just stand up for yourself" or "Go to the coach tomorrow and find out what happened" or "Report this to the guidance counselor," you risk your kid clamming up around you because they don't feel comfortable taking your advice. Worse, if you actually call the coach or guidance counselor yourself, you've almost guaranteed your child will cross you off the list of people to confide in. If you're not sure how to respond, imagine this is your coworker confiding in you. They need an opportunity to complain to you about their boss, and for you to listen as long as it takes to get it off their chest. Usually, they don't even want advice. *Never* do they want you to call their boss to fix it.

"Hey, are you sure everything is okay?" This sounds innocuous and, in some cases, it can be. But if you worry that your child is suffering after receiving negative feedback, a vague check-in like this sounds a lot like what Dr. Michael Thompson and Catherine O'Neill Grace call "interviewing for pain" in their book *Best Friends, Worst Enemies*. After an upsetting incident, it's enough to say to your child, "If you ever feel sad or want to talk through this more with me, I'm here to listen." Then leave it alone. We, as parents, often linger over our kids' pain for much longer than they do, and when we interview for pain points, we force them to marinate in it for a more extended period than they would otherwise.

"I'll be your friend." This impulse to be the thing your kid needs most comes from the softest place in your heart, but if it is your instinct to sub in as a friend when your child needs one, it's time to find a new response. What you feel you're saying is "I love you and think you're the greatest and you've always got me in your corner!" What your tween hears is "You aren't good at making friends with kids your age, so I'll play that part." There will be moments in your relationship with your child when you support and entertain each other just as friends would. I hope you'll cherish these lovely moments, but they don't replace essential peer-to-peer relationships. You can certainly model what a good friend would do in times of self-doubt: be supportive, listen, don't judge. Then encourage them to reach out to a friend or try a new activity to make a new friend.

In a Hurry? Here's a Crash Course

- People are constantly telling adolescents what to do and how to do it. It's important to recognize that everyone has different sensitivity to feedback, and to adjust your delivery to your child's temperament.

- We all have to find a balance between not caring what others think of us, and being cooperative community members.

- Kids benefit from being able to differentiate from constructive criticism (meant to help you improve) and destructive criticism (meant to make you feel bad).

- Remove your emotions from any situation when you learn about negative feedback your child has received. This will allow them to focus on how they feel and how they will cope, not how you feel or plan to cope.

- When giving a critique to a tween, avoid offering your opinion on their performance. Think of yourself as an instruction manual, not an editorial page. Instead of giving your opinion on how they're doing, just give them clear instructions on how to do a task.

- Research shows that traditional feedback (pointing out flaws) is not effective. People learn better when feedback highlights their strengths. We see more brain development when a person feels confident and competent.

- To help tweens cope with tough feedback, ask questions like "Which of your strengths can help you?" or "What has helped you before when you've faced a tough situation like this?"

12

Talking About Hard Work

In this chapter, you'll learn why it's important to evaluate hard work using flexible criteria, how four different types of motivation may affect your child's inclination to work hard, how to encourage and value effort even when the result isn't what your child hoped for, and the importance of talking openly about the increasing trend toward perfectionism and burnout.

You've heard the "joke" about your parents having to walk through the snow, to and from school, uphill both ways, more times than you thought possible. Despite your cynicism, you probably have a version of this yourself involving having to get off the couch to change the channel, your annoyance doubled by sometimes getting a static shock from touching the dial after dragging your feet across the shag carpet. The list of ways each prior generation had it harder than the next could fill a C-list comedian's entire set, and it often does.

This generational chest puffing (also known as "complain bragging") has long been a fun way for adults to bond over the memory of shared hardships. But I think we mainly do it to coddle a remote hope, that just *maybe*, if our kids knew the dues we've paid, they'd take us more seriously.

What we're really saying when we talk about the hard work we've put in is "I'm more than your chauffer, cook, therapist, and janitor! I worked hard all my life, as evidenced by this very story I am telling you now. I hope you see me in a new light."

This collective need of parents to mythologize hard work tells me three things. One, parents crave respect and they'll exaggerate the heck out of a story to get some. (Myself included.) Two, effort can be a source of real, lasting pride. And three, hard work is *entirely relative*.

Working Hard or Hardly Working?

Being cute about hard work is annoying to adolescents. Did you spend a summer laying brick in the sweltering heat, or cleaning bathrooms at an amusement park, or waiting tables at a tourist trap full of crying kids and cranky parents? It makes us midlifers feel tremendously proud to recall our youthful strength and stamina. We were Rocky punching sides of beef in the freezer! We had the Eye of the Tiger!

Your middle schooler will become a high schooler who, with any luck, will also get to do a terrible job some summer and have great stories to embellish over the years. Until then, try to resist poking fun at how hard *they don't work now*. Don't get me wrong. Make them do hard work. Just avoid comparing effort among people of varying ages, abilities, and opportunities.

Besides, what does hard work actually look like? A professional athlete will prioritize results over effort. You never hear a postgame interview where a player says, "I'm not disappointed at all. We tried hard and that's all that matters. Winning isn't everything." A researcher, on the other hand, will value exploration over outcome. You never hear a postexperiment interview with a scientist because our country doesn't care about that. But if you did, they might say, "It wasn't the outcome we were looking for, but we ruled out some important theories so today was a huge win!" A soldier would scoff at my idea of hard work, in the way I might reflexively roll my eyes when my child complains about having to walk the dog or put their dishes directly into the dishwasher instead of the sink. Hard work feels subjective.

I am someone who hates physical effort but loves mental exertion. Writing this book, I often sit in the same chair all day long, breaking only sparingly for the essentials (food and Facebook) to keep me going. But put me on a treadmill and at the first moment of discomfort, I'm done. My daughter, a state debate champion and never one to back down from hard work, once deadpanned about getting to the airport early. "I'll miss a flight before I run in an airport." I'm with her. I dread *that* kind of effort. My son needs lots of brain breaks when he's studying, but he's relentless at the gym. He'd run to catch a flight *and* carry his sister's bag on top of his. We all work hard, but if you evaluated us using the same criteria, we would all fail.

Parents want their kids to have a strong work ethic, but how do you ensure you're hitting the bull's-eye when you give your kid a hard work pep talk, especially when hard work is so subjective and personal?

Before you begin, ask yourself the following questions, intended to help you get clarity on your unique appreciation of what constitutes hard work. You can do this now in your head, but I think these questions make for rich conversations with a partner or friend, too.

- To what degree do you prioritize mental or physical hard work over the other?

- How do you know when it's time to quit working hard? When is hard work like a hamster wheel—keeping you busy but going nowhere?

- In her memoir, Barbara Bush wrote, "At the end of your life you will never regret not having passed one more test, not winning one more verdict, or not closing one more deal. You will regret time not spent with a husband, a friend, a child, or a parent." How do you balance hard work with your own thoughts on the larger meaning of life?

- How do you react when an outcome doesn't match your input? For example, if you worked hard, but didn't get the job, promotion, or recognition you wanted, how would you process the value of that hard work?

Contemplating your answers will help you frame how you approach this conversation with your tween, and doing this activity with someone else may give you a broader perspective into different types of hard work, since each of us tends to think our brand of hard work is the hardest.

Once you have your philosophy on hard work firmed up, check that you're leading by example. Kids are quick to point out when an adult has a "do as I say, not as I do" attitude, and they learn best when you demonstrate more than lecture. Since hard work is sometimes hidden, let them know what you're experiencing. "I wanted to give up on this because it was so hard, but I did x, y, or z to get through it." This is how your tween will start training their own inner voice as class work gets more complicated, teams get tougher to make, competition gets more serious, and you expect them to contribute more to the family. Now is the time to develop the habits needed to push through hard work, so that by the time your child is building their resume for college or work or whatever comes after high school, they have a work ethic philosophy of their own to lean on.

What Motivates You?

You know, this airport thing has me thinking: What are the optics of hard work? How is it perceived? If a tree falls in the forest and no one is there to hear it, does it still make a sound? I don't know. If a kid works hard and no one is there to praise them, does it still count? I'm not sure. I ponder this because a parent of an ADHD child recently told me about the extraordinary effort their child puts in each day, to do things like focus and listen, before that child can even begin the kind of hard work that elicits praise from others. This must be incredibly challenging and the parent, to their credit, makes it a point to *see* that effort and mark it with a comment or a pat on the back.

Some kids have to work harder than others to do what we consider normal, and we ought to acknowledge this. And all kids, from around age ten to about age fourteen, are working hard on the Middle School Construction Project I first mentioned in chapter 8. They're starting to build those three things they need to become adults: an adult body, an adult brain, and an adult identity. It's not the kind of hard work that parents get excited about, but it still is seriously hard work. I'm *extra* empathetic to the effort this takes, and maybe a little preachy about extending kids this age more mercy, patience, and recognition for the kind of hard work they're doing that we can't see.

Kids are conditioned to work hard for grades and praise, so your tween may believe that hard work without an admiring audience and a rewarding outcome is simply not worthwhile. For this reason, you should talk with your child about the motivation behind work. There are generally four classifications for motivation: internal, external, positive, and negative. By way of example, let's look at how these four types of motivation comingle in relation to academic effort.

1. Internal positive: This child works hard out of a desire to learn something new and to feel a sense of pride.

2. Internal negative: This child studies diligently to avoid not knowing the answers and being embarrassed in front of their peers.

3. External positive: This child is motivated by the end result of a good grade or a pleasing comment from the teacher.

4. External negative: This child fears being punished by parents for poor performance and possibly losing privileges.

You and your child both will benefit from exploring the root of their motivation, even if it isn't entirely clear to them yet. By talking about the different reasons for working hard, your tween can develop, at least intellectually, an appreciation for internal, positive motivation. Don't assume this means they will be able to suddenly transfer all their motivational energy into this category, but eventually it may become a self-fulfilling prophecy, as the more they are cognitively aware of recognizing internal, positive motivating factors, the more they are likely to unconsciously tune into it as they face new challenges. And you'll be able to support that by taking pride in their internal, positive inspirations for attempting a tough task.

At some point, your middle schooler is sure to argue against a tough task with this timeless refrain: "Why do I have to learn how to do this? I'm never going to use it." Let's look at how a conversation around the hard work of learning something "pointless" might sound.

BEGIN peacefully

Kid: *Algebra is such a waste of time. Who do you know who actually uses algebra as an adult?*
Parent: *Easy. Algebra teachers.*
Kid: *Ha ha. But you're proving my point. It's useless, so why do I have to waste my time learning it?*

RELATE to your kid

Parent: *Aah, the old Algebra Defense. I used to say the same thing when I was learning it.*
Kid: *Okay, so you agree with me. Then it shouldn't matter if I fail this class.*
Parent: *I absolutely agree with you that it's hard, and that I didn't understand the benefit of learning it when I was your age. But . . . give me a chance to change your way of thinking about it.*
Kid: *You can try! But unless you can show me how algebra will help me as an adult, I'm not changing my mind.*

INTERVIEW to collect data

Parent: *I love a good challenge! Okay, so let me gather some info before I lay out my argument. First, what do you think is the point of learning algebra?*
Kid: *I honestly don't know. That's my point. There is no point to it.*
Parent: *And, is algebra the hardest thing you've ever had to learn?*
Kid: *Yes.*
Parent: *Do you remember learning how to walk?*
Kid: *No, but I guarantee it was easier because everyone can do it.*
Parent: *Okay. Last question: what is the hardest part about learning algebra?*

Kid: *It makes no sense. I study and I pay attention, but I still don't get it. The teacher doesn't explain it either. Whenever I ask her a question, she says, "I already told you how to do this."*

ECHO what you hear

Parent: *This is helpful. So it's hard because the teacher expects you to learn it faster than you are, and because it's hard to keep trying when you aren't "getting" it. Am I understanding this correctly?*
Kid: *Yes. But you still haven't proven why I need to learn it.*
Parent: *True. Stay with me.*

FEEDBACK

Parent: *In some ways you are absolutely correct. Most people learn algebra in school without, in fact, using it in their daily adult lives (or as my math-ier friends would say, without realizing they're using it). I was just joking when I said only algebra teachers use it. Lots of adults use it: carpenters, welders, nutritionists, architects, electricians, and scientists. But let's say you don't want to be any of those things. It's still useful to learn how to learn it.*

Most kids assume the benefit of working hard to learn algebra is knowing algebra, but that's not the whole case. It's cool to learn how to solve problems when all the pieces of the problem aren't obvious at first. (If you ever become a spy this will be useful.) It's good to explore new things, 'cause you never know what you might like. (You might like spy work once you get hooked on solving these mysteries.) But seriously and most of all, it's good to exercise your brain.

Your brain is going through some intense growth right now and will continue through college. It's like a muscle. Learning makes it stronger in many ways and prepares you to be able to learn different new things. I asked you about learning to walk for a reason. When you were little, your leg muscles were like jelly. Walking was crazy-hard work for you! But you made those muscles stronger and now you can not only walk, but surf and bike and ski—all the stuff you enjoy more than "boring walking." My point is, don't give up on learning something new because it's hard and seems pointless. The point is you're doing yourself a huge favor by exercising your brain. And if the teacher isn't doing you any favors, I can help. Not with algebra, because I don't remember any of it, ha ha, but because working so hard to learn it thirty years ago made me a better problem solver. And that is how I know how to come up with all kinds of ways to get you the help and support you need. Whether that's a tutor or watching videos online, we can come up with ideas to help.

Okay, I've made my case. You don't have to be convinced, but just think about it. Fair?

With any luck, your kid will reflect on this and come to see the hard work of learning new things valuable, regardless of their difficulty or relevance at the time. You should anticipate one more late entry to this conversation, though, and it goes like this:

Kid: *Okay, so I've been thinking. If you're saying the point of learning algebra is to make my brain able to learn other things, it shouldn't matter what grade I get. Right? If I fail algebra, it shouldn't count against me if I'm only learning it as an exercise.*

Parent: *I like that you're thinking this through. You're thinking about the bigger questions of "Do grades really matter?" and "What's the point of getting good grades?" Grades matter in that they are a way for you to gauge whether you're learning the material or not. You might think you understand the math, or that you wrote a convincing history essay, but the grade tells you if your perceptions were accurate . . . or not. That's important when you're learning something new. I don't expect you to be good at everything, and I certainly don't expect perfection from you. I just hope you will want to try hard, even at stuff that's a challenge, so you can continue to get stronger. Grades can tell you when it's time to work harder—or sometimes, work differently.*

The Dark Side to Hard Work

At this point, I assume we all agree that, like with algebra, hard work for its own sake has value. By high school, though, some teens experience burnout on hard work, either by specializing in a sport or hobby with too much intensity, or by hyperfocusing on schoolwork, to the detriment of a balanced life.

Burnout comes from prolonged stress that causes a person to shut down both physically and mentally; it should not be taken lightly. It can weaken a person's immune system, making them vulnerable to serious and prolonged illness, persuade a person to seek comfort in drugs or alcohol, and spawn emotional isolation and cynicism.

Burnout has become so common that the medical field is paying attention. In the spring of 2019, the World Health Organization (WHO) added "burnout" to its International Classification of Diseases Handbook. The WHO attributes burnout to workplace stress, but parents of highly stressed adolescents know burnout isn't just for working adults.

It's tempting to glorify the fortitude of youth. Though we remember with awe our own strength and stamina from our teen years (I could stay up all night! I could lift so much more weight! I was unstoppable!), it is a mistake to think of adolescents as being superhumanly resilient. Yes, teen tiger blood is astonishing at times, but we can't take for granted that kids will always bounce back with some extra sleep on the weekends, more electrolytes, or a rousing pep talk. If your child, who normally excels at school, sports, or chess tournaments, tells you they need a break from that very thing, believe them. And if they don't tell you, ask from time to time. No one's health should play second fiddle to their talent.

Some kids bypass burnout, and that can be even more dangerous. They won't give themselves a break, churning out anxiety-fueled hard work that doesn't provide a real sense of accomplishment. This kind of perfection chasing sets tweens and teens up for long-term struggles.

Sometimes a parent will confide in me that they worry about their child who is never happy or satisfied with their accomplishments. This concern can spur parents to try endless "remedies," pursuing anything that might make their child feel better about themselves. "Maybe you should try ballet? You'd be great at that! Maybe you should try out for the play again, and this time you might get the lead! Maybe *this next thing* will finally make you feel better about yourself?"

The latest research on self-esteem indicates that this approach is not only unproductive, it's also contrary to how your child's brain works.

Doctors working with teens who have eating disorders, where perfectionism is a constant struggle, have long looked for ways to help patients stop chasing the ideal of flawlessness. Even when loved ones and casual observers can clearly see a teen is losing too much weight or has body dysmorphia, the teen still pursues "perfect eating." Researchers have discovered a major difference in brain function among people who pursue perfectionism and those who don't, and it has nothing to do with a person's drive, and everything to do with brain differences.

Some people naturally enjoy celebrating the results of their hard work. They make the team at school or get the promotion at work, and commemorate the occasion in some small but happy way. Whether treating themselves to something cheerful, or posting a happy announcement on social media, they want to mark their happiness with a reward. Other people, achieving the same, never feel that sense of pride and accomplishment. With each subsequent achievement, they'll downplay it as "not a big deal." Parents of children like this worry this behavior is rooted in low self-esteem, but it isn't. More accurately, people who gloss over their hard work and related accomplishments simply have inactive reward centers in their brain.

Recently, more attention has been paid to the danger of perfectionism, particularly among girls, though this is not a gender-blind phenomenon. It's disheartening when achievement isn't fulfilling. If you notice this trend in your child—a constant drive to do more or be more, but never the satisfaction of feeling more accomplished—you might look into Cognitive Behavioral Therapy (CBT), which research shows is effective in retraining reward centers. That's right: it is possible to retrain a person's reward center, even though they aren't naturally inclined to celebrate their achievements. For example, if your child makes the honor roll at school, before you let them blow off the accomplishment, stop for a moment and celebrate the achievement with them, *even* if they don't want to. You might say, "I know this doesn't feel like a big deal to you, but it is, and we want to recognize and enjoy this with you. Why don't you choose how we celebrate tonight?"

An alternate phrasing that might be helpful is "In this situation, I don't think you're experiencing yourself the way others are experiencing you. We are impressed and we'd like to commemorate this with [a round of applause, ice cream, a pat on the back, or however your family shows pride in one another's success]." By systematically stopping after an achievement, pointing it out, and having a small celebration, you can begin to recalibrate your child's brain to enjoy the reward of their hard work.

> By systematically stopping after an achievement, pointing it out, and having a small celebration, you can begin to recalibrate your child's brain to enjoy the reward of their hard work.

The Agony of Defeat

We all know someone for whom success seems to come easily, almost unnaturally. You know, the person who smiles and jogs around high-fiving everyone after the exercise class that made you almost puke your guts out. Or the colleague who keeps getting promoted at work despite "just kind of falling backward into the job, I guess!" Or the classmate from college who dropped out—despite your common-sense warning—to start a little passion project that is now on the verge of going global. And guess what? You're that person in someone else's eyes. While each of us is preoccupied with figuring out ways to compensate for our shortcomings, the rest of the world is admiring our virtues and good luck.

It's tempting to compare your success to others' and expect the same result for the same, or more, effort, but it's not realistic. For you, this can be frustrating. For your tween, it will be a massive injustice levied upon them. Talk with them about the normalcy of this experience. Point out that success and happiness are not limited resources. There is more than enough to go around, and neither bitterness nor resentment will help expand yours.

Incidentally, the four types of motivation I mentioned earlier can also help you explain why other people seem to reap disproportionate rewards in life. Perhaps the star athlete is motivated by the heavy hand of a parent trying to relive glory days, or the classmate who seems to always get the best grades is motivated by a crippling fear of failure that gives her a stomachache most days. It's easy to do an armchair assessment of results, but effort and motivation are not so transparent.

Finally, as with most things with life, timing matters. When my kids were in elementary and middle school, they participated on summer swim team. Some years they were excellent. Other years they were bad. To help them cope with this inconsistency, I would preface each summer by saying this is a winning season or this is a growing season. If they were at the bottom of an age group, it was a growing season. If they were at the top, it was likely a winning season. It helped to frame their expectations this way, so they didn't expect their efforts, which felt consistent to them each summer, to always manifest the same results. Understanding this pattern seemed to give them reason to continue working hard during the growing summers, even when they didn't have the ribbons to show for it. Many parents explain this by saying, "The seed you plant today is not the fruit you eat today."

Conversation Crashers

Normally, in this section of the chapter I offer a handful or more of phrases and approaches that might backfire on you with regard to the topic at hand. For hard work, I've got just one.

"If you work hard enough, you can do anything." Beware overselling hard work as a cure-all. You don't want your kids to perceive you as a snake oil salesman, hawking a magic cure for whatever ails them. It's worth mentioning that hard work is not the great equalizer we'd like it to be. Race, gender, geography, health, and wealth are just some of the many factors that influence a person's access to opportunities and success. Even with hard work, systemic injustices make it inherently harder for some than others. The saying "Some people are born on third base thinking they hit a triple" is a relatable way to talk with kids about how the luck and fortune of the circumstances you inherit at birth impact you throughout life.

We have invented a kind of folklore around the morality of hard work, reasoning anything is possible if a person has a bootstrapping work ethic. Like most people, I get teary eyed at those viral feel-good stories of a homeless teen getting a college scholarship, or an athlete fighting back to earn a spot on a team after having been cut, or a person investing their last dime in an idea that changes the world for the better and makes them rich at the same time. It makes for a compelling narrative when someone overcomes all odds with honest-to-goodness hard work, but these tales are exciting to us *because* they are extraordinary.

In everyday life, there will be many opportunities to talk about why hard work may not be the whole answer to life's problems. Take, for example, a homeless person asking for money. Your child might quietly assume that person doesn't want to work hard for money, that begging is easier. Tweens need to hear from you that hard work is an important part of taking care of yourself, but it doesn't guarantee success. Mental illness, family background, health, education, learning differences, and support systems all play a role in a person's ability to use hard work as a tool. Keep this in mind as you talk with your tween, and remind them hard work is not a stand-alone cure for everything.

Simple Ways to Build Appreciation for Hard Work

- **Do hard work side by side.** If your tween is overwhelmed with homework, sit next to them and work on a project of your own. Company makes hard work more tolerable.

- **Celebrate small wins.** Chunk hard work into smaller, more manageable pieces and revel in reaching milestones. A mom in my online parenting group wrote that when she was teaching her son to roller-skate, he got upset with himself for not picking it up as quickly as he expected. She told him to stop counting the number of times he fell, and to start counting the number of times he got up. Reframing this put him in a better place to celebrate his small wins and keep trying.

- **Recognize effort.** Talk specifically about what you notice when your child works hard and praise their attitude. They may not try as hard as you'd like . . . yet, but with encouragement, they're more likely to stay the course.

- **Find reasons to take a break.** In the immortal words of Ferris Bueller: "Life moves pretty fast. If you don't stop and look around once in a while, you could miss it." If the point of working hard is to enjoy a good life, be sure *you're* teaching your kids to actually do that. Don't delay joy. Rip up the to-do list, and take pleasure in doing no hard work at all with the people you love from time to time.

- **Play High-Low at dinner time.** Or anytime you're together near the end of your day. This game goes by many names, including High-Low, Happy-Crappy, and Roses and Thorns. The idea is to say one good thing that happened to you, and one bad thing that happened to you that day. Sharing like this is a nice way to realize everyone has ups and downs.

- **Consult the baby book.** When your child is down on themselves or their achievements, remind them they don't have to do anything to be special in your eyes. Tweens like being reminded from time to time that their worth isn't dependent on their success.

In a Hurry? Here's Your Crash Course

- Adults romanticize hard work (especially their own). It's fun to reminisce and take pride in your efforts, but comparison (and complaining) don't motivate tweens to work harder. On the other hand, kids take pride in their hard work when others do, too.

- Hard work is subjective and personal. Keep this in mind. For example, what comes easily to one child might be a huge effort for their sibling. Recognize these differences.

- You can help your tween build their own work-ethic philosophy by asking them the same questions you pondered in this chapter regarding hard work, including:

  1. To what degree do you prioritize mental or physical hard work over the other?

  2. How do you know when your efforts are effective or just keeping you busy without results?

  3. How do you balance hard work with enjoying relationships?

  4. If you work hard and don't get the results you hoped for, is there still value in the experience?

- Explain to your tween the four types of motivation (internal positive, internal negative, external positive, and external negative) so they can come to a better understanding of what motivates them now, and how they'd like to be inspired in the future.

- Beware burnout. If your child tells you they need a break from a beloved sport or activity, believe them. Too many adults gave up on sports or hobbies they once loved, and were talented in, because they were overexposed at a young age. We can't expect kids to trade the satisfaction of being happy, active, fulfilled adults for a narrow chance at early success.

- If your child is never satisfied with their own hard work and accomplishments, they may have an underachieving reward center in their brain. It may be possible to retrain this through therapy.

- Talk with your kids about how you cope when your hard work doesn't translate into the desired result.

13

Talking About Money

In this chapter, you'll learn the importance of having conversations about money that will help your tween separate emotions from finances before they become deeply entrenched, beginning with an understanding of why teens crave certain brands and how you can manage their expectations about having the right brands and still balance your family budget. You'll also learn tips for increasing gratitude and self-control, and how to talk about financial differences among families with respect and dignity.

When kids are little, if we teach them money lessons at all, they tend to be about savings. It's an easy starter lesson parents can make tangible with piggy banks or Pinterest-y mason jars labeled Save, Spend, Donate. It's good to talk about saving money, but you probably needn't worry about hammering that point. Most teens already understand. According to a National Consumers League 2002 survey, "Saving money is important to American teens; about nine out of ten save money, though 36 percent admit that they're saving for specific items they want to purchase. Almost one quarter (22 percent) are saving for college and 27 percent save for no particular reason. Four out of ten say they save half or more of their money, and three out of four have a savings account."

Teaching financial responsibility would be easy if all you had to explain were saving and spending. But most people don't find themselves in debt because they don't understand the simple math of "more in, less out." Math is the easy part. Consider how easy losing weight would be if the formula really were as basic as fewer calories consumed than burned. People struggle because that's an incomplete equation. Add in cravings, impulses, and emotions, and it's not the math that derails us. Similarly, when helping your tween develop strong financial health, focus on them understanding the emotional side of the equation. It's not hard to solve for x when x is a number, but when the factors are guilt, self-worth, or survival, the formula gets way more complicated.

Speaking of survival, a recent five-year study conducted by the Federal Reserve found that 39 percent of families, when faced with an unexpected expense of four hundred dollars, would not be able to pay it with cash, savings, or a credit card paid off on the next statement. While many of you are teaching your kids how to manage their pocket money and whether it makes sense to buy that jersey or those earrings, a large number of parents fear what will happen if they get a flat tire or if that toothache doesn't go away. Adolescents should understand the breadth of the financial landscape in their communities and beyond, and know that for well over one-third of families in the United States, the anxiety of barely making ends meet outweighs all other emotions.

It's unrealistic to expect anyone to completely unbraid their feelings from money matters, or to stretch a dollar further than many hardworking families are already forced to do, but there are ways to position your kid to think about money in a more functional, less stressful way. This begins with having open, honest conversations about how money makes you feel and recognizing how it makes them feel, too.

Brand Loyalty

Imagine yourself back in the seventh grade. Do you remember what you were wearing? The haircut you were trying to pull off? I bet most things about your appearance felt close to wrong. You believed you were too skinny, or too heavy, so you hid yourself in oversized sweatshirts, even on hot days. Your hair wouldn't hold a curl no matter how much product you coaxed through it. Or your hair was naturally curly and would only lie flat for an hour before it boinged back to life. Acne was fighting for more and more real estate on your body. You felt too tall, so you slouched to draw less attention to yourself, or too short, so you walked on tiptoe to see over the kids crowding the halls. Your voice cracked or still sounded like a child's. Your confidence plummeted.

How could you, with your uncooperative body, brain, and emotions, still telegraph to the kids at school that, despite all your lopsidedness, you were worth a vote of social confidence, a seat saved on the bus, a friendly calling of your name as you walked down the hall?

The answer is, and has always been, packaging.

At my school, Guess jeans (for the girls) and Adidas track suits (for the guys) told others that, despite being gangly, chubby, greasy, or goofy, you could still be trusted because you knew what was up. You controlled what you could and about all you could control was the "uniform," the great normalizer. Maybe at your school it was Tommy Hilfiger, Nike, Billabong, or L.L.Bean. During adolescence, certain brand names become the trusted workhorse, carrying the heavy load of fitting in on the backs of its pricey little labels.

As a parent, you may worry about a sudden and uncharacteristic rise in materialism during early adolescence, but "needing" a certain brand of clothing has everything to do with tweens signaling that they belong, not that they're greedy. Your tween is beginning to feel the weight of loneliness, insecurity, and doubt that comes from separating from you and finding a tribe among their peers. On the one hand, you'll do well to empathize with their urgent pleas for the same sneakers, sports equipment, or gaming systems as their friends, but on the other hand, be careful not to indulge their every whim, even if you have the means. You may remember Hebb's rule from your intro to psych class: "Neurons that fire together wire together." In this case, if your child has repeated, early success impressing people with their cool purchases, their brain might fuse the need for acceptance with spending money. I often tell parents, if you're able to spend a little money on a brand your kid craves, put that money toward shoes, a backpack, or a hoodie. These items are worn most days, so you get more bang for your buck.

Be Translucent, Not Transparent

In *Keeping Up with The Joneses: Middle School Edition*, your kid will maintain detailed comparisons of how your family stacks up to others. "Why can't our family go to Hawaii? Everyone goes on a cool spring break trip but us." "Why can't we get labradoodles?" "Why don't we move to a neighborhood with more kids my age and a pool?"

How do you explain family finances without laying all your cards on the table, knowing full well what you share with your tween may travel faster outside the family than a rumor in, well, middle school? This is where translucency helps. A shroud of secrecy around money does a disservice to kids. It's the reason so many of us (*ahem*) took out high-interest credit cards once we got to college. Your child may focus on other families' cool vacations or game rooms, but they have no idea who has credit card debt, who is or isn't saving for college, who has huge medical bills, or who inherited a starter house. Start explaining these concepts to them. When it comes to your own finances, you probably won't want to share specific salary or debt figures, but you could talk openly about the cost of groceries, average salary ranges for various professions, and rent or mortgage costs for different areas in your town, city, or state.

Kids can't understand value if they have no idea how much a pool, or game room, or labradoodle costs, and even then it helps to have the scope of that cost within a larger budget. You can start talking about the value of your purchases to help them understand how you make your own decisions. For example, if your kid begs you for a new game, saying, "But it's only twenty dollars! I know you have twenty dollars and it's on sale!" you can talk about what you perceive to be a good value within the context of your budget. "Yes, I have twenty dollars right now, and this is on sale. This one normally costs thirty dollars, but that isn't a good reason for me to spend twenty dollars. A good reason would be if we needed a new game, *and* I was planning on spending thirty dollars to buy one. Then this would be a great value. But since we don't, if I spent twenty dollars on this, I'd be using money I need for your field trip and that becomes a problem for our budget. You should put this game on a list of things to save for."

Fostering Healthy Feelings About Money

In addition to talking openly about emotions and finances, here are some approaches you can take at home to increase understanding of money matters:

Strengthen your gratitude muscles. A desire for more things and experiences can stem from feeling like you don't have enough (or aren't enough). Shine a light on the practice of gratitude in your home to help squelch those cravings. Research shows that grateful parents make grateful kids, so being expressive about your own gratitude is a great place to start. There are lots of clever ways to build appreciation for all you have. My favorite is keeping a family gratitude jar in the kitchen next to slips of paper and pens. Whenever someone feels thankful, they write down why and put it in the jar. Record gratitude for something as big as a nice trip or as small as a good quiz grade, yummy meal, or fun talk. A lovely New Year's Eve tradition can be reading and reflecting on a year's worth of nice moments, all together.

Gratitude is also tied to the feeling of being socially secure and supported. Kids ages ten to sixteen feel more gratitude when they feel more support from their parents, teachers, and peers. Keep in mind, it's hard to feel grateful when you feel constantly challenged or displaced. Make sure to ask your child to let you know how you can best support them these days.

Establish purchasing wait periods. Spending money isn't a bad thing, but spending out of impulsivity and insecurity can end up making you feel bad. Sit down with your tween and talk about reasonable lengths of time to wait before spending different amounts of money. Draw two columns on a sheet of paper. Label one column "Amount" and the other "Wait Time." If the amount is five dollars, the corresponding wait time might only be five minutes. If it's one hundred dollars, maybe the wait time is more like a week. You can offer your opinion, but let your tween decide what feels right. When your tween wants to make a purchase, refer them to this guideline before spending.

Explain how marketing works. Tweens need to know that some advertisers *want* them to feel badly about themselves. After all, if a person feels totally confident, they have no need for more stylish clothes, rebellion-scented body spray, or ultravolumizing shampoo. When an advertiser can make you feel bad enough about some part of yourself that you'll buy their product to fix it, they make more money. Explain also about the persistence of digital marketing messages with ads that pop up after you click on something once. When you start seeing those shoes you liked *over and over*, it begins to feel like you can't shake the need, but that's just some company's algorithms preying on you, not your own desire talking. The average person sees five thousand advertisements a day, giving you plenty of opportunity to talk about the emotional onslaught of sales messaging.

Track spending for a month. According to Piper Jaffray's annual Taking Stock with Teens survey of eight thousand teens, food is the biggest category for teen spending. I'm not surprised, since, for a relatively small amount of money, kids can buy not just a meal, but a complete social experience. Going to the mall food court or Starbucks is the tween equivalent of going to a bar in your twenties. Part of the fun is being seen, not knowing who you might bump into, and possibly meeting someone new. There are few other places for teens where they can gather to socialize like young adults without parents hovering. It's so fun and easy, adolescents (like lots of adults) might end up baffled where all their money has gone, not realizing how quickly a few five-dollar Frappuccinos and eight-dollar value meals add up. If your tween tracks the money they spend on food and realizes they can't sustain that kind of output, they don't have to stay in and miss all the fun. As a parent, recognize the value and draw of socializing like this, but if your child is bleeding money, suggest making a sandwich at home beforehand and then ordering a drink or fries instead of a whole meal with friends.

Balancing Excitement with Restraint

Once a tween feels the freedom of having their own money, they can feel jumpy to spend at every opportunity. This is how a BRIEF conversation about money, emotions, and financial independence might sound:

BEGIN peacefully

Parent: *So, I was thinking, between babysitting and the birthday money you got from Gran, you have a lot of cash these days!*

Kid: *I know! I'm rich.*

Parent: *Yes, relatively speaking, you are at the moment! That's pretty fun.*

Kid: *Want to hear what I'm gonna get?*

Parent: *I'd love to.*

RELATE to your kid

Kid: *Okay, I have a list. A new phone case. I'm gonna preorder a game that comes out at Thanksgiving. I told Evan I'd buy him lunch at the mall Saturday, 'cause he doesn't have any money. And I might get a new baseball hat when I'm there. I don't know. I'll decide when I see what they have!*

Parent: *That's a long list. You seem very excited and I'm happy you're getting your first big taste of financial freedom this year.*

Kid: *If you need anything, I can give you a loan.*

Parent: *You're very generous, that's for sure.*

INTERVIEW to collect data

Parent: *Sounds like you're planning on spending a lot of money at once. Have you given any thought to how you'll feel after you spend it?*

Kid: *Um . . . happy I have the stuff?*

Parent: *Yeah, maybe. Some people do. Some people like the feeling of getting new stuff, but then they feel guilty after their money is gone. They regret spending so much and miss the feeling of having freedom to choose. Do you think you like the feeling of choosing more, or having the stuff more? Because once you spend the money, the choices go away.*

Kid: *I don't really know. I want to preorder that download though! I really want that game.*

Parent: *I get that. It's your money, so it's your choice. You can get it all, if you can afford it. Or you can get it little by little to prolong the fun. You can even return something if it's unopened and you change your mind. But you have to ask the store rules on that first. Are you comfortable doing that?*

Kid: *What would I say?*

Parent: *You can just say, "If I need to return this, what's the policy?"*

Kid: *Okay.*

ECHO what you hear

Parent: *I'm glad you have income now through babysitting, and you're bound to keep making more money as you do it more often. It sounds like it will take some trial and error to figure out what level of spending and saving you're comfortable with since this is new to you. Do you think that's right?*

Kid: *Oh, yeah—saving! I forgot. How much should I put aside? Half?*

Parent: *I like the way you're thinking. I guess the answer depends on what's comfortable and uncomfortable to you, and that might take time to figure out. For now, it might make sense to start slowly with spending and save more. You can always increase spending and decrease saving, but it's hard to go the other way. Once the money is gone, it's gone.*

Kid: *But I made this list and now I really want all of it.*

Parent: *I completely understand. It's your choice, but can I give you a tip?*

Kid: *Yeah.*

FEEDBACK

Parent: *The excitement you feel now is fun. Can you think of a time in the past when you felt this excited about getting something new? I can! Remember how much you wanted an American Girl doll? They're expensive, so we waited and waited to get one, and you were thrilled when it happened! I know you love Samantha, and you're glad you got her, but you probably didn't feel the same intense excitement three months after you got her. Wanting something is its own form of entertainment, and it* *creates a sense of urgency, but you are in control of your money. Don't let your excitement make you think you have to act quickly. Take your time. Take a deep breath and wait awhile before you decide to spend the money you worked hard for. If you want, I can help you come up with a chart for how long to wait before making a spending decision. This can help you stay in control of your own spending habits. It's important for someone your age to learn more ways to manage their own resources.*

Young adolescents crave being in control of their own choices. Money gives them this chance. Frame learning new skills as opportunities for them to develop independence and they'll usually agree to hearing your tips, since they align with their goal of being more autonomous.

Notice the language in this conversation is heavy on the child's power. Young adolescents crave being in control of their own choices. Money gives them this chance. Frame learning new skills as opportunities for them to develop independence and they'll usually agree to hearing your tips, since they align with their goal of being more autonomous.

Don't Judge Other People's Choices

If you have tweens, you are certainly familiar with the absurdity of adolescent arrogance. A tween athlete watching a high school football game might say, "I could easily have scored three times by now." A voracious reader might say, "What's so hard about writing a novel? It's easy." Kids this age not only have an inflated sense of their own capabilities, they can't imagine why anyone else wouldn't be able to easily achieve what they can so expertly (fictionally) achieve (imagine).

This leads me to judgment. As you teach your child the basics of financial responsibility, they will learn just enough to be dangerous. At least, dangerously judgmental. Kids this age risk oversimplifying how money works. As I've said, finances are more than just math, and kids might assume that what one family can afford, another ought to as well, without taking into account things like college debt, medical bills, family members in need, or generational wealth. Step two of financial literacy should include the premise that other people's finances are personal and distinct, and it's not your place to police anyone else's activities.

I hear this kind of thinking come up when young adolescents ask questions like:

- Why do some kids always eat fast food if they can't afford to go on field trips?

- Why do they have such a nice car but live in a small apartment?

- How come that family can afford such a big house, but they don't send their kids to private school?

- Why don't both parents work if they need more money?

This is how a BRIEF conversation about being a money cop might sound:

BEGIN peacefully

Kid: *Did you know that a lot of the kids who get free and reduced lunch have crazy-expensive sneakers?*
Parent: *No, I hadn't paid attention to that.*
Kid: *Like three-hundred-dollar sneakers. If it were me, I'd just use that money to pack healthier lunches.*
Parent: *I think this is one of those situations that seems obvious, but is a little more complicated once you dig into it.*

RELATE to your kid

Kid: *What do you mean? It's just basic, like we talk about all the time. Don't buy things you can't afford.*

Parent: *Well, I appreciate you thinking about what we've talked about when it comes to money. In general, yes, that's a rule I believe in, but I don't think I've fully explained this outside the context of our family. Can I take a shot at that?*

INTERVIEW to collect data

Kid: *Okay.*
Parent: *So, obviously, every family has a different income, different spending needs, and makes different choices . . . yeah?*
Kid: *Yeah.*
Parent: *What if a celebrity came to your house and wondered why you didn't live in a mansion like them? You'd say you can't afford it. What if she said she knew how you could live in a mansion like her. Just stop taking vacations, stop eating at restaurants, don't buy new clothes, then sell your house and move into a tinier one so you could save more each year. In twenty years, you could buy a house that is three times more expensive than the one you live in now! Would you do it?*
Kid: *Probably not.*

ECHO what you hear

Parent: *Me either! How would you explain it to her?*
Kid: *It's just not worth it to only save up and never do anything fun.*
Parent: *I agree with you. It doesn't seem like being that restrictive is worth it—just to keep up with someone else's choices.*

FEEDBACK

Parent: *So, in the same way, just because someone might have less money than you, that doesn't mean they shouldn't enjoy things in life. We all allow ourselves some amount of that. And just as important, it's not our job to judge how other people spend their money or make their personal choices. I want you to be smart about your personal choices, but not get caught up worrying about other people's choices. Cool?*
Kid: *Yes.*

Remember that family finances are often a product of generational wealth. It's much harder to accrue wealth if your family hasn't already given you some opportunities to get ahead. I once heard this concept explained in a way that makes it easy for kids to understand. Imagine your friends have been playing Monopoly for a couple hours. You show up and want to play, too. They say, "Jump on in! Here, you can be the top hat. No one wanted that one. Here's your starting cash. You can roll next."

Great, you're in the game. But you notice some of the players have already put up hotels and almost all the properties have been purchased. "This isn't really fair," you say.

"No, it's fair," they say. "We all started with the same amount of money. It was totally equal. And we let you in. We can't help it that you started playing later than us."

This is a good opportunity to point out that what looks "even" or "fair" may not actually be so and that systemic injustices make leveling the playing field that much harder than it first appears.

Conversation Crashers

"You shouldn't care so much about expensive things." It never works to tell people what they shouldn't care about. In fact, it usually backfires in the same way as when you're really worked up about something and someone tells you to "calm down." Instead of dismissing the emotions your kid feels about strongly wanting more "stuff," engage them in conversation about their cravings: what do they really mean, how long do they last, how often, and so on. By doing this, you might help them conclude on their own what you were hoping for all along.

"That's a waste of money." The truth is, whatever it is, it probably *is* a waste of money. But—whatever your tween wants to spend money on feels important to them. This phase of financial freedom is new and exciting, and they will tune you out if you can't at least acknowledge this. Ask some questions to help your kid gauge whether they will be happy with the purchase in a few days or weeks, then follow up later to see if they predicted correctly. Over time, this is how they'll learn to think through emotional spending.

"You can get x when you get a job of your own." It's true. They can. There is nothing incorrect about saying this to your kid, but if you're trying to educate a tween about smart spending, statements like this won't get it done. Instead, acknowledge their desire, thank them for talking with you about the stuff they like, and then ask them how they plan to make it happen.

"That's private. Don't ask." It's wise to keep some details about your family finances private, but if a kid is asking you questions about money, use the opportunity to educate them. When we were little and our parents would say this kind of thing, they left us no choice but to sit back and wait for our own initiation into the world of paychecks, bills, and bank accounts. These days, answers—at least in a general sense—are a quick online search away. Tweens enjoy learning how the world works. Show them sites like Monster or CareerBuilder for salary information, Zillow for home pricing, Shipt or Instacart for grocery prices, and Travelocity for vacation costs. Learning to research expenses and income is a great skill and a fun way to spend time sleuthing online.

In a Hurry? Here's Your Crash Course

- Talk less about saving money (which teens already understand and practice) and more about the emotional aspects of spending money and accumulating debt.

- Tweens use name brands as a way to telegraph their acceptability to peers during a period of their lives when they fear social isolation and often experience heightened loneliness and self-consciousness.

- Be translucent, not transparent, about your family financial decisions. Keep personal financial information private, while still educating your kid about the general costs of mortgages, vacations, cars, health insurance, and other things they will need to understand as young adults.

- Set an example of being grateful for the things you already have, not sad about the things you don't.

- Retrain impulsiveness by asking your child their opinion on reasonable wait periods before spending, with suggested longer times for bigger amounts.

- Kids benefit from a high-level understanding of how marketing and advertising work.

- Tracking expenses, even as early as middle school, can show how multiple trips to the food court can add up.

- As your tween learns more about financial responsibility, make sure they understand the nuances of other people's situations and their right to make choices for themselves without judgment.

CHAPTER

14

Talking About Sexuality

In this chapter, you'll learn why it's important to identify what you believe are the ingredients for a healthy sex life before engaging in conversations with your adolescent about sex, sexuality, or dating. And, no, it's not too early to start talking about any and all of this. You'll understand why it's also important to address pornography (and how you can do that without too much discomfort), how to help your child start thinking about what it means to date someone, ways to talk about consent so it becomes second nature, how to bring up or respond to sexual identity and/or gender topics in a way that supports all kids, and finally, how to talk about sexualization and sexy dressing among younger adolescents.

Here we are. We've arrived at this chapter. Some of you are excited to do this. Many of you are praying for a miracle that I'll keep it brief, telling you "less is more," and "it's too soon to put this stuff on your kid's radar," and "you've probably already covered it all already—good job, yay, let's talk about independence and friendship again."

It turns out, 19 percent of parents aren't comfortable talking with their teens about sex, and 50 percent of kids aren't comfortable listening, according to a 2012 survey. Frankly, I'm not sure I buy that *only*

19 percent of you aren't comfortable talking about sex. Maybe that horrified 19 percent just come to all my talks!

Assuming that, for those of us who are adults and not asexual, we all agree that a healthy sex life is an important part of our human experience, we have a responsibility to educate young people about ways they can either intentionally prepare for good, meaningful sex as well as ways in which they may inadvertently self-sabotage. From my perspective, a healthy sex life includes: accurate information about anatomy and safety, mutual pleasure and consent, open communication with your partner, and the ability to reasonably handle unexpected emotional and physical outcomes. The tenets you believe are essential to a healthy and happy sex life will become the foundational messages you share with your tween about their developing sexuality. It's to your advantage to spend time thinking of your feelings about the end result you desire for your child as a healthy, sexually active adult, then work backward to figure out how to begin communicating those. If not, you'll find yourself dancing around messages without a clear target.

You'll find plenty of opportunities to share your values without talking about your child's impending sex life directly. For example, if you're watching TV when a male character brags how he never uses condoms, that's an opportunity to drop a comment about his ability to handle potential outcomes. If (when) a news story breaks about a person in a position of power taking advantage of someone sexually, that's when you can bring up both consent and reciprocation. By peppering these comments throughout your day-to-day interactions, you'll season the topic nicely over time, instead of dumping it all out at once and risking a "Too spicy!!" freak-out.

The more you talk about sex in an unflustered, unapologetic, and impersonal way, the more your child will be open to listening. As a matter of health and safety, not to mention happiness and fulfillment, I hope you'll be encouraged to share more information with your tween or teen, with consideration for what teens say works best. A recent study found parents' sex talks with teens fall into one of these six categories: "underdeveloped, safety, comprehensive, warning/threat, wait, and no talk." Teens reported parent talks could be improved if the parents were more specific (yes, more specific!), provided guidance, and took a collaborative approach (meaning listening, too). The teen subjects also noted that the *comprehensive* and *safety* categories were the most effective sex talks, and the study concluded that *safety* talks correlated with the lowest levels of teen risk taking.

On that note, let's just dive right into the hard stuff, shall we?

Pornography

You may be wondering, "Do I seriously need to talk with my sweet and innocent eleven-year-old about *porn*?" The average age a child first sees porn is debatable. Many people cite age eleven. I was one of them. But in researching this chapter, I found no strong data to support

The tenets you believe are essential to a healthy and happy sex life will become the foundational messages you share with your tween about their developing sexuality. It's to your advantage to spend time thinking of your feelings about the end result you desire for your child as a healthy, sexually active adult, then work backward to figure out how to begin communicating those. If not, you'll find yourself dancing around messages without a clear target.

this claim, just a generalized belief that this is when it happens. There is, however, research that shows the average age kids first start *looking* for porn is, you guessed it, fourteen. And if kids commonly start searching for porn at age fourteen, a large number of them probably stumble upon it accidentally much earlier. This means you'll want to get ahead of this topic, otherwise leaving your teenager's sexual health and development in the hands of a team of eager plumbers, pizza delivery guys, and naughty school girls. Bom chicka wah wah.

For the topic of pornography, I'm offering some short and critical points for you to cover, not a dialogue, because it is a rare and amazing child who would be willing to go back and forth on this topic. So, *phew*!

You're off the hook for a full dialogue, but you do need to make some simple statements. I recommend you do this side by side (in the car or on the couch during a commercial break) or in some other circumstance where you don't have to make eye contact and can easily jump from this topic back into a good distraction. You might even lead off with a guarantee to keep it short, like this: "Hey, I've wanted to bring something up and I wouldn't be doing my job as a parent if I didn't talk with you about pornography. I promise I can get through it quickly and then we can get back to what we're doing."

Whatever way you start, you'll want to get in and out without lingering. The main points to cover are that: 1) pornography isn't representative of real sex and 2) it can set you up for unhealthy behaviors and feelings. Again, this isn't a back-and-forth conversation, but here is a mini monologue you can tweak to sound like you.

"We live in a world where you are likely to see pornography. You may already have. You don't have to say. Sometimes it's by accident—it can pop up on your screen when you Google something, or sometimes you might click a link that looks fine, but it takes you to a weird website. My point is, you're bound to either run across it *or* hear people at school talking about it, so I want you to know something: Porn is not a representation of real sex any more than a Spider-Man movie is a representation of real crime fighting. This matters—that it isn't real—because if watching porn videos is how someone learns about sex, they could end up with an unhealthy and unhappy sex life by comparing real sex with these totally unrealistic portrayals, not to mention some porn can be violent and degrading. I want you to eventually have a healthy sex life with a respectful partner because it's an important part of being an adult. People need accurate information, and porn gives a lot of wrong information, which is why I will buy you books about sex you can read in private, or find answers to any questions you have on this subject."*

---

* Some of the great books out there for girls and guys include *For Goodness Sex* by Al Vernacchio, *Sexploitation* by Cindy Pierce, and *Queer* by Kathy Belge and Marke Bieschke. For girls only, try *Girls and Sex* by Peggy Orenstein. For guys only, try *Respect* by Inti Chavez Perez.

You'll need to assess your tween's squirminess around this subject before deciding whether to leave it at that. If you both have the bandwidth to carry on, there is another important point to make when it comes to looking at pornography: it can start off feeling good. As a parent, if you focus your message on pornography being wrong or gross or immoral, and your kid has actually seen porn and had a sexual reaction, that can send a mixed message or, in the worst-case, cause shame to grow alongside developing sexuality. Instead talk about the importance of having a healthy understanding of sex and sexuality. Acknowledge that sometimes things that start off feeling good (or at least intriguing) can become unhealthy. Think of it like this: Eating junk food can be a satisfying experience. But let's say you had *only* ever eaten junk food and then you met someone you liked, who asked if they could take you on a date. You show up at a nice little bistro, and on the menu are choices full of flavor and nutritional value, but they're all foreign to you. The easiest, most comforting thing is to stick with what's familiar. Given the choice between a bag of Cheetos and grilled chicken with green beans, the bag of Cheetos is going to win. You'll feel full after, but kind of sick and unsatisfied. Pornography is like this. If your ideas about intimacy are formed by what you learned from pornography growing up, this may affect how your brain and body will react to a more realistic and healthy sex life later.

There, we did it! Short and sweet, like I promised.

Dating

It's entirely appropriate for tweens to have romantic and sexual feelings in early adolescence. Businesses have made fortunes profiting on the curiosities and fantasies of tweens. Perhaps no one has understood this, or capitalized on it more, though, than the music producers who've introduced generations of boy bands to mobs of adoring fans. From the Beatles to One Direction to BTS, these bands are meticulously handcrafted so that groups of tween friends can each choose a favorite without causing infighting. There's the shy guy, the older brother, the goof, the bad boy, and, of course, the sex symbol who is disarmingly more pretty than hot, making him swoon-worthy without terrifying parents.

It behooves parents to accept what marketers have long understood about our kids: tweens think about sex, even if not in explicit terms. They have crushes, they fantasize, and they get aroused. Pretending these feelings don't or shouldn't exist is counterproductive. The conflict is in accepting this biological fact alongside our parental need to protect kids from being exposed to adult experiences for which they aren't emotionally or physically prepared.

To effectively do this requires a deep examination of your fears. By asking yourself, "What am I most afraid of?" you can zero in on how to give your young adolescent advice and limits *specific* to your concern, and not just issue blanket statements of disapproval. Some parents flat out say, "Middle school is too young to date." What does that mean, though? Too young to have feelings? (We know that's not true.) Too young to kiss? Too young to hold hands? Too young to bounce back from a broken heart? Too young to risk pregnancy or STDs? Once you've drilled down on your fears, you'll have a better road map for where your conversations need to take you. From there,

> Your child needs direction from you, but they'll tune you out if you talk about dating like it's a gateway to disaster. Keep your child's interest by balancing the nos with yeses, fears with hopes, and negatives with positives.

give guidance and set reasonable limits. "I'm okay with you 'going together,' but at this age you're too young for anything more than kissing." A guideline in their head might be a reassurance to them if they feel pressure to do more.

Remind yourself, too, not to get lost in your anxieties. Your child needs direction from you, but they'll tune you out if you talk about dating like it's a gateway to disaster. Keep your child's interest by balancing the nos with yeses, fears with hopes, and negatives with positives. This is how a BRIEF conversation about dating rules might sound:

BEGIN peacefully

Parent: *I noticed you've been on your phone a lot. Are you still texting Jordan a lot?*

Kid: *Um, yeah, I guess.*

RELATE to your kid

Parent: *He seems like a nice guy. What's he like? Does he play any sports or is he in any clubs?*

Kid: *He's nice. Smart. He runs track, but not until spring so he's not doing anything this season.*

Parent: *Is he good at track?*

Kid: *I think so! He says he is.*

Parent: *Ha! Well, confidence can be a nice quality.*

INTERVIEW to collect data

Parent: *So, what is it called now when people are a couple? I know it's probably not called "dating" anymore.*

Kid: *We're definitely not a couple. We're just talking.*

Parent: *Okay. Does talking mean you like each other?*

Kid: *I think so . . .*

Parent: *That's sweet. And besides being confident and smart, is he kind to you? And other people?*

Kid: *Oh, yes, he's super nice.*

Parent: *I'm glad. So, have you guys talked about doing anything in person, or is it just texting for now?*

Kid: *Can I? Do something with just him?*

Parent: *It depends. We can talk about what options are available to you. What would you like to do?*

Kid: *For now, just text. But if he asks me to go somewhere, I want to know if I can.*

ECHO what you hear

Parent: *I like that you're thinking ahead so you won't be caught off guard. And I'm happy you're willing to talk with me about it even if it's still kind of an unknown situation at this point. Should we go ahead and talk about a few guidelines now so you know how to answer if a relationship or a hangout comes up?*

Kid: *I don't know . . . it's not really a thing.*

Parent: *I get that and I respect it, too. I'm not trying to rush you. But if we talk about this before it happens, it'll be less embarrassing than me having a reaction in front of someone you like. Does that make sense?*

Kid: *Okay, yeah, I don't want you to embarrass me.*

Parent: *Same.*

FEEDBACK

Parent: *I'm probably going to use a lot of the wrong words, so I apologize in advance, but I'll just call it "hanging out," which is what I would have called "dating" in my day. When you have a crush on someone and you start hanging out, it can affect your heart, brain, and body, so here are some quick starter rules for each of those.*

Your heart: When it comes to your heart, at this age you can feel happy and excited by someone and two weeks later feel completely different. Your emotions will change a lot, and so will the other person's. It's nice to open your heart up to that happiness, if you can handle the sadness when things change. From experience, that sadness is usually temporary, but if the feelings become overwhelming for you, or keep you from doing well in school, or being nice to people, or if they affect your health, the rule is you have to talk with me or a professional about how to cope with those feelings. Okay?

Kid: *Okay.*

Parent: *Your brain: When you like someone, it can feel like your entire brain is taken up by them. It feels fun to think about someone all the time,* *and to know they're thinking about you, until you realize you've left no room for other friends and family and things you enjoy. The rule is, you can spend time talking to, or thinking about, the person you're hanging out with, but not all the time. You have to balance it out with the rest of your life, and if I see that isn't happening, I will have to limit time spent texting or going places. Okay?*

Kid: *Okay.*

Parent: *Your body: Speaking of going places . . . if the two of you want to go somewhere together, at your age it needs to be bright and public, not dark and private. I'm thinking yes to the pizza place for lunch, and no to the movies. When you're in high school, we can revisit these rules. If your friend comes here or you go to his house, you need to stay in the main living area with a parent nearby. For privacy, you can sit on the porch and talk, or play a game in the living room, but I'll occasionally walk through. This is because you're both young and new to these feelings, and it takes time to figure out what's comfortable. I don't want either of you to rush. The rule in middle school is you can hold hands or hug if you both want to, and I wouldn't lose my mind if you kissed at some point, but you're too young for anything more than that. (But out of respect to the family, not in the living room.) Also, it's normal to have physical feelings now, but if someone pressures you to do more than you're ready for, or pressures you to break your family rules, that's probably proof they aren't a good match for you.*

Alright. Those are the basics. I'm happy you have someone nice to like who likes you, too. If you want to talk more about these rules, we can. If not, do you want to help me figure out where to order takeout from tonight for dinner?

Consent Comes First

I attended college at a small midwestern liberal arts school in the early 1990s. In the town next to my college was an even smaller, even liberal-ier, even artsier college. My freshman year, that school announced that they were implementing a new policy around sex and consent, which included, among other rules, that a student must obtain verbal permission before kissing another person. Every time! Back in the '90s! It doesn't sound so radical now, but at the time, you could hear the students on my campus laughing all over the quad about this. It felt absurd, stiff, impractical, and highly unromantic. Hadn't anyone at that other college ever seen a rom-com? How was a hot guy supposed to sweep you off your feet if he had to stop the momentum of the unexpected and thrilling first kiss with a child-like request for permission? Yuck.

Thankfully, we've come such a long way. Consent isn't the punchline it used to be and has instead become a normal and essential component of sexual education. That *other* college, it turns out, was a pioneer and like most, had to suffer being the butt of the joke before everyone else eventually caught on.

> If you talk early about consent, starting with nonsexual situations, your tween will develop comfort and proficiency with the concept, which will position them for safer sexual encounters later in life.

What you should know about consent and tweens is that it isn't just about sexual contact. It's simply about having the right to decide who touches you and when. It's about establishing boundaries toward touch. If you talk early about consent, starting with nonsexual situations, your tween will develop comfort and proficiency with the concept, which will position them for safer sexual encounters later in life.

People who haven't yet wrapped their minds around the concept of consent may downplay it as absurdly restrictive. "Oh, so people aren't allowed to *touch* anymore?" If you have a family member who disagrees with teaching consent to kids, who insists they hug Grandma out of respect, for example, remember, it's not that people aren't *allowed* to touch. To be accurate, the question should be "Oh, so now you have to ask somebody every time before you touch them?" And the answer is "Yes." "So, I can't high-five someone without getting permission? 'May I have permission to give you a high five?' That's stupid." To which the reply would be "Nope. You just put your hand in the air like normal. But if someone doesn't want to high-five back, they won't. And then you can't force them."

Below is an example of how a conversation about consent could sound using the BRIEF conversation model. It refers to a viral video of a kindergarten teacher with a chart outside her classroom door. Each kid coming in the classroom points to the greeting they want: a hug, fist bump, handshake, high five, or dance. If you haven't seen it, take a moment to Google it when you can. [Google search: kindergarten teacher lets students pick greeting]

BEGIN peacefully

Parent: *Have you seen this cute video?* [Parent shows video on phone.]
Kid: *Aw, it's so cute.*

RELATE to your kid

Parent: *I thought you'd like it.*
Kid: *I wish we had that when I was little.*
Parents: *Me, too! I kind of wish I had one at work.*
Kid: *What? Why?*
Parent: *Just because some people still think it's okay to touch other people. It's not like they're being perverted, but I don't want someone I don't know well grabbing my shoulders when they walk by or squeezing my arm whenever they say hello.*
Kid: *Ew, that's so weird.*
Parent: *Isn't it? That's why I'm glad these kids are learning this early.*

INTERVIEW to collect data

Kid: *Well, they're learning how to say hello to their teacher in the morning, but I don't think they're going to have a chart like this at their jobs.*
Parent: *Ha! No, they won't have a chart at work, but it's basically an early lesson in consent and I love that. Do you know that word consent?*

Kid: *It's like saying "I agree," or giving permission.*

Parent: *Yep. Or like saying "I don't agree" or give permission. Is this something your teachers ever talk about?*

Kid: *Not really. Do you mean like "Do you agree to behave in class?"*

Parent: *It can be used generally like that, but it's more often used to talk about your personal boundaries.*

Kid: *No, we don't talk about that in school. It's probably more of a home thing anyway.*

ECHO what you hear

Parent: *I see why you'd say that. School feels like it should be more structured and focused on learning, doesn't it?*

Kid: *Right.*

FEEDBACK

Parent: *I get that. Although boundaries are something we take with us everywhere. And I like that these little kids get to make the choice for themselves about how they'd like to be touched or not. And they're at school.*

Kid: *Do you think a kid in that video could choose none of the choices?*

Parent: *I do. I don't know why it is, but in middle school kids can get handsy. You'll see guys jumping on each other's backs and girls hanging on each other. And there's always that person who loves giving out hugs to everyone. I know lots of people do this to show pure joy or to spread happiness, but it can still cross a line. Some people hate it and don't know what to say. You just have to be aware of that and respect people's space, and give them a chance to say whether they want a hug or a piggyback ride, or whatever.*

And I want you to know your boundaries and what makes you feel comfortable so that if someone makes you feel uncomfortable, you can say something.

Some kids are naturally proficient at saying no, or stop, or I don't want to. Others need encouragement to understand that saying no isn't rude.

Be sure to talk with your child about ways they can communicate their own boundaries that feel comfortable.

In my leadership camps, for example, I help middle schoolers practice saying no when a friend asks them to do something they don't want to do. Nine times out of ten, tweens will lie to avoid conflict. A child who is too tired to play, or who needs a break from a needy friend, or who would prefer to stay home and finish a game or book, will, when pressed by a friend to hang out, say something absurd like "I'm grounded for a month!" Or "My aunt's cat died and I have to go to her house today for the funeral or something." Encourage your tween to give a simple, straightforward no when they don't want to do something, and when pressed, to repeat their answer without resorting to bigger, bolder lies in hopes that will convince the person asking to leave them alone. It's enough to say, "I can't today, but I hope you find someone who can. Have fun!" and, if pressed, "I *really* can't today but I hope you have fun."

Another way to teach consent at home is to speak up about your own need for spatial boundaries. All humans need to experience touch, known as "touch hunger" or "skin hunger," and in early adolescence that need often goes unmet. The kid you once nuzzled countless times a day is now a tween who bristles at your touch, yet their need for physical contact hasn't waned. Some kids satisfy touch hunger by acting overly affectionate or playful with each other at school. Others will ignore you for as long as they can at home, then climb onto your lap unexpectedly. Does your tween sometimes hang on you too much or invade your space? It's important you don't deny them affection and that they know they're not too old for hugs or snuggles, but there will be times when you need your space. Clearly articulate your boundaries to show them how it's done. "I love snuggling when we watch a movie, but you can't have your legs on me the whole time. Let's sit side by side."

Finally, don't overlook personal property as a way to teach consent. Siblings, in particular take a "what's yours is mine" approach to communal living, at least when it's to their benefit. Establish family rules about respecting people's things and asking for permission to use them. Even if you've paid for all your kids' possessions, they need to feel ownership over their personal items so they can practice this early form of consent.

LGBTQ+: Understanding and Accepting New Labels

Most people say they don't like labels, but those people aren't tweens. Starting around middle school, kids embrace labels because they can be used to organize and explain their confusing new social environment and where they belong within it. Though adults might perceive this as limiting, tweens and young teens see it as reassuring. At an age when kids are starting to examine their emerging adult (to be fair, *very young adult*) identities, they seek out the precise vocabulary to define and express how they feel and identify.

If words like *cisgender, binary, fluid, trans,* or *pansexual* sound confusing, startling, or unnecessarily complicated, you're sharing common feelings with many people over age forty. But these words aren't made up and they aren't superfluous. They represent real people who are authorities on their real selves and the onus is on all adults to keep up with the evolving vernacular. Not only it is relatively easy to stay educated, but it's also important to the health and safety of our kids that we respect and celebrate the many ways people can be in this world. The Internet has you covered. Whenever you hear a new term, look it up. Then, assuming you're reading from a site that supports the LGBTQ community, believe the definition. The CDC reports that "most lesbian, gay, bisexual, (LGB) youth are happy and thrive during their adolescent years. Having a school that creates a safe and supportive learning environment for all students and having caring and accepting parents are especially important."

But even though things have gotten better for LGBTQ adolescents in the United States, they are still subject to bullying, harassment, and displacement, and in the worst of cases are sent to conversion therapy or kicked out of their homes. The CDC cites a heart-wrenching statistic that almost one-third of LGB youth had attempted suicide in the previous year and the American Academy of Pediatrics reports that up to 50 percent of transgender youth attempt suicide. Clearly, we need to do more to let kids in these groups know they are loved just as they are.

Even among the understanding and open-minded parents I work with, I still see discomfort when young people talk openly and confidently about sexual identity. I find it's not the terms that make parents bristle, but the age at which kids want to introduce them. Labeling, as we all not-so-fondly remember, is a popular pastime in middle school, so perhaps it should come as no surprise that the practice now extends to classifying who is gay or bi or transitioning, or to announcing one's own identifying category. Some parents worry that declaring sexuality at a young age is inappropriate, or inaccurate, or a potential source for future regret. Even if you share these concerns, don't discourage open identity talk whenever it happens. Even the smallest comment can unleash the internalized fear of homophobia in a questioning tween's mind and heart. Definitely make sure your child understands the vocabulary they're using though, as some kids claim a label erroneously because they misunderstand the meaning.

If your child comments on their sexual identity, don't ask whether they really know, are old enough to know, or might regret making an announcement if they "change their mind" in the future. More important than your child being correct, or consistent, or regret-free when it comes to how they identify, is that they feel able to express themselves. A tween might be bisexual today and gay or straight some day in the future, and that's okay. Here's the good thing about labels: they aren't permanent. Despite the proliferation of Valley girls, preps, jocks, and goths in my middle school, I know next to none as an adult. (Only the nerds have stood the test of time. This is, in fact, the only endurance event I could possibly have participated in, even if unwittingly, and I'm enjoying this feeling of triumph right now.)

> More important than your child being correct, or consistent, or regret-free when it comes to how they identify, is that they feel able to express themselves.

This isn't to say your child's identity *will* change. Sexuality shouldn't be dismissed as a phase your child will outgrow, but it *can* evolve, so don't get caught up worrying about labels changing.

Your tween may openly talk about someone else's identity, if not their own, around you. Even when they're talking about another kid, react with the same sensitivity as if they were sharing about themselves. In this way, you are always laying groundwork for trust. This is what a supportive conversation about sexual identity and labels could sound like using the BRIEF conversation model:

BEGIN peacefully

Kid: *Do you remember Abbie from last year?*
Parent: *Of course! It's been a while since I heard her name.*
Kid: *So, she was in this group text someone started and she told everyone she's bisexual now.*

RELATE to your kid

Parent: *Yeah? Were people respectful of that?*
Kid: *Yes, it's not weird, Mom.*
Parent: *Of course not. When I was your age, this wasn't something people discussed so openly, but your generation has done a lot to improve on that.*
Kid: *Her parents are super-upset though, and they don't agree with it. They told her she's too young to know and that she's just looking for attention.*

INTERVIEW to collect data

Parent: *I'm sorry to hear that. Do you think people say this kind of thing to get attention?*
Kid: *I guess some people would, yes. But she seems honest.*
Parent: *It must be hard for her. Have you thought about how you can be a good friend through this?*
Kid: *We all told her it wasn't fair of her parents to say that.*
Parent: *That's good. And just to be sure, do you feel you understand what it means to be bisexual?*
Kid: *You like girls and guys.* [Kid looks at you like you're an idiot.]

ECHO what you hear

Parent: *Well maybe that's an easy one, but there are other terms I'm still learning as an adult. I'm just saying if you happen to come across a term*

you don't know, about identity or anything related to sex, I can give you
resources for correct information. As far as Abbie is concerned, sounds like
her parents aren't willing to give her support or reliable information now,
so she may need extra help from outside her family.

FEEDBACK

Kid: *I know! What can we do to make them accept her?*
Parent: *I don't know that you can make her parents feel differently. I do*
want to reassure you though that you're already doing the most important
thing by supporting her.

I know her parents said she's too young to know, and sure it's possible
she is misinterpreting some feelings, but I don't think that matters. I think
it's damaging to tell someone what they feel is not "correct," whether that
feeling stays the same forever or changes in a month. Humans are complex
and there isn't just one right way to be. For you, and your friends, I'll
always be a safe space to talk about these things.

A Word About Appearance

I can't close out a chapter on sexuality without covering appearance.
There will come a day when your child walks into the room and you realize it. They're dressed a little bit . . . sexy. More often, because of our cul-
tural obsession with young female attractiveness, we see this with girls.
What do you say when your tween daughter's attempts to look grown-up
and cool make her look racy, especially when her age hasn't caught up to
her appearance? We all worry about creeps and predators. You will want
to protect her from any unwanted attention she'll receive, but at the same
time avoid causing her shame about her body or sexuality.

You should be honest with your daughter about your internal conflict. Tell her that she should never be ashamed of her body and can
make her own decisions about what she wears. She is not responsible
for other people's reactions to how she looks. However, I would also
tell your daughter that she is getting old enough to sense when she is
not comfortable with the kind of attention her clothing choices may

(or may not) cause. Sometimes that attention may even make her feel unsafe. That's not fair, but it's reality. Outside of meeting a reasonable school dress code and being respectfully dressed for other events, such as babysitting, a choral concert, or going to the theater with Grandma, she can wear what she wants. She can start to make those choices for herself, within the bounds of what's appropriate for certain settings, as long as she can process the scope of how others may respond to her choices. Ripped jeans and a tight tank may read edgy and rebellious at the mall, but a tad disrespectful at her dad's Rotary speech. And even at the mall, edgy and rebellious might be cool to her crush who works at the food court, but also draw comments from his lone, lurking boss behind the counter.

Both appearance and style reflect an array of fascinating personal choices, but they should be made with regard to a general social contract we all enter into as community members. Give your child the authority to make decisions about their appearance, but teach them to also take into consideration whether the vibe they're going for works in the given context.

Conversation Crashers

"I check the search history on all devices and if I see you looking at anything inappropriate I'm taking away the Wi-Fi." This feels harsh, especially if it's a warning and not a reaction to a serious, existing problem. Kids will take in the tone of condemnation, and be unlikely to share with you if they come across, even accidentally, unsafe messages or images online. Instead, let them know if they stumble onto pornography online, or someone asks them to look at or send a nude photo online, they can safely come to you and you'll help.

"You don't realize the message you're sending wearing that." It's embarrassing to have put effort into a look and be told you don't understand what you've done. Instead of *implying* the message, try this:

"You look grown-up. You look *so* grown-up, you might get reactions from adults that make you feel uncomfortable. Before you leave the house, let's talk for a minute about how to deal with that, and then you can decide what you'd like to do."

"Love the sinner, not the sin." When parents grapple with their kid's sexual or gender identity, especially those raised in a strict, conservative faith, I hear them rely on this line of thinking. My guess is it feels like a way to resolve two seemingly unreconcilable forces: love for a child and a religious belief that condemns that child. The problem with this is twofold. First, it doesn't reconcile anything. At best, it might buy a conflicted parent time to decide which they will choose: the whole child or the doctrine. At worst, it tells a kid your love for them is conditional on them not being themselves. That's because the second problem with this approach is it excludes gender and sexuality as parts of identity, and identity is not something you do, it's something you are. "Love the sinner, not the sin" works perfectly if your child has stolen something or (God forbid) committed murder, but not when your child has done nothing other than be themselves. If you are struggling with this as a parent, I know no amount of data, or scripture, or anecdotal evidence that I offer will convince you. All that will help resolve your conflict around this is in your own heart. Every religion is rooted in love and compassion. Immerse yourself there.

"You're too young to be thinking about girls/guys/dating." When parents say this, I don't think they actually mean you're too young to *think* about these things. Obviously, no one can put controls around what a person thinks and when they begin having romantic feelings. Not to mention, sometimes these are the same parents who joked in preschool, "Aw, look who has a little girlfriend!" I think this is less about being too young and more about fearing that thinking will become doing, and lots of parents aren't comfortable defining what's allowed to be done and what's not. Remember, kids want adults to be specific. It's usually not okay to establish rules around romantic feelings, but fine to set expectations regarding physical intimacy.

In a Hurry? Here's Your Crash Course

- Teens report parent sex talks could be improved if they were more specific, provided guidance, and were collaborative.

- Teaching safety during sex talks correlates to less risk taking.

- The average age a person first searches for porn is fourteen. Get ahead of this by talking about pornography early. Don't focus your message on pornography being immoral or gross, or you run the risk of shame mingling with developing sexuality. Instead, talk about how porn doesn't represent real sex and the implications of that on a healthy sex life later in life.

- When your child wants to start dating (or whatever they call it), establish guidelines for what's acceptable in terms of physical touching, coping with new emotions, and staying attentive to school, family, friends, and interests.

- Stay educated on new terms related to sexuality and identity.

- It's normal and okay for tweens to label their sexuality. Labels may or may not last, unlike the feeling they get when you accept and support them.

- Talk about consent early and often, starting with nonsexual scenarios. Establishing rules about asking permission before touching someone's things and articulating your own preferences for space and touch preferences are two ways to begin teaching consent at home.

- Middle schoolers, especially girls, may start dressing in ways that feel, to you, provocative or sexy. By this stage, tweens need to feel authority over their own bodies and how they dress or adorn them. Talk openly about whether they're prepared for the attention they may receive (wanted and unwanted) and how to react to that.

Talking About Reputations

In this chapter, you'll learn how to talk about reputations in a way that recognizes the complicated nature of this subject, as well as how to encourage your child to think about their future in a way that will best serve them down the road. You'll also understand why asking your tween to be honest isn't as straightforward a request as you think, and how to talk through the rise of a major reputation breaker among young adolescents—asking for and sending nudes.

Universally, people love rooting for the underdog, the nonconformist who bucks societal expectations and embraces revolutionary self-acceptance. Hollywood has long been printing money off our rebel worship. From Jim Stark to Ren McCormack, and Jo March to Katniss Everdeen, the idea of a teenager, especially, who breaks convention is exciting and emboldening, in part because it's a bit of a fantasy. (It's worth noting, Hollywood teen rebels are almost universally white. It's dangerous for teens of color to rebel against authority and it's often disliked by white audiences. Nonwhite teens must be more subtle in their rebellion to remain safe, by being antiestablishment in their choices of clothing, language, or music.) Most of us, and especially teenagers, are locked in by peer expectation and approval. We lack the finesse needed to break the right rules without crossing into the kind of different that results in being shunned. Knowing when it's appropriate to meet or ignore people's expectations is a big part of reputation management during adolescence.

We don't make this easy on kids. For one thing, adults unwittingly send kids mixed messages when it comes to reputations. From one side of our mouths we say, "Who cares what other people think?!" and from the other we say, "Don't do that! What will people think?!"

To complicate matters, wrestling with the concept of reputation relies on some forethought about how you want to be perceived in the future, a skill most young adolescents haven't got down. Tweens live in the moment. They are famously egocentric in the way they think of themselves and their needs first, and they are also present-centric in how they think of time. To a young adolescent, now is the only time that matters. It's as if the future will happen to someone else entirely.

One way to begin nudging your child out of present-centric thinking is to explain that it's smart for "current you" to do "future you" favors. In terms of building a reputation, think of it like starting a bank account. Your Reputation Savings Account starts with a zero balance. When you do something that adds to your good reputation, it's like putting money in the bank. When you do something that subtracts from your good reputation, it's like withdrawing money from the bank. People will look at the balance of your savings account to make decisions about you in the future. For example, let's say a teacher accuses you of cheating on a test and then sends you to the principal. The principal has to decide what to do, but she wasn't in the room and doesn't know if you cheated or not.

> Tweens have trouble connecting the dots between what they do and how they're perceived because they think of a reputation as something that just *happens* to you, as opposed to something you consciously and incrementally build over time.

All she can do is look at your savings account. Have you made a lot of deposits by being a good student generally, or too many withdrawals by being a frequent visitor to her office? She's going to use that to help make her decision.

No, this isn't always fair or accurate. It's just what happens.

Tweens also have trouble connecting the dots between what they do and how they're perceived because they think of a reputation as something that just *happens* to you, as opposed to something you consciously and incrementally build over time. This is our fault. Think about how often we warn kids that one mistake could derail them forever. By trying to scare them into making good choices, we may inadvertently be sending kids the message that a good reputation is built through years of careful, perfect behavior, and a bad reputation is just one slipup away.

Responding to Gossip

Gossip plays a big role in influencing reputations. For one thing, how adults react to gossip matters, because the weight of adult opinion can send a kid's reputation in the wrong direction, and for another, when adults gossip, they judge kids from inside a vacuum. When the parents at a middle school softball game pass whispers through the bleachers about the third-base player who got caught giving a blow job, what messages reverberate out to the kids about mistakes, reputations, and consequences? Adults think talking about scandals will raise awareness and deter other kids from making the same choices. But gossip is less a deterrent than you'd like. Gossip, like tragedy, feels like the sort of thing that happens to *other*

> In general, when you talk with your kids about reputations, high points should include that it's a good idea to make choices they think will help them in the future, and it's a bad idea to either condemn or glorify someone based on an incomplete picture.

people. That flattened perspective makes it easier to think "things like that don't happen to people like me." What kids need to hear is that people are complex. That third-base player might have made a different choice than you want your kid to make. She also works hard for her teammates and is kindhearted. It's complicated. Similarly, when kids hear all the parents at graduation praising the winner of the student athlete award, not knowing how he treats other kids when no adults are around, they learn that a reputation is a pretty shallow assessment.

If your child comes to you with gossip, this is a good opportunity to talk about our ability to protect or impugn someone else's reputations. Help them separate the person from their actions by asking questions like:

- "Does this person often make choices like this, or was this an unusual mistake?"

- "This sounds like a bad decision. What do you think this person can do to move forward instead of getting stuck?"

- "How will your reaction help or hurt this person in getting through this?"

- "Do you have all the information, or is this person getting a bad reputation based on hearsay and assumptions?"

In general, when you talk with your kids about reputations, high points should include that it's a good idea to make choices they think will help them in the future, and it's a bad idea to either condemn or glorify someone based on an incomplete picture.

"Decide What to Be and Go Be It"

This is a quote from one of my favorite songs, "Head Full of Doubt/ Road Full of Promise," by the Avett Brothers. It's a good sentiment for this chapter because it's a simple mantra for a complicated topic. Kids should understand that a reputation won't give you full control over what people think of you, but it can be a useful tool you use to shape what people think. If you ever find yourself in a friendly, quiet moment with your tween, you might ask them, "When people think of you, what three things do you hope come to mind?" Explain that you're not looking for adjectives like *funny* or *athletic* to describe what they can do, but traits that describe who they are on a deeper level. Whatever traits they pick—reliable, trustworthy, generous, loyal, kind, open-minded—those will be a touchstone for them throughout their life. Once they know the kind of person they want to be, they can use those words as a benchmark to help respond to the hard situations that are peppered throughout early adolescence.

The Trouble with Honesty and Reputations

Who stole the cookie from the cookie jar?
Your middle schooler stole the cookie from the cookie jar!

And then denied it, right to your face.

Tweens are pretty big liars, and this adds another dimension to the reputation conversation, since adults and tweens, unfortunately, have different opinions about what makes for a good reputation. For example, adults often say being honest is critical to building a good reputation. After all, it's a sign of integrity. For young teens, integrity has a much more specific definition. It looks more like loyalty and reliability *among their peers* than truthfulness toward parents. Let's say you discover your child was at a sleepover where someone dared them to climb out a window and ding-dong-ditch the neighbor at 2 a.m. If you insist, as a matter of integrity and trustworthiness, they be honest with you about who dared them to do this, you will find yourself locking horns on completely different issues. To a tween, integrity means *loyalty* at all costs. To you, integrity means *honesty* at all costs. To answer your question, your kid will have to betray their values to answer for yours.

Let's look more closely at how an "honesty at all costs" philosophy can derail a family from open communication. According to a study conducted by researchers at Stanford University, the Catholic University of America, and the University of Maryland, a vast majority (as high as 82 percent) of teens lie to their parents, usually on at least one important matter. Not all lies, however, are created equal. When parents approach honesty as a moral absolute, it backfires and encourages kids to stretch the truth because they can't meet an impossibly high standard.

Knowing why kids lie can help you determine how to have conversations about honesty. Sometimes, kids lie to protect a friend or to spare someone's feelings. Sometimes, it's because a parent's rules feel arbitrary or unfair. Sometimes, it's an impulse toward protecting themselves from consequences. Often, it's just because kids are aging into a deeper, and normal, need for privacy and don't want to reveal *everything* to their parents. If you can get to the root of why your child lies, you can have more productive and analytical conversations, rather than repeatedly professing "You should never, ever lie."

Importantly, while adolescents tend to agree that the types of lies mentioned above are justifiable, researchers found teens also tend to agree that two kinds of lying to parents are not acceptable, namely: lying to get even with parents who have lied to them, and lying to see how far they can push boundaries. In other good news, as teens get older, they lie less and less to their parents when their parents give them increasing freedom and privacy. Lying does not decrease in teens whose parents remain controlling and rigid in their approach to raising teens.

If honesty matters to you most of all, avoid putting your kid in a position where they might lie to sidestep an undesirable outcome. One way to set yourself up for success: don't ask questions when you already know the answer.

James, a dad I work with, was upset that his son, JJ, kept taking his fidget spinner to school, despite the teacher saying they were against the rules. One morning, JJ ran upstairs and when he came back down his fidget spinner was poking out of his back pocket. "What's in your pocket?" James asked.

"Nothing," JJ replied, looking his dad in the eye.

"No fidget spinner?"

"Gotta go—I'm gonna miss the bus!" JJ hollered, as he ran out the door.

Later that day, James e-mailed the teacher and got confirmation that JJ had, in fact, been busted for distracting the other boys in class with his spinner.

I asked James to consider taking more direct action instead of beating around the bush and giving JJ the opportunity to lie. The next time JJ ran downstairs at the last minute with his contraband, James told JJ to empty his pockets onto the counter so he could see what he was taking to school. Then he said, "You know the rules. No bringing fidget spinners to school. I'll keep this on the counter and you can put it back in your room later." Problem solved.

The parents I work with worry a lot about catching their middle schoolers in a string of little lies. Are they raising sociopaths? Of course not. This is the age when kids start fibbing about things that seem unworthy of wasting a lie on, such as "I already brushed my teeth" (they haven't), and "I didn't have to do that assignment because we had a sub" (they did). The conundrum is that experimenting with dishonesty is both a normal part of growing up (phew!), *and* it can lead to a bad reputation (ugh!). Let's look at how a conversation about these types of annoying lies might go in your house.

Note: Since this is a topic that speaks directly to a kid's character, it's a quick trigger for defensiveness. The best way to work around this is to initiate this conversation as either a reflection on something that happened a couple days ago, or about another child. In the example below, the parent waited a few days to bring up an incident.

<u>B</u>EGIN peacefully

Parent: *Hey there! How was swim practice?*
Kid: *It was good! We didn't have to do dryland training today.*
Parent: *Nice! Do you have much homework?*
Kid: *Not really.*
Parent: *Okay, great. Do you have ten minutes after dinner to touch base with me on some household things?*
Kid: *Sure . . .*

RELATE to your kid

Parent: *[After dinner] So, I was tidying up in your bathroom a few days ago and I found your shampoo bottle was empty. I'm assuming it's still empty?*
Kid: *Oh, probably.*
Parent: *I know you have a lot to remember and you might have forgotten to mention it whenever you came downstairs. Are you having a tough time keeping up with your toiletries?*
Kid: *Yeah, I just keep forgetting.*
Parent: *I understand.*

INTERVIEW to collect data

Parent: *The thing is, I've been asking you if you washed your hair because it hasn't been looking clean, and you've said yes every time. So, we need a better system. Do you have any ideas on how to remember to tell me when you need shampoo?*
Kid: *I'll just remember.*
Parents: *Well . . . that hasn't worked. How about if I put a supply list on the hall closet, and you can just put a check mark there when you run out of deodorant or toothpaste or shampoo?*
Kid: *Yes, that would work because I'll see it whenever I walk by.*
Parent: *Great! Any idea why you were dishonest about the shampoo before?*
Kid: *I didn't want you to make me go back and shower again when I already did it.*
Parent: *Ohhhh.*

ECHO what you hear

Parent: *So you kept forgetting to refill your supplies, and then to cover that up you lied about washing your hair to avoid me making you take another shower.*
Kid: *Yeah, sorry.*

FEEDBACK

Parent: *It's okay. I'm not mad about you forgetting because I know you're new to managing your own toiletries. But I'm not thrilled with the lying,* *although it helps me to know why you did it. Can you understand how the lying seemed to me?*

Kid: *It looks bad.*

Parent: *It looks bad. And that's the thing about telling little lies. They usually make things seem worse than they are. Now that you're in middle school, you're old enough for two things to start happening.*

Number one: I am not going to be the person to make you take showers and wash your hair. If you forget, you don't have to lie to me about it. You'll just have greasy hair and smell bad. Eventually, someone might point it out at school, or talk about it behind your back. If it gets to the point that you're so stinky we can't be in the same room, I may have to make shower rules, but I don't want to do that.

Number two: You're getting to the age where you're interested in more and more freedom and I want you to have it. But . . . if I feel like you're lying about little things, then I wonder if you can be trusted with bigger things. You lied here to avoid the consequence of having to redo your shower when you wanted to relax. But now, you've created an even bigger consequence for yourself, which is that I might have some doubts about whether you're being truthful in the future.

As far as the shampoo goes, you're generally good at taking care of yourself. I trust that you can keep up with the new system for replenishing the products you need. As far as the little lies go, you should make a choice: do you want to be trusted and given more opportunities? If so, then you need to choose to be honest. If you make the choice that lying is easier than being truthful, you have to be okay with the reputation you're building around that.

Now, I'm adding shampoo to the shopping list. Is there any new brand or scent you'd like to try?

Dealing with Bigger Problems

Skipping shampoo is one thing, but what should a parent do if they discover their tween has done something that puts their mental or physical health at risk? In general, my philosophy is that kids should be given the opportunity to take risks and learn from them, until or unless they do something that becomes dangerous to their long-term well-being. If you find out, for example, that your eighth grader drank alcohol at a friend's house and puked all over the basement, you've got to take strong action. I like this mantra: "When your kid's world gets too big, make it smaller." This is the kind of situation that requires a strict tightening of freedom first, and benefits from meaningful conversations second. In this circumstance, I'd advocate for a memorable grounding, including an apology to anyone affected (presumably the parent who hosted the kids), followed by some educational discussions about the effects of alcohol on a growing brain and body. I'd tie active and meaningful participation in these types of discussions to good behavior that the child could use to earn back certain privileges during the grounding. Their ability to talk openly with you about hard things is one way they can earn back your trust. Make it possible for them to do this by being a patient and nonjudgmental listener.

Once you've handled the situation in your home, you'll also want to give some thought to reputation management. My advice is to give your child the same respect and privacy you would want from others if you made a mistake. *Don't talk about it publicly.* You might think you can say something to people that would help explain the situation, advocate for your child, or rebuild your child's reputation, but when you say anything, you only open the door for others to keep talking. This is not to say you won't need or deserve a way to process what happened, and it's fair to have a confidant or two you can talk with, but choose wisely the people you can trust most to maintain your minor's privacy. This is your child's narrative and they have a right to discuss it or not with people outside of your family. Encourage them to share only with the few people they trust most and to talk with you *anytime* they want to process what happened. If anyone asks about your kid, you can simply say, "Thanks so much for checking on us. That was rough but they are learning a lot and we are all going to be fine." If pressed, you can say, "We've agreed this is their story and we won't talk about it out of respect for their privacy." Then change the subject.

Develop a Growth Mindset

There is no such thing as perfect parenting and, even if there were, no amount of it would keep a kid from going off the rails at some point in middle or high school. Your kid is going to make mistakes. My kids have made (big!) mistakes. Every parent I know has kids who step off the path in both tiny and terrible ways. Good parenting isn't about keeping your kids from screwing up. It's about teaching them how to pick themselves up and move forward when they do. This will be easier if, today, you start talking about mistakes as a part of learning. This promotes what's known as a "growth mindset," when a person can see an error as an opportunity for moving forward instead of a setback.

A kid who makes a public mistake shouldn't resign themselves to having a bad reputation. They should view it as a time to do a little positive PR work. One of the best lessons you can teach your child when they inevitably make a mistake is how to deliver a good apology. If your kids watch the news or engage with social media, they are already exposed to a steady stream of bad examples from politicians, business leaders, athletes, and entertainers issuing apologies intended to save their reputations and paychecks, but that make them look callous and childish instead. Kids need better examples of apologizing with a growth mindset.

A good apology does not:

- blame other people for misinterpreting your actions
- blame others for feeling hurt or offended
- blame circumstances for clouding your judgment
- waste words convincing people you're a good person who just made a mistake

A good apology does:

- explain what you did wrong
- acknowledge who you've hurt and how
- say what you will do differently
- accept consequences

The easiest way for your tween to learn this valuable skill is by watching you show them how it's done. You don't have to wait for a grand-scale mistake to teach this point. If you make a quip about your kid's outfit, and it hurts their feelings, show them how a sincere apology works (even if you *still* hate the ratty T-shirt they tried wearing to the awards banquet).

Nudes: A Reputation Maker or Breaker

If I had to pull a metaphorical rabbit out of a hat, my magic trick would be to face an auditorium full of both elementary and middle school parents and distinguish the two groups by asking one simple question. (And no, the question could not be "What grade are your kids in?") Facing one hundred parents in a room, evenly split with fifty parents of elementary schoolers and fifty of middle schoolers, I would ask, "Who wants to talk about kids sending nudes?" The elementary parents would gather their things as they stood up to leave in a hurry. The middle school parents would look at me like "Yep, let's talk about it."

It's difficult to find current, accurate data on the prevalence of adolescents sending nude or seminude photos. As it's a relatively new phenomenon, and relies on self-reporting, there isn't a lot of reliable research yet. But in pop culture, kids hear about sexting and sending nudes, *a lot*. The wildly popular, if controversial, *13 Reasons Why* miniseries on Netflix explored the tragic consequences of private photo sharing, and the critically acclaimed coming-of-age movie *Eighth Grade* honestly addressed the pressure girls feel to share photos so boys will like them. Even family sitcoms give a nod to the ease with which people share nudes these days. Whether adults or kids are sending pics with such regularity, kids get the message that it's a part of growing up. Furthermore, in real life, kids watch celebrities not only recover from breaches of their private photos, but become more famous after the "scandal."

A 2018 study from the *Journal of the American Medical Association Pediatrics* found that 14.8 percent of American teens were sending sexts, and 27.4 percent were receiving them. Whether this number seems high or low to you, the tweens and teens I work with tell me "everyone is doing it." Parents, too, seem to feel the numbers are much higher than what's being reported, based on communication from administrators at their own schools. In my online parenting group, most parents echo one mom who recently posted, "It's not a matter of *if* a girl will get asked to send nudes in middle school. It's a matter of when." Without more reliable ways of gathering data, we can use the *JAMA Pediatrics* statistics as a baseline, but know the numbers probably skew higher. Again, that's not to say everyone does it, but it is certainly a part of the climate for kids this young.

It's not only boys requesting and girls sending pics, but the trend leans that way. I've spoken with lots of parents who say their daughter was pressured so relentlessly she finally gave in just to make the pressure stop. In one case, where I knew the kids involved, the guy who begged for the first picture then used it to blackmail the girl to get more, an unexpected and damning twist for the girl. Some boys ask for nudes as a way to build a reputation for being experienced, powerful, mature, and manly. Girls might say yes as a way to build a reputation for being desirable, pleasing, and popular.

Whether sending or receiving, being involved with nude pics is a surefire way to damage one's reputation, if word gets out. I've seen both classmates and parents turn against kids for doing it. Once exposed, kids often have to switch schools and hope the rumors don't follow them. If you want to share a story with your kids that illustrates how ostracizing someone can end in tragedy, do an online search for Amanda Todd, who made a YouTube video using flash cards to tell her awful story about being blackmailed into sending a topless photo in seventh grade. She later died by suicide. I am heartbroken for her family and hope her story compels people to treat kids who make this mistake with compassion.

I recommend all parents talk with their kids about this trend well before high school, ideally at the beginning of middle school. This conversation is a good one for the car or while watching TV, since it's cringeworthy for kids to talk about this subject while making eye contact. Here is how this one might sound:

BEGIN peacefully

Parent: *Now that you're in middle school, I realized one of the things we should talk about is kids asking for and sending inappropriate photos.*

Kid: *Oh my god.* [Kid buries head in nearest blanket.]

Parent: *It's okay. It won't be a lecture. I just won't be doing my job if I don't cover a few things with you. I'll make it quick, but you can come back and ask me questions or talk about it some more if you ever want to.*

Kid: [Crickets]

RELATE to your kid

Parent: *I'll just dive right in. The first thing I want to say is I'm not bringing this up because I think you've done it or that you will do it. I'm mentioning it because, statistically, kids in middle school have a good chance of being asked to send a photo without their clothes on, and you should be prepared for that ahead of time. I know how hard it is to say no to someone when they catch you off guard, so I want to be sure you have given this some thought.*

Kid: *This is the worst.*

Parent: *Stick with me.*

INTERVIEW to collect data

[The kid has provided some clear feedback that they aren't on board for this talk, so I'd skip over the interview and go straight to what you need them to know.]

Parent: *I'm not going to ask you what you know or what your thoughts are about this topic because I know it's an awkward one. I'll cut to the chase.*

Kid: *Ugh, can we just be done?*

ECHO what you hear

Parent: *Soon! I know you are uncomfortable and I promise I won't drag it out.*

FEEDBACK

Parent: *This is what I want you to know on this subject. It's not wrong to be curious about how people look. But no one your age should ever ask someone to send them a nude photo. I know it's almost common now and that might make it seem normal. We've even seen it on TV or the movies. But those stories follow a script where everything works the way the writer plans. In real life, unexpected things happen. I want to be sure you've heard from me the ways this goes wrong.*

Think about how hard it is to keep a secret. The person you trust and share the photo with may show the picture to only one person. Just as you believe you can trust your person, they believe they can trust their friend. If everyone just trusts one person to share the photo with, pretty soon it's far out there and a lot of people have seen it.

And another point is revenge. You may never believe that it's possible, but people change, especially at this age. A person who you trust now can be a different person in six months. It's not worth the risk that they could use your photo to embarrass or hurt you if you break up.

Lots of parents spot-check their kids' phones or monitor their social media. Even if you think the image you send on Snapchat is going to disappear, it's still stored somewhere, and it can be captured in a screenshot. They can tell other parents about what you've done. News travels fast, and you could feel isolated by that.

Then there's blackmail. Once you send a single photo, the person who received it can use it to force you to send more. Sometimes people say, "If you don't send more, I'll send this pic to a lot of people." Maybe you think the person you sent it to would never do that, but if their phone is lost or one of their "friends" gets a copy of it, they can use it to pressure you.

I recommend you think about what you'll say if someone asks you. I've seen lots of funny responses online, so we can look up ways to respond with humor if you want. Just be prepared in case it does come up for you or a friend.

I'd also like you to know that people who ask for the pics are the root of the problem. No one should pressure someone else that way. People often blame the person who took the photo more than the person who asked for it and that's not right. And never forward a photo if someone sends you one. If you receive one, delete it right away.

Finally, if you know someone who is suffering because they made this mistake, don't make it harder for them. Don't treat them like they're sick and contagious. Everyone makes mistakes and everyone deserves the chance to recover.

Okay, I hope you see you can trust me to talk about this, even if it's a weird and complicated subject. I'm done! You're free! Thanks for listening to me. I'm going to water the garden now.

If you can, try to carve out some space to reinforce that feeling curious about seeing nude pictures is totally normal at this age. You're not saying it's wrong to be interested, just that too many things can and will go wrong. Incidentally, people are always curious about things before they're ready for them. I may be curious about outer space, but I'm not competent to go there! Along these lines, be clear that if friends or schoolmates pressure your child to ask someone for nude photos, that's wrong. Your child can assume when people do this, they want to look cool or get some pressure off their own back to do this by convincing someone else. An appropriate response to peer pressure like this would be "Nah." That's all it takes. Or if they can carry off a joke, "Oh, sure, want me to rob a bank and bring you the money, too?"

Conversation Crashers

"It only takes one bad decision to unravel a good reputation." Why even try then? Kids need to understand that making a mistake doesn't make someone a bad person. A good reputation can be built on how well you recover from your mistakes.

"Honesty is always the best policy." Your ninety-four-year-old Great Aunt Elmira wants to know what you think of the sweatshirt she made you. You know, the one with her favorite, and your least favorite, president on the front. Is honesty the best policy here? By middle school, your kid is old enough to appreciate the nuance of honesty. Instead of drilling clichés, talk about how complicated the idea of honesty can be.

"You can get convicted of child pornography and be sent to jail!" On the subject of nudes, this is the go-to warning issued by many parents. (Even outside of this topic, I often hear parents advise each other to scare their kids with a worst-case scenario like this so they don't get into trouble.) It's not that I'm against trying to scare kids out of making big mistakes, it's just that this isn't actually scary to tweens because it doesn't ring true. Most young middle schoolers will have at least heard about other kids sending nudes and older middle schoolers will know kids who've done it. Chances are high that none of these kids have been convicted of child pornography. A more realistic (and scary) consequence than jail is social ostracization. Talk about how sending nudes can backfire when classmates find out and ridicule or blackball the sender. But also, keep in mind, this is an embarrassing and vulnerable topic. We've seen too many national news stories about kids dying of suicide after adults found out they were sexting, especially when adults threatened legal action that might "ruin their lives." Be tuned in to whether you are being too heavy-handed. Adults tend to make these conversations about shame and embarrassment and breaking the law, when these are really just tender young humans trying to figure out who they like and how they fit in and what sex makes them feel like—things that are really, really normal.

In a Hurry? Here's Your Crash Course

- Adults send mixed messages about when and whether kids should care what others think of them. We also confuse kids when we say good reputations take a long time to develop and a moment to derail.

- Building a reputation can be a hard concept for tweens, who have a present-centric way of thinking about time.

- Gossip has a huge effect on reputation, and how adults respond to gossip is important. Ask kids questions to make sure they consider the whole picture and the full character of a person, instead of focusing on one mistake.

- Kids lie for lots of reasons and not all lies are created equal. Lying to protect a friend or spare someone's feelings, for example, is different from lying to hurt someone.

- As adolescents experience increased freedom and privacy, they lie less.

- Protect your child's reputation by guarding their private mistakes. Don't share details without their permission.

- Learn the components of both good and bad apologies. Practice making good apologies in front of your tween.

- Taking, sending, and receiving nudes is now part of the modern adolescent experience. Not for all teens, but for enough that it merits its own conversation with regard to reputation. Be wary of sounding too heavy-handed and always lead with empathy. Yes, nudes can be reputation breakers, but less so if we understand that at the heart of these scandals are tender young humans who are trying to navigate new feelings in a new environment.

CHAPTER

16

Talking About Impulsivity

In this chapter, you'll learn why impulsivity isn't necessarily a bad thing when it comes to teens, the two most common ways impulsivity shows up in adolescent behavior, how to react to impulsive—even dangerous—behavior in a way that won't compound the effects, and how to talk with your child about their impulsive behavior in a way that encourages more critical thinking without shame, or if your child is unwilling to take any risks, encourage a bit more spontaneity.

The movie *We Bought a Zoo,* based on Benjamin Mee's memoir, tells the story of how he and his children coped after losing his wife, their mom, to cancer. (Spoiler: they bought a zoo.) It's a terrific film, and unlike countless family movies I forgot soon after the credits roll, this one stuck with me. I relished the many ways Mee's character, played by Matt Damon, showed his children that life relies on some level of impulsivity to be rewarding. Recounting the story of how he first asked out their mother, Mee says, "You know, sometimes all you need is twenty seconds of insane courage, just literally twenty seconds of embarrassing bravery, and I promise you something great will come of it." The message was aimed at the kids, both in the film and on my couch, but I tried to internalize his pep talk, too.

I'm someone who needs quite a bit of encouragement when it comes to being impulsive. Shortly after I started dating my husband, Travis, we were driving through downtown Charlotte, North Carolina, one evening when a car crossed traffic, careened through a plaza and up the steps of an office building, crashing to a stop only when its front windshield wedged under the stair's metal handrail. Travis pulled the car over immediately, threw it into park, and sprinted up the steps after the car. First on the scene, he assessed the driver's condition and called 911. While I . . . watched. Frozen in the car. What he did was heroic. And impulsive. These two traits have a wonderfully symbiotic relationship, and I'm grateful there are people in this world who embody them.

Unlike my husband, I have an impulsivity handicap. I overthink most things. This is great when I come up with a creative solution to a nagging problem. It's helpful when I'm preparing for a presentation. It's irritating when something basic, like shopping online for a pair of dress pants, spans weeks of revisiting the same websites. And it's never, ever useful during a crisis.

My husband, as you now know, is amazing in a crisis. He's also the most fun on a family vacation. But, he's not so great with a well-planned to-do list on the weekends. "Let's scrap it and go camping instead!" he'll say. And I'll remind him we can't. (The to-do list, after all.) Happily, we've figured out a pretty good balance. He'll slow his roll long enough for me to put together a solid packing list and shop for car snacks, and I'll agree the laundry can wait until we get back home. Sometimes, he heroically and impulsively rescues me from my analysis paralysis. And sometimes, I thoughtfully and patiently rescue him from being woefully ill-prepared. We need and enjoy each other's balance. There's that wonderful symbiosis again.

The point is that we all need a certain amount of impulsivity as well as restraint, and part of growing up is figuring out the right balance of each. Experts in adolescent development often talk about the impulsive nature of the teenage brain, causing many parents to worry about the multitude of ways their adolescents can get into trouble. I encourage you not to be put off by this explanation of brain development, and instead look for opportunities to talk with your tween about *how* to make decisions. Do you slow down and take a breath first? Do you consult someone with experience? Do you make a pros and cons list? Sometimes, in the case of the car accident for example, it's terrific to have quick instincts. Other times, in the absence of being taught how to make thoughtful choices in practical and clear ways, it's not. As you explore ways to talk with your middle schooler about this topic, remember that the goal is to foster a better understanding of what compels your child, and to encourage them to contemplate what kinds of situations require restraint and forethought, and which benefit from spontaneity and bravery.

Impulsivity!

"You keep using that word. I do not think it means what you think it means."

Remember when Inigo Montoya, played by a young and terribly handsome Mandy Patinkin in *The Princess Bride*, questions Vizzini's understanding of his own catchphrase, "Inconceivable!"? I think of this iconic scene every time I witness a disconnect in parent-child communication. They almost always stem from *vocabulary confusion*.

We all have different tolerances for what constitutes impulsive behavior and, therefore, a blurry understanding of what *impulsivity* actually means. Let's begin by getting on the same page about the function and form of impulsivity in an adolescent's life.

Impulsivity isn't simply acting without thinking. More accurately, it's "a form of decision making that is overly sensitive

> Impulsivity isn't simply acting without thinking. More accurately, it's "a form of decision making that is overly sensitive to immediate urges without adequate consideration of consequences." Pause on that. Impulsivity isn't a *lack* of decision making. It's a *form* of decision making.

to immediate urges without adequate consideration of consequences." Pause on that. Impulsivity isn't a *lack* of decision making. It's a *form* of decision making.

What matters isn't whether your child is spontaneous or deliberate, but that over time, they learn to manage their decision making in a way that works for them *and* the people with whom they have important relationships. Try to think about impulsivity as neither intrinsically good nor bad. Your tween will make countless decisions daily, within countless complicated contexts, which means their relationship to impulsivity will be built during a long, slow learning process that will inevitably drive you nuts. When your tween pours all your new, fancy essential oil into a bubble bath without asking (really?!), or gives away the new jacket you just bought them (WTH?!), or sends out invitations to host a friend's birthday party for thirty kids at your house without asking you (#$@&%*!), you will want to scream, pound a stiff drink, pull your hair out, or maybe all of the above. If any or all of those don't help, I recommend you form a close tie with your nearest meditation app, empathetic friend, or therapist for help coping with a kid whose choices makes you crazy. (Not to say that the drink of your choice or pillow-screaming session aren't also fine ways to decompress sometimes, too. But if you need more, don't deny yourself that support.) And remember, these wacky (infuriating) behaviors probably don't reflect the kind of adult your kid will become. Deal with them appropriately by teaching your kid what they should have done and having reasonable and related consequences, but don't freak out too much about your kid's ability to make good decisions longer term.

Impulsiveness takes us by surprise, but you can prepare a little bit with an understanding of how and when it's most likely to show up during adolescence. The most recent research on impulsive behavior among teens provides insight into two types of impulsivity, as well as ages when impulsivity peaks and wanes.

You should be familiar with these two kinds of impulsivity:

1. the kind that comes from an inability to delay gratification

2. the kind that comes from a drive to try new things

Know that the first kind, the impulsive behavior that drives your middle schooler to choose immediate, though lesser, gratification over waiting for a more satisfying reward later, actually declines steadily throughout adolescence. Parents despairing regularly about your tween putting off studying to play video games, or begging for rides to the store every time they have a five-dollar bill burning a hole in their pocket, should remember that, like that Flock of Seagulls haircut you insisted on getting in the eighth grade, this, too, shall be outgrown.

Different from the need for immediate gratification, but still a major reason why teens make rash and irrational decisions, is the drive toward sensation seeking, which does not decline as teens age, but instead spikes for girls at age sixteen and for boys at age nineteen. In other words, the need for instant gratification declines steadily among adolescents as they get older. But the "need for speed," or at least for new and exciting encounters, does not.

Sensation seeking, a term coined in the 1960s by psychology professor and researcher Dr. Marvin Zuckerman, refers to the amount of stimulation a person requires for fresh experiences. In the 1990s, the sensation-seeking scale was modified to reflect a more accurate portrayal of sensation seeking among children and adolescents. New research indicates tween decision making is largely driven by a need to acquire new experiences. This makes sense, given that novel experiences will help adolescents obtain new knowledge, as well as develop and practice new skills, all of which they need to become successful adults. The brain endorses this by sending out a surge of dopamine when it experiences something new. Dopamine directs the development of the prefrontal cortex, the part of the brain that does all the stuff you want your child to be good at, such as risk analysis, problem solving, and critical thinking. So, the idea that we should protect kids from experiencing new things because their brains aren't ready creates a catch-22. Young adolescents *need* more experiences to make their brains more capable of handling new experiences.

When you understand that impulsive decision making is often a response to one of two things: either the inability to delay gratification, or the desire to seek out new sensations, then you can visualize the trajectory each follows throughout adolescence, and you can tailor your expectations to their age and stage, and your conversation to their motivations. Kids do better when they understand what drives their behavior. It's embarrassing to do things that upset other people, and not even know why you did them in the first place. If you explain both kinds of impulsivity to your child, you can help them understand what makes them tick. Then, you can use that as a way to talk about what they might do differently next time.

We've All Been There

As you consider the consequences of your child's poor choices, be aware of how guilt and shame can comingle with impulsivity and risk taking during early adolescence. Psychologists often describe the difference between guilt and shame this way: *Guilt is the feeling that you* did *something bad. Shame is the feeling that you* are *something bad.* Guilt helps us become better, whereas shame paralyzes growth.

Now would be a good time for you to go back to middle school. Take a moment to recall when you did something dumb or dangerous or uncharacteristic. For most of us, the mistakes we made in middle school are still front and center in our minds. The impulsive decisions we made as young people are often closely tied with regret and other uncomfortable emotions, and those kinds of memories—the ones rooted in feeling bad—erode more slowly than happy memories.

I asked the parents in my online parenting group the same question I just asked you. Their replies were quick, plentiful, and insightful. They spanned a full range of experiences, from the funny: "The one that comes to mind is the one my mom *still* mentions, because my siblings and I did it all the time—poured a huge glass of milk only to take a few sips and then let it sit on the counter untouched. Got yelled at for wasting milk. Did it again a million times, seemingly unable to stop and think about how much milk I actually wanted."

To the painful: "I was in eighth grade at a small private school and was being bullied by a powerful, very mean popular girl. I found myself in the bathroom with a marker and started writing 'I hate _____.' A friend of hers walked in and discovered me before I could write her last name (I must have not closed the stall door?) and I lied about who I was writing about. Impulsively said another girl with the same first name who I actually liked. Got in trouble for the whole thing and had to apologize to the girl I liked. I still feel shitty about it."

To the death-defying: "I was bored with some kids from my neighborhood. We made up a game where we sat in a circle on the blacktop, broke the sticks off bottle rockets, and threw them, one at a time, into the circle. You never knew which way it was pointing and basically hoped it would pass between two people and not hit you on the way out."

I was especially moved by a parent who shared a time when she broke a big rule at school and ended her confession with: "It was humiliating, and a little exciting, and I've never told another soul about this until right now!"

Shared stories like these remind us that a full range of impulsivity is a universal part of growing up, and this normal part of being a tween shouldn't fill you with disproportionate concern for your child. All the parents who shared stories in my group grew up to be safe and responsible adults. Even bottle-rocket kid, who is, incidentally, now a police officer.

How You React Matters

When you discover your tween has made a bad decision, whether it's overpouring the milk or graffitiing the bathroom, check yourself before you react. (If it's fireworks as weaponry you stumble onto, by all means, feel free to momentarily lose your mind.) But, if your child isn't in imminent danger, imagine you are twelve again and think of how a parent, teacher, or coach might have reacted to you. What would have worked or backfired? How can you help your child learn from their experience, instead of shutting down? How can you let their own guilt work *for* them, instead of fostering shame that will work *against* them?

Here are some phrases to help you start a conversation that will encourage reflection:

- So, something unexpected has happened. What do you think should happen next?

- What would you do differently next time?

- That was something you *did*, not who you *are*.

- There will always be consequences for your actions. Consequences don't tell you you're a bad person. They just tell you you're human. You should use them to think about whether you need to make changes in your actions next time.

- I can see you feel bad. If I could say anything to make you feel better right now, what would it be? Could you say that to yourself? Is there someone else in this situation who needs to hear from you?

- If you had to guess, would you say this happened because you didn't slow down to think, or because you really wanted to do this? (This is a way to talk about the difference between the inability to delay gratification, and the drive toward sensation seeking/new experiences.)

Impulsive Outbursts

If you have multiple children, no doubt you've been witness to countless arguments between them that inevitably devolve into impulsive outbursts. Let's look at how a conversation about impulsive outbursts might go.

BEGIN peacefully

Parent: *Got a minute? I heard you and Caleb getting loud earlier.*
Kid: *You need to talk to him, not me! It was his fault!*
Parent: *Okay, yes. I plan on talking to him, too. But first, you and me.*

RELATE to your kid

Parent: *Listen, I know he gets on your nerves sometimes.*

Kid: *Sometimes?*

Parent: *You're entitled to all your feelings about having a brother. Being in a family is hard occasionally and we all can relate to feeling overcrowded.*

INTERVIEW to collect data

Parent: *So, this morning when I heard you two, it sounded worse than regular bickering. I thought I might have heard a loud thud . . . ?*

Kid: *Okay, he would not let me in the bathroom and I was going to be late for school. He was taking so long for no reason.*

Parent: *How did it turn into yelling?*

Kid: *I told him he needed to hurry and he called me an idiot and purposefully slowed down in there.*

Parent: *And the thud?*

Kid: [Pause] *I threw my book bag at the door because he wouldn't listen.*

Parent: *Did it work?*

Kid: *Did what work?*

Parent: *Throwing the bag? Did he hurry up after that?*

Kid: *No. But it made me feel better.*

ECHO what you hear

Parent: *So, your main frustration is Caleb being in the bathroom too long makes you late.*

Kid: *And that he slows down on purpose when I nicely ask him to hurry up.*

Parent: *That would be frustrating. You said it made you feel better to throw your bag, but it sounds like what would feel best is if you didn't have to wait for the bathroom at all.*

Kid: *I wish I had my own bathroom!*

FEEDBACK

Parent: *I know. And I know you wish you had more control over Caleb's morning routine and his response to you. I can tell you from experience* *it's almost impossible to make other people act the way you want them to. But there might be some things you can try to give you more control over the situation. Maybe you could get in the bathroom before him, since you get up first. Or you could try talking to him about it when you are both in a good mood. Or you could put your toothbrush in the downstairs bathroom. You can probably come up with some ways of managing the situation even if you can't manage him.*

But let's talk about that book bag. When you chucked it at the door, nothing happened, except that it upset me. What else could have gone wrong?

Kid: *I could have broken something in my bag.*

Parent: *Yes. Or Caleb could have opened the door and you could have broken his nose. Or you could have broken the door. That was pretty impulsive and it didn't make him hurry up, but it sure upset my morning hearing that and worrying what was happening. Next time you're angry with Caleb, I want you to delay your reaction by ten seconds. After a week, see if you can go to fifteen seconds. Then thirty. Your whole life, you're going to come across people who cause problems for you. The best thing you can do is pause before you act out of anger. If you do this, you give yourself time to think of the* best *response, not the* first *response. If you start practicing now, you'll thank yourself when you're great at it in high school.*

Confronting your kids about their fights probably plays out like small-claims court on television. The plaintiff will cry victimization and claim emotional distress, presenting evidence of the defendant's bad character along with their blatant disregard for the rules. The defendant will stand there with a "prove it" smirk. You will long for a gavel to pound and, lacking such a dignified way to silence them, will scream at the top of your lungs to "stop being so petty!!" Each kid will beg for you to make a fast and firm ruling in their favor. Don't. Change the channel from court-room drama to a detective show. Put each suspect in a separate holding area and talk with them about their experience only. Doing this helps you avoid being told "You always take his side!" and gives you the opportunity to help them with personal skill building, instead of deflecting. As a friend's wise therapist once told her, and she lovingly passed on to me: "When it hits the fan with your family, don't rush into a shitstorm. Sit back, detach, and watch the show."

Temptation

I can resist anything except temptation. —Oscar Wilde

Delaying gratification is a skill measurable by time, making it easier to teach than how to withstand the urge to experience new things. You can say, "Wait two minutes before you eat this. It's hot." With the help of any watch or timer, you can say, "Not yet!" keeping your kid from impulsively burning the roof of their mouth. But you can't measure impulsivity driven by sensation seeking, and when things can't be quantified, they're harder to teach. You might say, "Don't do things that could get you in trouble just because they're exciting." Eh. This kind of instruction or advice feels wilted. A better approach is to get as specific as possible.

Imagine, for example, you see a tiny happy face drawn in ink pen on your eighth grader's ankle. It's cute, but sloppy, and you hope it washes off before your family photo shoot this weekend. That night you're in bed on the laptop, and you click the down arrow on search history. Nothing out of the ordinary until near the bottom. You see it and your stomach drops. Last search: Stick-and-poke DIY tattoos.* Just a few seconds into the video, you realize that smiley face is not drawn on and *NOT temporary*! What's your next move?

Let's listen in on how a conversation about this kind of impulsivity might sound. Taking a deep breath, you head to your kid's room and knock on the door.

---

* Stick-and-poke tattoos happen to be a thing where I live, at the moment. This conversation can apply to any trend or challenge that involves bodily harm. It seems there's always a new one popping up—from rubbing an eraser on your arm 'til you bleed or jumping out of a car and dancing at a stoplight to eating suffocating amounts of cinnamon or burning your skin with salt and ice.

BEGIN peacefully

Parent: *Hey, mind if I come in for a second?*

Kid: [Excited to see you] *How come you're still up?!*

Parent: *Couldn't sleep. I have something on my mind. Can we talk?*

Kid: [Nervous now] *Is everything okay?*

RELATE to your kid

Parent: *I hope so. I noticed the smiley face on your ankle this morning and I didn't say anything because I thought it was just pen. But tonight I saw something on the laptop about homemade tattoos, so I wanted to come talk with you about it.*

Kid: *Are you mad? Am I in trouble?*

Parent: *I haven't figured out how I feel yet. I think we have a lot to discuss, though. Can I sit with you in bed and talk?*

[Kid lifts covers to let parent in.]

INTERVIEW to collect data

Parent: *I'm feeling shocked and don't even know where to begin. Can you show me your ankle first?*

Kid: *It's really small. I'm so sorry. I just thought it would be fun and I wanted to try it. Then once I started, I had to finish or it would look dumb.*

Parent: [Biting tongue to stop from saying it looks dumb now] *Do you like it?*

Kid: *Kind of.*

Parent: *How did you do it?*

Kid: *Camryn's sister and her friends do them all the time. So they did them for us.*

Parent: *From what I read, it's permanent.*

Kid: *Well, yes, but they do fade out after a while.*

Parent: *Hmm. So I guess the biggest question is* why? *Can you walk me through this decision?*

Kid: *I kind of like them. And I wanted to see how bad it hurt, because I might get a real tattoo someday. And I don't know. I just know a lot of people who do it and I kind of wanted to try it.*

ECHO what you hear

Parent: *I'm hearing a lot of "kind ofs" and "I don't knows," and I'm not sure if that's because you are worried about getting in trouble, so you're trying to soften this, or because you did this without thinking it through.*
Kid: *I know. I'm not sure what to say.*

FEEDBACK

Parent: *Well, this is a big deal to me. Wanting to try new things is totally fine. But making a choice to do something permanent to your body when you're this age is not. You risk infection, which is my biggest concern. But my other concerns are that you made a decision with permanent consequences that you didn't think through. I don't want you doing this in other ways where you could get seriously hurt.*
Kid: *People can get tattoos removed.*
Parent: *Yes, but that becomes an expensive and painful proposition. Tomorrow, we need to see a doctor to make certain there is no infection. And after that, we will talk a lot more about your decision making on this one. I know you want to experience new things, especially those that feel more grown-up, but this shows me you need some help figuring out what's okay and what's not. For starters, I want you to work on a list of questions you can ask yourself before you decide to try something risky like this. Type them on your phone, then show me when we talk tomorrow. Now try to get some sleep. I love you.*
Kid: *Um, am I in trouble?*
Parent: *I haven't had time to figure out the consequences here, but I can say for now, no going to Camryn's or hanging out with her sister until I do. What I want you to know is that I think this was a bad decision, but I think you're an amazing person. I just want to make sure you are prepared to make better decisions that will keep your body safe and your heart free from too much regret, so that's what we'll work on.*

There's no way a single conversation could solve all the problems this situation brought up, which is why I approach big events like this with a triage approach. In an emergency room triage, the intake nurse will assess who is seen, in what order, based on whether their situation is 1) immediately life threatening, 2) urgent but not life threatening, or 3) less urgent. Applying this methodology to your home, you might establish three similar stages of triage for dealing with the aftermath of teen impulses: 1) immediate threats to health, 2) serious, but less immediate, dangers, and 3) possible complications. This should reduce the pressure to cram everything into your first conversation.

In the case of the DIY tattoo, I'd see the immediate threat to health as twofold: first, a risk of infection, and second, a risk of this happening again right away. In my first conversation, I'd apply a tourniquet, so to speak, by getting a doctor involved to assess any damage (and to be a second voice of reason), and then limiting access to the people who enabled or encouraged this.

Once I'd addressed the immediate crisis, I'd have more time to think. In my follow-up conversation, I'd talk about the serious, but less critical, issues this raises. In this specific situation, I'd want to talk about how my child views their body's autonomy with respect to "everyone else was doing it." I'd listen for any clues to self-esteem and to whether my child might benefit from a therapist. Was the pain from the tattoo a release for emotional pain, for example? I'd also want to talk about the sneakiness of the incident, whether my child thought I really wouldn't notice a homemade tattoo, and whether they thought begging for forgiveness instead of permission indicated this was, in fact, not a good choice to begin with.

Lastly, once the immediate threats were handled, I'd take the time to explore possible complications for the future. Here, I'd focus less on the literal complications of the tattoo (like, "You're gonna regret this weird smiley face thing!") and more on the broader complications (like, "You seem drawn to excitement and I think you may continue to make choices like this if we don't get you involved in something that will fulfill your sense of adventure").

What About the *Other* Kind of Kid?

When I speak at schools, there is almost always one parent who tentatively raises their hand to ask, "Should I be worried if my child *isn't* impulsive?"

Most parents fret over where their child sits on the "normal" scale and upon hearing me talk about the normalcy and necessity of impulsivity and risk taking, the parents of kids who always dot their *i*'s and cross their *t*'s become nervous. Will their child overthink decisions to the point of paralysis? Will they miss opportunities because they aren't willing to jump at them?

What I tell parents is that some kids take risks boldly, in public, and others do so quietly, in private. One is not better, or worse, than the other. Asking to borrow a pencil from the cute kid in class may not look like a crazy-impulsive move, but it can feel like a giant risk to a nervous tween. Don't assume your child isn't impulsive, just because you don't see it. But, if you're worried your child is too rigid, you can encourage impulsivity by trying things like this:

- Model fun: "I just cooked this dinner but, what the heck—let's cover it up and go get ice cream first! Why not?"

- Tell me what to do: Whatever action your kid is debating, change roles. Cast yourself as the main character and ask them to tell you what to do.

- Consider worst-case/best-case scenarios: Ask your kid to imagine the worst thing that could happen if they took a risk. For example, what is the worst-case scenario if you run for class president? What is the worst-case if you don't? What's the best-case scenario if you do? Best-case if you don't?

- Leave it to fate: If making decisions is too overwhelming, put choices in a hat and pull one out.

Conversation Crashers

Keeping in mind that tweens probably feel embarrassed or guilty after they've been caught making an impulsive mistake, the quickest way to derail a conversation on this topic is to take away any shot they have at saving face. A few phrases that might unintentionally do this:

"What were you thinking?!" By nature, impulsivity means not thinking and just going for it. Your child will probably have an impossible time answering this question, so they're likely to go quiet. For better insight, try: "Walk me through what you were feeling as this happened."

"I raised you better than this." Well, it happened, so . . . you did raise someone who did do the thing. If you're hoping to convey disappointment, just say that. Then offer a lifeline. "I'm disappointed that you did this. Where do we go from here? Do you need any guidance from me in making this right?"

"Well, this is going to screw up your chances/plans/future." I understand the need to convey the weight of some mistakes. Saying it like this, though, can be so damning that kids just shut down. Instead of a blanket statement of doom, talk about specifics. Ask what they think this will affect, and fill in the blind spots they're not seeing.

"You're smarter than this. I thought you knew better." This is just a dig at intelligence. Even smart people make bad choices. Even experienced people do, too. Instead, try this: "You're smart. So I don't think this happened because you *couldn't* think this through. I think it happened because you didn't slow down enough to consider the possible outcomes. Tell me how you can do better next time."

In a Hurry? Here's Your Crash Course

- Impulsive behavior gets a bad rap, but impulsivity isn't inherently unhealthy or naughty. Without impulsive people, we'd have fewer heroes and innovators.

- You don't need to squelch your teen's impulsivity, but you should explain it to them and help them figure out which situations benefit from fast action, and which benefit from careful analysis.

- Impulsivity isn't a lack of decision making. It's a form of decision making.

- Impulsivity during adolescence is a result of one of two things: the inability to delay gratification (which gets increasingly better over time), or the drive to try new things (which peaks at around age sixteen for girls, and nineteen for boys).

- Tweens and teens should be given the opportunity to experience new situations independently. The surge of dopamine that comes from "sensation seeking" actually helps the teen brain develop and become capable of handling more complicated experiences.

- There is no need to harbor disproportionate fear for your impulsive tween's safety or future success. Almost all people do impulsive (crazy/dumb) things growing up, and almost all end up totally fine.

- When reacting to your child's impulsive actions, it's okay if you evoke feelings of guilt, but be careful you're not triggering shame. Focus on what they could do differently next time and remind them their actions represent what they did, not who they are.

- Use a triage approach for dealing with the aftermath of teen impulses: 1) immediate threats to health, 2) serious, but less immediate, dangers, and 3) possible complications. Handle anything that falls under the first category immediately and swiftly, but take your time figuring out the rest.

- You can't change your child's personality, but if they overthink things to the point of missing out on opportunities, you can encourage a little flexibility and even impulsivity by showing them how it's done, and rewarding spontaneity.

17

Talking About Helping Others

In this chapter, you'll gain an understanding of why it's so hard for young adolescents to balance other people's best interests with their own—especially when speaking up for someone else may put them at risk, how speaking to your child with empathy translates to their ability to care for others (not to mention the surprising connection between showing empathy and fostering grit), the three essential ways humans need and give help to one another, how gentle conversations about standing up for others can inspire your kids (if you're patient), and how talking to tweens about compromise can bring them back into family holiday traditions as they're starting to pull away.

How proud would you feel if you found out your kid picked up litter when they passed it on the playground, or cleared a path for a classmate in a wheelchair trying to get through a crowded hall, or refused payment after cat sitting for an elderly neighbor?

Incredibly proud! Me, too. Raising good humans includes teaching them to recognize and respond to the needs of others. I want my own kids to care for the earth, their community, their extended family, their friends, and, frankly, me someday. I already rely on my kids to explain lots of things to me, including most often, our TV. If I continue on my current path of obsessing over good TV shows, and tech continues on its current path of dividing and conquering my entertainment through the likes of Netflix, Hulu, Amazon, YouTube, Disney+, and Apple TV, my beloved hobby is going to be outpaced by my ability to find it. Of course, I want my kids to be strong and generous warriors for social justice. I just don't think that needs to be mutually exclusive with making sure, in my old age, I am properly logged in to watch my stories on my Holographic Content-a-Vision from my floating BarcaLounger.

Is it easier to imagine a floating BarcaLounger than this selfless, future adult of yours?

It can be difficult, especially because at this age your kid's energy is trained on the extremely specific and personal affronts they alone face, like how you could have possibly forgotten to pick up pizza bagels at the store again, or why you can't skip your work thing to pick them up early from their friend's because it stopped being fun like ten minutes ago.

How do you begin guiding your child's thoughts away from their own needs, toward having a positive effect on others? This chapter will give you some ideas to open your child's eyes to the importance of, and satisfaction in, service over selfishness.

Raising a Prosocial Person

Prosocial behavior is when you do something for the benefit of others, not for personal reward. Neat, but . . . when it feels like a Herculean feat to get your middle schooler to acknowledge your tenth request to take their junk pile from the bottom of the stairs to their bedroom, it's kind of hard to imagine inspiring them to make the world a better place.

Should you just wait until they've gotten past the "me, me, me" phase to point out the effect they can be having on "us, us, us"?

The answer is: "sort of, but not really."

The early adolescent social ocean is exhausting, complicated, unpredictable, and, at times, vicious. You can teach your kid how to swim, tell them how far out to go or when to stay on the sand because the waves are just too big, and keep a watchful eye from the shore, but there will still be times when someone plays too rough, or they get caught in a riptide, and they will forget all you've told them. Though we have high hopes our kids will be their best selves when they are wading into their teenage years, we can't expect them to handle the torrent of this new environment without making impulsive decisions and big mistakes. And while we want our kids to be kind and courageous on behalf of others, often they're just too preoccupied with treading water to stay afloat that they don't have the presence of mind or wherewithal to simultaneously throw someone else a life preserver.

> As you continue to support your child, you'll strengthen their ability to think outside of themselves. Developing compassion for others starts with self-kindness.

Kids can be prosocial when they feel confident, safe, and secure themselves, and most early adolescents don't feel this way. As you continue to support your child, you'll strengthen their ability to think outside of themselves. Developing compassion for others starts with self-kindness. These years will feel like a very self-focused, self-indulgent time in your child's life, but fighting that won't help. Instead, nurture their ability to take care of themselves as the first step in being able to care for others.

The Case for Empathy

I recently polled 312 parents of adolescents, asking them to identify which of the following five characteristics they most want their kid to exhibit: empathy, grit, respect, honesty, or gratitude. The poll instructions explained that parents might want their kids to embody all of these traits, but to identity the one trait that was most important; 55 percent chose empathy, 28 percent chose grit, 9 percent chose gratitude, 6 percent chose honesty, and 2 percent chose respect.

If you're like the majority of parents I polled who chose empathy as the most important trait, you may be interested to learn that empathy isn't inborn. It's a learned skill that has to be taught. But how?

Empathy may seem like an easy thing to demonstrate to your child. You might initiate a dinner discussion about the plight of the homeless, or raise money for St. Jude Children's Research Hospital, or drop off baked goods at an assisted living center. These are wonderful things to discuss and do. Keep in mind that if this is your approach, a young person can begin to associate empathy with people who are "other." I sometimes hear parents say that if a kid is acting ungrateful or privileged, the solution is to take them to volunteer at a homeless shelter so they will realize how good they have it. Yes, it's a wonderful thing to volunteer at a homeless shelter. But doing it to show your kid how good they have it feels like crisis tourism. It creates an "us" and "them" mentality about helping. Perhaps this "othering" is even a superstitious way of guarding against misfortune. "This wouldn't happen to me because I'm not like those people." In this way, we sympathize with someone's "hard luck" without empathizing with their full experience.

This kind of distance is the enemy of empathy, and it's not limited to people who feel foreign to us. Within the microsocieties of our families, it can be hard to make room for empathy when so many other emotions (bitterness, resentment, jealousy, and so on) take up space. If you are raising siblings, consider how hard it can be to convince one kid to see a problem from the other's point of view. When it comes to developing empathy, I hope parents will continue to push their kids outside of their comfort zones and show them they are more alike than different from others, despite their circumstances. I also hope they will begin with modeling hyperlocal empathy by listening to, and compromising with, the people with whom they share a bathroom, refrigerator, or Xbox.

Recently, I watched an online discussion unfold around a common parenting dilemma that I thought tied pretty tightly to empathy development: when to let a kid quit an activity. Amy's twelve-year-old daughter, Rachel, begged for horseback-riding lessons, and Amy agreed to buy a package of lessons. Five lessons into the ten-lesson package, Rachel started making excuses about why she couldn't go and, after much prying, admitted to her mom that she wanted to quit. Amy was angry because she'd shelled out the money. Rachel thought she'd like riding, but didn't. She was overwhelmed and nervous on the horse. What to do?

Parents online chimed in quickly, with approximately 95 percent of them urging Amy to make her daughter finish.

"How will she learn to finish what she starts?"

"It's called *commitment*."

"She'll never understand financial sacrifice if you let her quit."

But I tend to think about money already spent like food served on a plate. You don't need to be a member of the clean-plate club to have gotten what you need out of a meal. You also don't have to finish an activity just because you paid for it. I can't even count the number of movies I had to leave with my kids when they were little because they couldn't sit still, or they promised they could handle it but then they got scared, or they puked midway through with a stomach bug. *You don't always get what you paid for with kids.*

Money aside, the concern with this scenario seems to be teaching perseverance. How can Amy teach Rachel to find the resolve and courage she needs to finish what she started? It helps to think of middle school like a buffet. It's not necessarily about finishing everything, but bravely trying new flavors. Some kids, when they go out to eat, order the butter noodles or chicken tenders without fail. They're afraid of being stuck with something new in case it turns out to be inedible. But in early adolescence, when kids start the job of figuring out their own personal likes and dislikes (apart from what their parents have routinely chosen for them), it's time to belly up to the buffet. They need to try a whole bunch of little bites of new things to figure out what they like without the pressure of having to eat a heaping plate of something they may hate. Maybe those bites look like auditioning for a play, or wearing a bold outfit, or joining a new club. If kids are told they have to finish everything they start, that can dissuade them from trying anything new.

That said, kids should also develop the ability to push through challenges. So how do parents balance these seemingly conflicting notions of developing grit and taking new risks? I tend to think of grit as growing out of an accumulation of experiences, and as a byproduct of learning, again—over time, that you can trust yourself in challenging circumstances. How do you learn to trust yourself? By tuning in to your inner voice and having that validated by the people you trust. Grit grows best when fertilized with empathy.

If Amy's only message is "you have to finish what you started," Rachel may hear that she can't trust her instincts. She may find that confusing later when she's in an uncomfortable situation and doesn't know how to tune in to her inner voice. Does she take the dare to jump off the bridge into the river below? They hiked all this way . . . Or does she trust her gut? Kids need to learn grit, but they also need to hear from us that they can stop something when they realize it doesn't feel safe or right.

Whether your kid is struggling with an elective activity, a class at school, or a fight with a friend, *begin with empathy*. "That sounds like a tough situation. I'm sorry you're going through this. How can I support you?" This will show your child how to check in with their emotions and find a way to cope. My suggestion would be to then listen to them share the details of what's hard and to validate those emotions. Then ask when in the past they have done something hard and surprised themselves. Remind your kid how hard they worked to learn to tie their shoes, or ride a bike, or get to the next level in Minecraft. Then ask how they pushed through when it got hardest. What special talents or skills can they rely on when things get hard? Sometimes this kind of coaching will encourage your kid to keep trying. Sometimes they will quit anyway.

> Grit grows best when fertilized with empathy. . . . Kids need to learn grit, but they also need to hear from us that they can stop something when they realize it doesn't feel safe or right.

I can't know for sure whether letting Rachel drop the lessons would teach her a valuable lesson that she has agency over what causes her discomfort, or if making her continue would teach her a different but also valuable lesson that sometimes things become more comfortable when we stick them out. I do know for sure, whatever Amy decides, the key will be to lead with empathy and not anger, so the "lesson behind the lesson" is that when someone is struggling, we offer our support. In this way, empathy becomes the stone that grinds grit to its sharpest.

Types of Help

Dr. Kristen Dunfield, a researcher into prosocial behavior at Concordia University in Canada, has created a categorization of basic human needs and prosocial behavior. People generally need three types of help:

1. Instrumental need: assisting someone with an action they can't do on their own. This might look like holding open the door for someone when their arms are full.

2. Unmet material desire need: realizing that not everyone has the same resources and trying to rectify the distribution. This could mean making sure each person has gotten a slice of pizza before piling your plate full.

3. Emotional distress need: recognizing when someone is experiencing distressing emotions and attempting to soothe them. This might look like sitting next to your child when they're stressing out over a project and offering encouragement.

In response to these three categories of need, Dunfield has identified that the three ways to be prosocial are helping, sharing, and comforting.

For our own kids to grow up wanting to help others beyond themselves, first their family, then their friends, and then their community, they need to identify what it feels like to be on the receiving end of prosocial acts. Parents who model prosocial behavior at home, then out into the world more broadly, set kids up to be increasingly prosocial themselves. We do this by supporting kids as they try to do new things for themselves, sharing our resources with them (food, clothing, and shelter are nonnegotiable, but this one is also about the little acts of sacrifice, such as taking off your jacket and passing it across the booth at dinner when you see your kid is cold), and recognizing their emotional distress and offering your support. You will have plenty of opportunities to practice that last one during the middle school years.

Raising Upstanders, Eventually

Parents tell me all the time they hope their children will be kind to other kids at school, especially to kids who most need social support. Schools, too, have embraced the importance of encouraging kids to be *upstanders*, not bystanders, when they see a classmate being picked on. An upstander is someone who speaks up or intervenes when someone else is being targeted, as opposed to a bystander who, obviously, just stands by.

This emphasis on, and appreciation for, a child's whole experience at school is a fairly recent and welcome approach to education. I love the intention behind encouraging kids to stick up for others who are targeted or disenfranchised, but we also need to recognize, out loud, to our kids, that this is not as simple as it seems. For one, kids this age worry a lot about drawing the anger of the aggressor in their direction, causing the bully to turn on them either through physical retaliation or social retribution. For another, bullying isn't usually done right out in the open. When it's subtle, manipulative, and sneaky, a kid can't always tell when to step in.

Let's look at how a conversation on this topic might go.

BEGIN peacefully

Parent: *Can I ask you for your thoughts on something? There is always a lot of talk in the news about bullying and I'm curious if you think it's a problem at your school, or if it's being hyped up.*

Kid: *I think it depends. It can be a big problem for some kids. But not everyone gets bullied.*

Parent: *Do your teachers talk about it? Have you ever heard of the term* upstander, *for instance?*

Kid: *We have had assemblies, but our teachers don't really talk about it. But I know an upstander is supposed to stick up for the person.*

RELATE to your kid

Parent: *Yep. When I was your age, people talked about bullies differently than they do today. There wasn't even the concept of an upstander. I think it would be hard to stand up for someone, even if you know it's the right thing to do because if someone is a jerk, you don't know if you'll make it worse for yourself by saying something.*

Kid: *It's more that you don't see it happening. Usually when someone is being mean, it's not face to face, or it's not in front of a crowd.*

Parent: *That's such a good point.*

INTERVIEW to collect data

Parent: *So how do you see kids being treated badly at school?*

Kid: *Sometimes people make bad jokes about someone. But kids usually laugh that off. Like if someone calls another kid a name, no one would say, "Hey! Stop that!" You just kind of laugh it off and then they stop.*

Parent: *There can be advantages to not giving someone the reaction they want, not giving them the satisfaction of hurting you. Do you think laughing when someone makes a mean joke encourages them to keep making those jokes?*

Kid: *Probably.*

Parent: *What do you think you would do if you heard someone make fun of someone's weight, for example?*

Kid: *I feel like ignoring it is probably the best idea. Not laughing is good.*

Parent: *What about when it's not in person. Do you ever see people being ganged up on online? Like in a group text or on social media?*

Kid: *You sometimes see a mean comment on someone's post, like "This is dumb," but then someone would probably jump in and say, "This is not dumb." And then other people would add, "You're dumb" to the person who wrote the first thing.*

Parent: *So when it's online and public—people chime in. What about when it's a group text or something?*

Kid: *No one is going to say something mean to someone on the text. They would just start a side group without that person.*

Parent: *Oh, so you wouldn't know if someone was saying bad things about you on a group text because you wouldn't be included.*

Kid: *Right. Unless someone told them about it later.*
Parent: *Does that happen?*
Kid: *Sometimes.*

ECHO what you hear

Parent: *It sounds so much more complicated than when I was in middle school. Actually, we called it junior high. It sounds hard to know when it's safe to say something.*
Kid: *Yeah.*

FEEDBACK

Parent: *Thanks for talking with me about this. I worry about kids who are left out, but I also know it's hard to know how to support them.*

Just so you know, I hope you, and everyone in our family, will help people when they're hurting. If you see a kid at school who is being left out or teased, and you just aren't sure what to do, you can talk with me about it. I may not have the answer either, but I can help you think it through. What I do know is that if no one says anything, the bad behavior doesn't stop. And if just one person says something that lets people know what's happening isn't okay, more people always join in.

And look, when it comes to helping the kids around you, you don't have to do big, heroic things. You can smile at the kid you think looks lonely. If you hear someone making a mean joke and you're not comfortable speaking up right then, you can go up to the kid they were making fun of later, and say, "Hey, that wasn't right what that person did. Don't listen to them." If people are talking behind someone's back on a group text, you can say, "We shouldn't talk behind their back," and then change the subject. It takes one person to change the conversation and I think that person could be you.

Look for incremental ways your child can practice being an up-stander. It may not happen in a dramatic fashion—although some older teens tend to do better at grand gestures after they've gotten some experience under their belts. In the meantime, look for more manageable ways kids can step up to help others with tasks, share resources, and provide emotional comfort to those in need.

The Holiday Blues

The topic of helping others probably comes up during the holidays more than any other time of year. Many of us wrestle with the mixed messages (and mixed feelings) around materialism and spirituality, community and family, wish lists and giving back. I felt this confusion heighten to holiday malaise when my kids were in middle school.

I could tell my tweens still craved being wowed, but nothing quite did it anymore, not the presents, not the singing bears downtown, and not co-zying up to watch holiday specials in our PJs. As a parent, this time can feel lonely, but take heart that in high school your kids will come back around. In the meantime, don't stop all the lovely traditions and baking and Charlie Brown specials. As your older teens reminisce, you'll find out they're glad you made them stick certain traditions out.

One of my favorite quotes about being a parent comes from Claire Dunphy on *Modern Family*: "Raising a kid is like sending a rocket ship to the moon. You spend the early years in constant contact, and then one day around the teenage years, they go around the dark side and they're gone. And all you can do is wait for that faint signal that says they're coming back." The holidays in middle school feel like your kids have traveled out of range, but how you talk with them about their voyage can make them seem closer than you first thought.

This sample conversation can be modified to your holiday or family traditions, whether Christmas, Hanukkah, Kwanza, Diwali, Festivus, or however you celebrate family and community.

BEGIN peacefully

Parent: *I was checking the calendar and you get out for winter break on the twentieth this year.*
Kid: *I can't wait!*

Parent: *Me, too! It will be fun to have some time off together.*

Kid: *Are we doing anything fun?*

RELATE to your kid

Parent: *Well, I hope so. I guess we should talk about what would be fun for the family this year.*

Kid: *Can we go skiing?*

Parent: *That would be fun, but it's also expensive and not something we can make happen this year. I'd love to find some other things that each of us would like to do. Let's start with you.*

INTERVIEW to collect data

Parent: *Besides skiing, are there other things you can think of that would make this holiday fun?*

Kid: *I don't want to just sit around the house. I want to do something active, like skiing. Can we just try to go?*

Parents: *I understand that it's important for you to be active. Should I look up some less-expensive options that I think you'd enjoy? Maybe we can get a group to go sledding and drive somewhere with better hills? Or go tubing one day?*

Kid: *Yeah, can we do that?*

Parent: *I'll look into it! Will you help me plan out a calendar for the break so everyone gets to pick an activity? You probably don't want me to do it by myself, because then you get less of a say in it. I want to bake cookies as a family. You want to sled or tube. We can see what everyone else wants to do and make a schedule.*

Kid: *No, let's not bake cookies. It takes too long. Can we just buy them?*

Parent: *If I said yes to only what you want to do and not what me, your dad, or your sister want, it wouldn't be fair.*

So let's talk about some of the traditions we usually do at the holidays. We don't have to do them all. But the ones that are most important—for me, it's cookies—we do have to keep. Which ones do you like the most?

Kid: *Presents, obviously. And I like when we make the paper chain of days counting down to the big day.*

Parent: *Funny—that's one I'd skip! But I won't, since I know it's special to you.*

Kid: *But I really, really think it's embarrassing to get our picture taken in matching pajamas. Can we please not do that? It's so embarrassing.*

Parent: *Oof. That's one I love. But . . . since I love the cookie activity more, I will take the matching outfits off the table this year. I'll do that if you agree to be flexible with me, too, on some things.*

Kid: *Yes!*

Parent: *So we have two weeks off. In addition to making our list of favorite fun activities over break, we should also think of something we can do as a family to give back to others. There will be lots of people who can use help this time of year. So maybe start thinking about what area would be good for us to focus on: helping people who need warm clothes or food, helping kids who might not get presents, helping elderly people who need companionship . . . you tell me which one sort of gets you in the heart the most and that's where we'll focus.*

Kid: *Right away, the saddest one to me is the kids not getting gifts.*

ECHO what you hear

Parent: *That's so kind. It sounds like we have a good place to start then. As a family, we will help make sure some kids get gifts who otherwise wouldn't. And as a family, we'll also come up with a list of each person's favorite activity to do this break, and if it's in the budget, each person can claim that activity. Does that sound good?*

Kid: *Yes, can I start looking up places to go tubing?*

FEEDBACK

Parent: *Of course! That would be helpful. Before you do, I want to say one more thing to help set your expectations for this year. The holidays are probably going to feel different to you for the next couple years because you're growing up. I don't want it to take you by surprise. I've heard this is what happens at this age and it's totally normal. You probably won't feel the same crazy excitement you did when you were little and that can be disappointing at first. Have you ever seen a seven-year-old flip out over a* *cheap plastic toy? Or some candy? It's hard to carry that same excitement over when you're eleven or twelve or thirteen. But, here's the good news— you have me, and a loving family, and we will continue to find ways to feel the magic of the holidays. We'll carry on some traditions and we'll make some new ones. You'll start to take on the role of making magic for other people, like the kids we'll buy presents for, and that's amazing. And you'll start doing other, more grown-up things and that's fun, too. Like, if you want to go gift shopping with friends and not a parent, you can do that this year. Gifts are fun. And you'll always get them. But they'll start to feel less and less magical and the good feeling you get from having a positive effect on others will* eventually *start to make you feel even better than toys.*

It's hard on parents when kids don't feel the magic anymore. But don't forget, it's hard on kids, too. You can soften the family mood of resentment and disappointment by acknowledging that things are changing and appreciating how that can be uncomfortable, while also recognizing that change can open the door for fresh adventures and gratitude to enter.

Conversation Crashers

"I expect you to do the right thing." Your kid's social life happens in a nuanced environment. Often, things aren't black and white, and even when your child senses someone is being treated badly, the right response isn't immediately clear. There's nothing wrong with setting expectations that your child find ways to help others, but it's the "how" that trips kids up. Instead, acknowledge the difficulty of being a helper, and invite your kid to talk with you or a trusted member of your village, such as a neighbor, relative, or family friend, when they need help figuring out what to do. So often, kids keep these stories from us because they're afraid we won't understand, or that we'll make them do something embarrassing to help. Assure them you are there to listen and, if they like, suggest ideas, but not to enforce actions.

"You need to start acting more grateful!" I am certain I've said a version of this a hundred times, and a hundred times it did not make my child more grateful. Not once did they have an epiphany and say, "Oh you're right, Mom. I was thinking selfishly." It's hard to fill someone else's bucket when you feel your own needs haven't been met. When your child is being ungrateful, try asking, "What do you need most right now?" When they tell you, acknowledge it. Then state what you need most. Then ask how you can both get your needs met. What compromises can be made on both sides? This is one way to get your child to think beyond their own needs.

"Try thinking of someone else for a change." Unless your child has always been remarkably self-centered, this is probably less of a long-term character flaw and more of a stage they're passing through. It helps to recognize that they are going to have a few years of extraordinarily self-focused behavior as part of the growing-up process. Rather than pointing out their shortcomings in this area, work hard to find the moments when they do something for someone else, and praise them for that. "It was a huge help to me when you brought down your laundry from your room. Thank you for saving me the trip because my back has been hurting. You're a thoughtful person." Yes, it's laying it on a bit thick, but tweens respond well to, and grow from, your praise, whereas they shut down to criticism.

Being a contributor might not come naturally during early adolescence, but by later high school, if you've modeled empathy toward your child's own problems, given them the chance to collaborate with you on problem solving at home, and arranged for opportunities where they can have some say in how you support people outside of your family, your teen will be ready to step into a bigger role in helping others. This is how they develop the trifecta of emotional intelligence, resolve, and courage needed to advocate not just for themselves, but for others who need that support.

In a Hurry? Here's Your Crash Course

- We all want to raise prosocial kids (kids who do things for the benefit of others, not just themselves). Young adolescents are naturally self-centered (that's okay!), but it means sometimes they lack the capacity to think outside themselves. This gets better as they grow up.

- Work on developing empathy to get kids thinking outside themselves. Focus on the three ways we build prosocial behavior: helping, sharing, and comforting.

- Be careful not to "other" people who need help. Avoid using people's misfortune to make your child feel grateful.

- Empathy ties closely with grit. Grit, the ability to trust yourself to get through challenges, is learned by tuning into your inner voice. That voice is nurtured through parental empathy.

- Being an upstander, someone who sticks up for someone else, is not as easy or straightforward as it sounds. Start with baby steps. If your child isn't comfortable confronting a bully, they can privately say something kind to the target. With practice, they'll be able to do and say more.

- Holidays with young adolescents always bring up feelings of loneliness for parents and a loss of "magic" for tweens. Try negotiating on important traditions with your tween, and be open to new ways they can create the magic for others.

Now What?

At the beginning of this book, I described your experience reading this as a kind of Choose Your Own Adventure. Now that you're done reading, I hope you'll take that to heart again as you consider the days and years ahead. The later years of high school are when teens settle into more comfortable friendships, identify new activities they find interesting, get jobs, engage in more community events, and begin to plan seriously for independence. They'll talk with you about these things, if you've shown yourself to be nonjudgmental, supportive of their decision making, and interested in their thoughts.

Some things to keep in mind as you venture forward:

Perfect, as they say, is the enemy of good. When my children were little and they spilled water on their shirt or accidentally knocked over a block tower, I taught them to shrug and repeat a mantra we'd all do well to say more often: "Oh, well!"

Did your child only make it through half a conversation before they walked out on you? Oh, well!

Did you hope your child would open up more, but they only gave one-word answers? Oh, well!

Did you expect to be better at this, then found yourself sounding robotic or unable to find the right words? Oh, well!

These conversations are not a test you or your child need to pass. They are a practice, and much like the practice of yoga, force is the enemy of progress. Take pride in baby steps. Allow your relationship to gradually and comfortably bend to a new shape. One day, without realizing exactly when it happened, you'll realize you've begun having good conversations together. Just keep talking, and more importantly, keep listening.

In the meantime, tune your ear inward, too. As your child begins to prioritize people and interests outside of you, it's time for you to start listening to your own needs and wishes. Rediscover old hobbies or new interests. Connect with your friends or partner. Pay attention to the things you enjoy outside of being a parent. Think of all the fun things you'll have to talk about.

Finally, if you've enjoyed what you read here, we can continue our conversation, too. You can find me in my private Facebook group, Less Stressed Middle School Parents, or on my public page, Author Michelle Icard. I hope to see you there.

Small Talk Conversation Starters

Getting to know someone better through small talk can be a fun, productive, and meaningful way to forge closer ties. Below are questions and conversation prompts you can use to have quick, entertaining, and sometimes revelatory chats with your kids. In addition to the fun prompts, I've also included a section on preferences. As you prepare for your changing parent-child dynamic, it will be helpful to reestablish preferences around handling conflicts, emotions, and expectations.

Parent to Child:

- Given where we live, what do you think will be your first job?
- If you were giving a tour of your school to a new student, what part of the school would impress them and what part would you just skip?
- What do your friends like about coming to our house and what do you like about going to theirs?
- Which song would most kids get hyped up for if it came blaring over the loudspeaker during lunch?

Child to Parent:

- What was your first job? What was your worst job?
- What was your best subject in high school? And/or what was your college major and why did you pick it?
- What is something cool you did before I was born?
- What is something your parents could have done better? What is something they did well?

Parent to Child and Child to Parent:

- If you could spend time with anyone outside of our family, who would it be?
- What is something that makes you laugh, but probably shouldn't?
- What are you the best at in our family?
- What do you wish your friends would do more of?
- If you suddenly had a free day tomorrow with zero responsibilities, what would you do?
- What's your least favorite chore?
- What was the most recent scary thing you saw on TV or read in a book?
- What's something about our house that maybe only you know?
- If you could redesign one thing about our town, what would you change?
- What famous person do people say you look like?
- If you won a contest and got to meet a mystery celebrity, who would you be wishing for? Who would you be hoping against?
- Think of the people you spend time with outside of our family. If you could pick one to be more like, who would it be and why?

Preferences

- When something good happens to you, do you like a lot or a little attention? Is it different depending on where it happens? (In public versus home, for example.)
- When you feel sad, do you want me to check on you or leave you alone?
- When you've had a hard day, what could I do to make it easier?
- When I appreciate something you've done, how would you like me to let you know? A hug, high five, nice text, in-person compliment, or expensive gift and lavish vacation?
- When I want to brag about you, who can I tell? Just family, certain friends, the whole world on social media?
- When we've had an argument, do you prefer to talk about it right afterward or later? How much later?
- When I need you to do something, do you want me to tell you or write it down for you?
- When we need to talk about a problem, do you want to do it in your room, in my room, in the car, or somewhere else?
- When you have friends over, how much do you want me to talk with them?

Endnotes

Chapter 1

"Suicide rates have risen"

Sally C. Curtin et al., "Increase in Suicide in the United States, 1999–2014," NCHS Data Brief, no. 241 (April 2016), https://www.cdc.gov/nchs/products/databriefs/db241.htm

"By age fifteen"

Substance Abuse & Mental Health Data Archive, "National Survey on Drug Use and Health 2018." Accessed February 22, 2014, https://www.datafiles.samhsa.gov/study-dataset/national-survey-drug-use-and-health-2018-nsduh-2018-ds0001-nid18758

"Middle schoolers who tried vaping"

News Release, "Results from 2018 National Youth Tobacco Survey Show Dramatic Increase in E-Cigarette Use Among Youth over Past Year," U.S. Food and Drug Administration, November 15, 2018, https://www.fda.gov/NewsEvents/Newsroom/PressAnnouncements/ucm625917.htm

"Diagnoses of clinical depression in adolescents"

R. Mojtabai, M. Olfson, B. Han, National Trends in the Prevalence and Treatment of Depression in Adolescents and Young Adults," Pediatrics 2016; doi: 10.1542/peds.2016–1878

"A study of males"

Stephanie Burnett et al., "Adolescents' Heightened Risk-Seeking in a Probabilistic Gambling Task," *Cognitive Development* 25, no. 2 (April 2010): 183–96, https://www.ncbi.nlm.nih.gov/pmc/articles/PMC2896475/

Chapter 6
"For the 1 percent of you"
A. C. Hartl et al., "A Survival Analysis of Adolescent Friendships: The Downside of Dissimilarity," *Psychological Science* 26, no. 8 (August 2015): 1304–15, https://www.ncbi.nlm.nih.gov/pubmed/26187246

Chapter 7
"A 2010 survey of 1,500 CEOs"
IBM Institute for Business Value, *Redefining Competition: Insights from the Global C-suite Study—The CEO Perspective* (Somers, NY: IBM Global Business Services, 2016), https://www.ibm.com/downloads/cas/L5QQOADW

Chapter 8
"According to a 2010 study"
Kristen G. Anderson and Sandra A. Brown, "Middle School Drinking: Who, Where, and When," *Journal of Child and Adolescent Substance Abuse* 20, no. 1 (2010): 48–62, https://www.ncbi.nlm.nih.gov/pmc/articles/PMC4543295/
"While we were enjoying"
Kathleen A. Ethier et al., "Sexual Intercourse Among High School Students: 29 States and United States Overall, 2005–2015," *Weekly* 66, no. 5152 (January 5, 2018): 1393–97, https://www.cdc.gov/mmwr/volumes/66/wr/mm665152a1.htm
"A 2016 study reported"
E-Cigarette Use Among Youth and Young Adults: A Report of the Surgeon General (Rockville, MD: U.S. Department of Health and Human Services, 2016), https://e-cigarettes.surgeongeneral.gov/documents/2016_SGR_Exec_Summ_508.pdf
"I first wrote this chapter"
"Outbreak of Lung Injury Associated with the Use of E-Cigarette, or Vaping, Products," Centers for Disease Control and Prevention, https://www.cdc.gov/tobacco/basic_information/e-cigarettes/severe-lung-disease.html
"Research has found that"
P. L. Kerr et al., "Nonsuicidal Self-Injury: A Review of Current Research

for Family Medicine and Primary Care Physicians," *Journal of the American Board of Family Medicine* 23, no. 2 (March–April 2010): 240–59, https://www.ncbi.nlm.nih.gov/pubmed/20207935; and John Peterson et al., "Nonsuicidal Self-Injury in Adolescents," *Psychiatry* 5, no. 11 (November 2008): 20–26, http://www.ncbi.nlm.nih.gov/pmc /articles/PMC2695720/

"Talk of suicide is another big"
"10 Leading Causes of Death by Age Group, United States—2016," National Center for Injury Prevention and Control, https://www.cdc.gov /injury/wisqars/pdf/leading_causes_of_death_by_age_group_2016 –508.pdf

"In other words, you can"
T. Dazzi et al., "Does Asking About Suicide and Related Behaviours Induce Suicidal Ideation? What Is the Evidence?," *Psychological Medicine* 44, no. 16 (December 2014): 3361–63, https://www.ncbi.nlm.nih.gov /pubmed/24998511

Chapter 9

"A 2017 study out of Dartmouth"
"Study: Teens' View of Fairness Shifts as Brain Develops," Dartmouth College Office of Communications, September 20, 2017, https://news .dartmouth.edu/news/2017/09/study-teens-view-fairness-shifts-brain -develops

Chapter 10

"The Journal of Emergency Medicine"
Gary Smith, "Knife-Related Injuries Treated in United States Emergency Departments, 1990–2008," *Journal of Emergency Medicine* 45, no. 3 (September 2013): 315–23, https://www.ncbi.nlm.nih.gov /pubmed/23849364

"Common Sense Media has published"
Technology Addiction: Concern, Controversy, and Finding Balance (San Francisco, CA: Common Sense, 2016), https://www.commonsense media.org/sites/default/files/uploads/research/csm_2016_technology _addiction_research_brief_1.pdf

Chapter 11

"A 2017 study out of"

Paul Green Jr., Francesca Gino, and Bradley Staats, "Shopping for Confirmation: How Disconfirming Feedback Shapes Social Networks," Harvard Business School, Working Paper No. 18–028 (September 15, 2017), https://www.hbs.edu/faculty/Publication%20Files/18–028 _5efa4295-edc1–4fac-bef5–0111064c9e08.pdf.

Chapter 12

"More accurately, people who"

Walter Kaye, "Neurobiology of Anorexia and Bulimia Nervosa," *Physiology and Behavior* 94, no. 1 (April 22, 2008): 121–35, https://www.ncbi .nlm.nih.gov/pmc/articles/PMC2601682/; and Suzanne N. Haber et al., "Reward-Related Cortical Inputs Define a Large Striatal Region in Primates That Interface with Associative Cortical Connections, Providing a Substrate for Incentive-Based Learning," *Journal of Neuroscience* 26, no. 32 (August 9, 2006): 8368–76, https://www.ncbi.nlm.nih.gov /pubmed/16899732

Chapter 13

"Speaking of survival, a recent"

Report on the Economic Well-Being of U.S. Households in 2018 (Washington, D.C.: Board of Governors of the Federal Reserve System, May 2019), https://www.federalreserve.gov/publications/files/2018 -report-economic-well-being-us-households-201905.pdf

"Shine a light on"

William A. Rothenberg et al., "Grateful Parents Raising Grateful Children: Niche Selection and the Socialization of Child Gratitude," *Applied Developmental Science* 21, no. 2 (2017): 106–20, https://www.ncbi.nlm .nih.gov/pubmed/28943753

"Gratitude is also tied"

Hannah Reckart et al., "A Preliminary Study of the Origins of Early Adolescents' Gratitude Differences," *Personality and Individual Differences* 116 (October 1, 2017): 44–50, https://www.researchgate .net/publication/316356012_A_preliminary_study_of_the_origins_of _early_adolescents'_gratitude_differences

"The average person sees"
Louise Story, "Anywhere the Eye Can See, It's Likely to See an Ad," *New York Times,* January 15, 2007, https://www.nytimes.com/2007/01/15/business/media/15everywhere.html

Chapter 14

"It turns out, 19 percent"
Press Release, "Half of All Teens Feel Uncomfortable Talking to Their Parents About Sex While Only 19 Percent of Parents Feel the Same, New Survey Shows," Planned Parenthood, January 30, 2014, https://www.plannedparenthood.org/about-us/newsroom/press-releases/half-all-teens-feel-uncomfortable-talking-their-parents-about-sex-while-only-19-percent-parents

"A recent study found"
Amanda Holman and Jody Koenig Kellas, " 'Say Something Instead of Nothing' ": Adolescents' Perceptions of Memorable Conversations About Sex-Related Topics with Their Parents," *Communication Monographs* 85, no. 3 (2018), https://nca.tandfonline.com/doi/full/10.1080/0363377521.2018.1426870

"There is, however, research"
Michele Ybarra and Kimberly Mitchell, "Exposure to Internet Pornography Among Children and Adolescents: A National Survey," *Cyberpsychology and Behavior* 8, no. 5 (October 2005): 473–86, https://www.ncbi.nlm.nih.gov/pubmed/16232040

"Having a school that creates"
"Lesbian, Gay, Bisexual, and Transgender Health," Centers for Disease Control and Prevention, https://www.cdc.gov/lgbthealth/youth.htm

"The CDC cites a"
Laura Kann et al., "Sexual Identity, Sex of Sexual Contacts, and Health-Related Behaviors Among Students in Grades 9–12—United States and Selected Sites," *MMWR Surveillance Summaries* 65, no. 9 (August 12, 2016): 1–202, https://www.cdc.gov/mmwr/volumes/65/ss/pdfs/ss6509.pdf

Chapter 15

"According to a study conducted"

Lene Arnett Jensen, "The Right to Do Wrong: Lying to Parents Among Adolescents and Emerging Adults," *Journal of Youth and Adolescence* 33, no. 2 (April 2004): 101–12, http://www.jeffreyarnett.com/articles /articles/ARNETT_the_right_to_do_wrong.pdf

"A 2018 study from"

S. Madigan et al., "Prevalence of Multiple Forms of Sexting Behavior Among Youth: A Systematic Review and Meta-Analysis," *JAMA Pediatrics* 172, no. 4 (April 1, 2018): 327–35, https://www.ncbi.nlm.nih .gov/pubmed/29482215

Chapter 16

"Impulsivity isn't simply acting"

Daniel Romer et al., "Beyond Stereotypes of Adolescent Risk Taking: Placing the Adolescent Brain in Developmental Context," *Developmental Cognitive Neuroscience* 27 (October 2017): 19–34, https://www .sciencedirect.com/science/article/pii/S1878929317301020?via%3 Dihub?xid=PS_smithsonian#bib0945

"Know that the first kind"

Wouter van den Bos et al., "Adolescent Impatience Decreases with Increased Frontostriatal Connectivity," *PNAS* 112, no. 29 (July 21, 2015): E3765–74, https://www.pnas.org/content/112/29/E3765

"Different from the need"

Romer et al., "Beyond Stereotypes," https://www.sciencedirect.com /science/article/pii/S1878929317301020?via%3Dihub?xid=PS_smith sonian

"Dopamine directs the development"

Lauren M. Reynolds et al., "DCC Receptors Drive Prefrontal Cortex Maturation by Determining Dopamine Axon Targeting in Adolescence," *Biological Psychiatry* 83, no. 2 (January 15, 2018): 181–92, http:// biologicalpsychiatryjournal.com/retrieve/pii/S0006322317316694

"The impulsive decisions we made"

Elizabeth A. Kensinger, "Negative Emotion Enhances Memory Accuracy: Behavioral and Neuroimaging Evidence," *Current Directions in*

Psychological Science 16, no. 4 (August 1, 2007): 213–18, https://www2 .bc.edu/elizabeth-kensinger/Kensinger_CD07.pdf

Chapter 17

"Dr. Kristen Dunfield, a researcher"
Kristen A. Dunfield, "A Construct Divided: Prosocial Behavior as Helping, Sharing, and Comforting Subtypes," *Frontiers in Psychology* 5 (2014): 958, https://www.ncbi.nlm.nih.gov/pmc/articles/PMC4151454/

Acknowledgments

Thank you to everyone who helped me during the writing process, especially:

Quinn Davidson, who helps me run the business behind the book, for defying a job title because you do it all, and for taking on even more so I could write uninterrupted. This ship stays afloat because of you. You are the Leader of Loyalty and I feel grateful every day to work with you.

Anna Sproul-Latimer, my literary agent, for believing in this project from the beginning, for being my pop culture soulmate, and for taking me with you to Neon where I love being intimidated by all the cool, smart, edgy kids at your lunch table, and still can't believe you patted the seat next to you and said you saved me a space.

Marnie Cochran, my editor at Harmony, for saying yes so enthusiastically to my proposal, for replying to my emails with lightning fast speed, for having a New England sensibility that makes me feel right at home, and for having wicked smart answers to my questions.

Betsy Thorpe, my longtime editor extraordinaire, for being an enthusiastic cheerleader, for knowing and nurturing my voice, and for convincing me I'm funny when I don't believe it. I trust your feedback implicitly.

Jill Dykes, my publicist, for knowing the best tricks of the trade, for always seeing the hook, for making my NYC and TV dreams come true, and for being an all-around delight of a person.

Members of Less Stressed Middle School Parents, my private Facebook group, for being a huge part of my daily motivation, for being a fun part of my daily procrastination, and for spending your valuable time talking with me, and each other, about the joys and challenges of raising adolescents.

Erin Mills and *Wendy-Marie Norwood,* for coming to my home on alternate days to take dictation when I was too dizzy to type, and to the team of doctors who made their jobs obsolete by figuring out how to make me better.

Drs. Kristin Daley, Dawn O'Malley, Melissa Miller, and *Amanda McGough* for being brilliant psychologists and for letting me consult with you so often on these topics.

Drs. Trish Hutchison and *Melisa Holmes,* cofounders of Girlology, for your friendship and insight into raising young people with healthy ideas about bodies, sex, and sexuality.

And last but most, thank you to the other three members of the core four, *Travis, Ella,* and *Declan,* for being the best people I know, fixers of all things broken, masters of comedic timing, indulgers of list-making, loyal walking companions, brave adventurers, fanatic binge watchers, extremely reluctant followers of the Dirty Dishes System, and professional pep talkers. I am grateful for your support and so proud of our family.

Index

About the Author

MICHELLE ICARD is an internationally known speaker, author, and educator who helps kids, parents, and teachers navigate the complicated social world of early adolescence. The author of *Middle School Makeover: Improving the Way You and Your Child Experience the Middle School Years,* Michelle is also a member of the *Today* show parenting team and NBC News Learn. Her work has been featured in *The Washington Post, Chicago Tribune,* CNN, *Time,* and *People* magazine. Her middle school leadership programs, *Athena's Path* and *Hero's Pursuit,* have been implemented at schools across the country and she speaks around the globe at schools and parenting events. She lives in Charlotte, North Carolina, with her husband, Travis, and her children, Ella and Declan.